LIFE AND LETTERS OF
JOHN GREENLEAF WHITTIER

By SAMUEL T. PICKARD

IN TWO VOLUMES
VOLUME I.

LIFE AND LETTERS

OF

JOHN GREENLEAF WHITTIER,

1807 – 1892

BY

SAMUEL T. PICKARD, *1828 – 1915.*

IN TWO VOLUMES
VOLUME I.

HASKELL HOUSE PUBLISHERS Ltd.
Publishers of Scarce Scholarly Books
NEW YORK, N. Y. 10012
1969

First Published 1907

HASKELL HOUSE PUBLISHERS LTD.
Publishers of Scarce Scholarly Books
280 LAFAYETTE STREET
NEW YORK. N. Y. 10012

Library of Congress Catalog Card Number: 68-24941

Standard Book Number 8383-0191-6

Printed in the United States of America

PREFACE

THE thought that at some time the story of his life would be called for was not a pleasant one to Mr. Whittier; but fearing that, in the absence of correct data, a biography full of inaccuracies might be given to the public, about ten years before his death he authorized the collection of material for such a work, and assisted the friend to whom it was confided by suggestions of a general character. He had never kept a journal, nor charged his memory with dates, but he remembered his correspondents, and gave information which resulted in a large collection of letters, illustrating nearly every year of his life. The editor has regarded the use of this material as a sacred trust, and in accordance with Mr. Whittier's wish has allowed him, as far as practicable, to speak for himself.

In editorial work, and in his correspondence, he always expressed himself freely upon every subject which interested him. His familiar and unstudied letters have special value, revealing as they do the warmth and steadfastness of his friendships, the genuineness of his sympathy, his earnestness in philanthropic reforms, the spontaneity

of his humor, and his constant interest in public
affairs.

Mr. Whittier's editorial work upon partisan
papers developed a taste for politics and ambition
for political preferment, as shown by letters now
for the first time published.   These letters do not
fairly represent him when judged by the tenor of
his later life, but without them we could have no
true idea of his early manhood, and of the great
change which marked his religious, literary, and
political life when about twenty-seven years of
age.   Previous to this time, while irreproachable
in morals, no deep conviction of duty seems to
have nerved him to self-denying, heroic action.
He was evidently looking forward to a political
rather than a literary career.   Comparatively little
has hitherto been known of the first thirty years
of his life, beyond the fact that he edited political
papers in Boston, Haverhill, and Hartford, and it
may surprise his friends of the present generation
to find that he was an aspirant for congressional
honors, which, but for the constitutional limit as
to age, he had a fair prospect of obtaining, in a
district where he enjoyed exceptional popularity.
As a power in politics, even when working in a
small minority, Whittier has never been rightly
estimated.   In several of his poems he speaks of
his consecration to the cause of freedom as involv-
ing a change in all the motives of his life; but

this has not hitherto been taken so literally as it will now be seen was intended. While his serious work at this period was in politics, he was at the same time winning reputation as a poet, by verses which, though highly complimented by poets and critics of national repute, were suppressed by the more cultivated taste and judgment of his later years.

At the age of twenty-five we find him entering upon a contest in which every talent was to be used as a weapon of assault against a system which he had no reason to suppose would be overthrown in his day. In this field, the skill he had acquired in politics was not thrown away, and we can readily understand why he favored the political wing of the anti-slavery forces. With his genius for statecraft, nothing else could have been expected, and the reader can but admire the skill he exercised in keeping his despised cause before the people, and compelling the unwilling help of able men, who at heart were opposed to his aims and measures. As the trusted adviser of statesmen, the extent of his influence has never been fully appreciated beyond the circle of his intimate friends.

To those who have loved Whittier as a poet whose utterances have quickened their religious spirit, and given expression to their highest and holiest aspirations, the pages of this memoir devoted to his political activities, and a reform long since happily accomplished, may seem of small interest, and yet it must be admitted that the experience and labors of the years thus spent, with their important bearing upon the development of his character, could not be lightly passed over.

The editor would express his sincere thanks for the kind courtesy of relatives and friends of Mr. Whittier, in placing at his disposal letters and other interesting material for the preparation of this memoir. He would also acknowledge the valuable assistance of Mr. Whittier's cousin, Gertrude Whittier Cartland. No one now living enjoyed longer the intimate friendship of the poet, or was more fully in his confidence and in sympathy with his religious, philanthropic, and literary work.

S. T. P.

PORTLAND, MAINE, *September*, 1894.

CONTENTS.

VOL. I.

LIST OF ILLUSTRATIONS.

VOL. I.

LIFE AND LETTERS

OF

JOHN GREENLEAF WHITTIER

CHAPTER I.

ANCESTRY AND CHILDHOOD.

1807–1826.

JOHN GREENLEAF WHITTIER was born on the 17th of December, 1807, in a house built by his paternal ancestor, in the East Parish of Haverhill, Mass. This ancestor, Thomas Whittier, was the first of his name in America, and is supposed to have been of Huguenot descent. He was born in England in 1620, and came to this country when eighteen years of age. He sailed from Southampton, England, for Boston, Mass., in the ship Confidence, April 24, 1638. Among his companions on this voyage were his uncles, John and Henry Rolfe, and a distant relative, Ruth Green, whom he married a few years after his arrival, and whose name appears in every subsequent generation. He settled in Salisbury, Mass., on land now within the limits of the town of Amesbury and bordering on the Powow River, a small tributary of the Merrimac. The hill which to this day bears his name was included in the grant he received. It is a tradition in the family that he was a man of gigantic size, weighing more than three hundred pounds before he was twenty-one years of age, and he was possessed of great muscular strength. It is certain also that he had a high degree of both moral and physical courage.

He was sent as a deputy to the General Court from Salisbury, and served his town in other offices of trust. Removing across the Merrimac, he lived for a short time in the town of Newbury. In 1647, he took up his permanent residence in the town of Haverhill, and was again on the north side of the Merrimac, about ten miles above his former home in Salisbury. As before, he settled a mile or two from the "great river," and upon the bank of a small affluent now known as "Country Brook," but then as "East Meadow Brook." His first house was built of logs, and situated about half a mile southeast of the present "Whittier homestead." Here all but the eldest of his ten children were born. He had five sons, all possessing the stalwart proportions of their father, each of them being more than six feet in height.

In this log house he lived with his large family until about sixty-eight years of age, when he began to hew the oaken beams for a new and more capacious dwelling. The site which he selected was near by, upon the bank of a pretty rivulet, tumbling in a series of cascades through a ravine running along the north base of Job's Hill. In this retired and picturesque spot he built the house which he occupied until his death, November 28,

1696, and which has sheltered generation after generation of his descendants. The erection of the new house is supposed to have been in 1688. The foundations of the log house built by his pioneer ancestor, the poet used to see in his youth, but he was unable to find them when last visiting the place, in 1882.

Haverhill was first settled in 1640, and was for seventy years a frontier town, an unbroken wilderness stretching to the north for more than a hundred miles. During the first forty years of the settlement, there was no trouble from the Indians who fished in the lakes and hunted among the mountains of New Hampshire; but during the next thirty years they were frequently hostile, and Haverhill suffered all the horrors that accompany savage warfare. When these hostilities began, in 1676, Thomas Whittier had been living in his log house on East Meadow Brook for nearly thirty years, receiving frequent visits from the Indians, whose respect and friendship he won by the fearlessness and justice he displayed in his dealings with them.

When friendly intercourse with the pioneers was broken, and the savages began to make their forays upon this exposed settlement, several houses in the town were fitted up as garrisons, and we find that in 1675 Thomas Whittier was one of a committee appointed to select the houses that should be fortified as places of refuge. But though many of his townspeople were killed or carried into captivity, he never availed himself of this shelter for himself or his family, and it is the tradition that

he did not even bar his doors at night.   His frame
house, now standing, was built in the midst of the
Indian troubles, and he had occupied it several
years before the principal massacres, the records of
which make the bloodiest pages in the annals of
Haverhill.   The Hannah Dustin affair occurred in
1697, a year after the death of the pioneer.   The
Dustins lived in the western part of the town, re-
mote from the Whittiers, and nearly all the tragic
events of these troublous times in Haverhill were
beyond the limits of the East Parish.   But the Indians in their war paint occasionally passed up the
Country Brook, and the evening firelight in the
Whittier kitchen would reveal a savage face at
the window.   But this household was never harmed.

Thomas Whittier was a contemporary of George
Fox, and appears to have had much respect for
the doctrines of the new Society of Friends.   In
1652, he was among the petitioners to the General
Court for the pardon of Robert Pike, who had
been heavily fined for speaking against the order
prohibiting the Quakers Joseph Peasley and
Thomas Macy from exhorting on the Lord's Day.
The meetings of the Quakers had been held in
their own dwelling-houses.   A petition against this
order had been signed by many of the residents of
Haverhill, and when it was presented in the General Court, a committee of that body was appointed
to wait upon the petitioners, and command them to
withdraw it or suffer the consequences.   Some of
them did retract when thus called upon, but two of
the sixteen who refused were Thomas Whittier and
Christopher Hussey, both of them ancestors of the

poet. The only punishment they received was withdrawal for some years of their rights as " freemen." The disability in the case of Whittier was removed in May, 1666, when he took the oath of citizenship. The franchise at this time was granted only to those who were named as worthy by the General Court. He not only had the right to vote, but was an office-holder and a man of mark in Salisbury and Newbury for many years previous to his residence in Haverhill, and had also been a member of the General Court; and there can be little doubt that the delay in conferring upon him the full rights of citizenship in the last-named town was due to doubts respecting his orthodoxy. It may be that his interest in the doctrines of the new sect carried him beyond the point of desiring for its preachers fair play and freedom of utterance, but there is no evidence that he joined the Society of Friends. Indeed, we find him in his later years acting upon the ecclesiastical committees of the church then dominant in the colony.

His capacity for civic usefulness was recognized for years before the right to vote was conferred upon him. In laying out roads, fixing the bounds of the plantation, and in other ways, his engineering skill was drawn upon. When he came to Haverhill from Newbury, in 1647, it was considered of sufficient importance to note in the town records the fact that he brought with him a hive of bees that had been willed to him by his uncle, Henry Rolfe. This incident seems emblematic of the industry and thrift which have so largely characterized his posterity ; and it has furnished **a** device which has been woven by some members of the family into the Whittier monogram.

His youngest son, Joseph, through whom we trace the poet's lineage, married, in 1694, Mary Peasley, granddaughter of Joseph Peasley, the leading Quaker in the town, and one of the exhorters for whom Thomas Whittier asked in vain the clemency of the General Court forty-two years earlier.[1] In the mean time, George Fox had been preaching in America, and his adherents had so increased in numbers in all the colonies that further persecution was out of the question. For four generations nearly all the descendants of Joseph Whittier retained their connection with the Society of Friends, but that some of them lost their membership is shown by the fact of their holding military titles during the wars of the eighteenth century.

The East Parish of Haverhill is one of the most rugged and hilly sections of Essex County. Two centuries ago, as now, this county was more thickly populated than any other on this side the Atlantic that included no great city. And yet, here in its northeast corner was a spot so isolated that from the date of the erection of the Whittier mansion to the present time no neighbor's roof has been in sight. Whittier refers to the seclusion in " Snow-Bound," where he says : —

> " No social smoke
> Curled over woods of snow-hung oak."

[1] The house of Joseph Peasley, Jr., the father of Mary, was built of bricks brought from England, and is still standing near Rocks Village in the East Parish. It was used as a garrison house in the French and Indian wars.

While thus shut in from the busy world, there have always been neighbors within half a mile, and when the wind favors, the bells of Haverhill and Newburyport, and the roar of the storm waves breaking on Salisbury beach, are heard in this secluded valley.

In a letter written in 1881, Mr. Whittier says of the Ayer house, which is the nearest to the old homestead, that it was built within his remembrance, and that he recollected well the old garrison house that stood in the same place. It was of two stories, with only a single room below, and two small diamond-paned windows. The door was of massive oak plank, and the entry was paved with rough flat stones. The fireplace occupied nearly one side of the room. The ceiling was unplastered.

The principal settlement of Haverhill, now a city of about 28,000 inhabitants, is three miles away. The town originally stretched twelve miles along the north bank of the Merrimac, and was six miles wide. But when the long-disputed boundary between Massachusetts and New Hampshire was settled by royal commissioners appointed in 1737, a strip only three miles wide north of the river fell to the share of Massachusetts, and the northern half was given to New Hampshire. The windings of the Merrimac are to some extent followed by the boundary line, with the result that the East Parish is inclosed in an elbow of the river. Three beautiful ponds separate it from the city proper.

The rounded, dome-like summits of the gravelly hills were in the days of the pioneers, and indeed down to the poet's time, covered with a heavy hardwood growth, the oak predominating. In Mr. Whittier's youth there were no evergreens on the farm, except a few hemlocks. But upon clearing an acre of oaks there sprang up a growth of white pine covering the whole tract, — the only pines in the neighborhood. The noble elm not far from the house, centuries old, but still flourishing, its trunk eighteen feet in circumference at the smallest point, and casting a shadow at noonday a hundred feet in diameter, is known as "the Whittier elm."

Thomas Whittier's widow died in July, 1710. After the estate had been divided among the ten children, Joseph, the youngest, bought most of the land that was apportioned to his brothers and sisters. He died at the age of seventy, December 25, 1739, leaving nine children. His youngest child, also named Joseph, born in March, 1716, married Sarah Greenleaf, of West Newbury, July 12, 1739, and died October 10, 1796. They had eleven children, of whom five died in infancy or in youth, and only three of the others were married. The three who were married were Joseph, Obadiah, and John. Five of Joseph's children settled in Maine; seven of Obadiah's nine children settled in New Hampshire; and John, the youngest son who married, remained upon the Haverhill farm, with his younger brother, Moses. In April, 1802, John and Moses, in partnership, bought the interest of the other heirs in the estate, paying them therefor about $1700. The partnership continued until the death of Moses, in 1824.

John Whittier, father of the poet, was born November 22, 1760, and died June 11, 1830. He was forty-four years old when he married Abigail Hussey, October 3, 1804, and she was twenty-one years his junior. Abigail was a daughter of Samuel Hussey, of Somersworth (now Rollinsford), N. H., and Mercy Evans, of Berwick, Me. She was born in 1781, and died December 27, 1857. John and Abigail had four children : Mary, John Greenleaf, Matthew Franklin, and Elizabeth Hussey.

Those who are curious in vital statistics may find something of interest in the following summary : Thomas Whittier was forty-nine years old when his son Joseph was born, and he lived to be seventy-six years of age. Joseph was forty-seven years old when his son, the second Joseph, was born, and he died at the age of seventy. The second Joseph was forty-five years old when John was born, and he lived to be eighty. John was in his forty-eighth year when John Greenleaf, the poet, was born, and he lived to be nearly seventy. These five lives extended over the unusual period of two hundred and seventy-two years. Although each Whittier in this list lived to good old age, they each passed away without seeing their grandsons. The poet's grandfather, who lived to be eighty, died eleven years before the birth of his grandson. His father died in good old age, when he was a young man of twenty-two. These were all accounted stalwart men, while he who seemed to have the frailest physique lived to be five years older than either of his Whittier ancestors. The

delicacy of his physical frame and the unusual development of intellectual and spiritual force may
be taken as confirmation of the theory that the
older children of a family inherit a larger share
of physical strength, while the younger ones come
into possession of a corresponding share of nerve
and brain power.

Abigail Hussey, mother of the poet, was a descendant of Christopher Hussey, who was in early
life, as we have seen, a leading citizen of Haverhill, and a contemporary and friend of Thomas
Whittier. The Husseys came from Boston, England, and were people of distinction in both the
English and American branches of the family.
Christopher Hussey, before he came to this country, married Theodate, daughter of Rev. Stephen
Bachiler. As some of the personal characteristics of
Parson Bachiler were transmitted to recent generations in several branches of his family, and were
particularly observable in the subject of this
memoir, a brief sketch of his rather remarkable
career may not be out of place here.

Rev. Stephen Bachiler, born in England in
1561, was educated at Oxford, and in 1587 was
made vicar of a church in Hampshire, where he
remained until 1605, when he was deprived of his
living because of nonconformity. He preached in
England for twenty-five years thereafter, and then,
at the age of seventy-one years, came to America.
He arrived in Boston, June 5, 1632, and at once
proceeded to Lynn, with the little company who
had made the voyage with him. His daughter
Theodate, who had married Christopher Hussey,

was already settled in Lynn. Mr. Bachiler, a
stanch nonconformist in old England, retained
his independent ways during his twenty-two
years' residence in New England. Notwithstanding his advanced age, he caused much annoyance
in the Puritan community. Prince speaks of him
as " a man of form in his day, a gentleman of
much learning and ingenuity." Governor Winthrop in his journal tells some strange stories about
him, which for more than two centuries have be-
clouded his reputation; but recent investigations [1]
show that the scandals, which were inherently im-
probable, were false accusations growing partly out
of religious bitterness, and partly out of the intrigues
and aggressions of the Massachusetts Bay Colony
which were being resisted by the New Hampshire
settlements. While residing in Lynn he was
brought before the court for some irregularity,
and enjoined from preaching or teaching for a
year because of his " contempt of authority, and
until some scandals be removed." These " scandals," as it now appears, did not affect his moral
character, but refer to his independence of Massachusetts Bay authority. He received a grant of
land in Ipswich in 1636, and removed thither, but
difficulties arose and he did not remain. Soon
after, the town of Newbury made him a similar
grant, but his stay was equally short. In 1639, at
the age of seventy-eight years, with his son-in-law,
Christopher Hussey, he planted the town of Hampton, N. H., and was the first minister settled there.

[1] See article by Charles E. Batchelder in *N. E. Hist. and Gen.
Register*, January, 1892.

He was excommunicated on a charge for which he was never tried, though he demanded trial, and in three years restored to communion, but not to the ministry. The people of Exeter called him to be their pastor, but the court refused permission. At the age of eighty-nine he married his third wife, from whom he soon found abundant cause for separation. But the court passed a stringent order requiring them to live together. This order was maliciously unjust to Bachiler. Whereupon, at the age of ninety-two, he returned to England, and died at Hackney, near London, in 1660, in the one hundredth year of his age. Probably the passage in "The Wreck of Rivermouth" which indicates the poet's belief in the guilt imputed to his ancestor would have been revised, if the evidence now found in his favor had earlier come to light.

To this remarkable man several New England families of note trace their origin, and he seems to have transmitted to his descendants some marked physical and mental peculiarities that are still discernible, after a lapse of several generations. It was the Bachiler eye, dark, deep-set, and lustrous, which marked the cousinship that existed between Daniel Webster and John Greenleaf Whittier. Susannah Bachiler, the grandmother of Webster, was a daughter of one of the sons of the eloquent nonconformist clergyman whose troublous old age has been sketched, and Whittier was a descendant of his oldest daughter. In several other families descended from Bachiler, the physical peculiarity referred to is quite noticeable. The eyes which first saw the light before Shakespeare was born have repeated themselves, generation after generation, to this day.

Mr. Whittier was named for his father and for the family of his father's mother, Sarah Greenleaf.[1] His grandmother was descended from Edmund Greenleaf, who was born in the parish of Brixham, Devonshire, England, about the year 1600. The

[1] The home of Sarah Greenleaf was upon the Newbury shore of the Merrimac nearly opposite the home of the Whittiers. The house was standing until a recent date. Among Mr. Whittier's papers was found the following fragment of a ballad about the home-coming, as a bride, of his grandmother, Sarah Greenleaf, now first published : —

> " Sarah Greenleaf, of eighteen years,
>   Stepped lightly her bridegroom's boat within,
> Waving mid-river, through smiles and tears,
>   A farewell back to her kith and kin.
> With her sweet blue eyes and her new gold gown,
>   She sat by her stalwart lover's side —
> Oh, never was brought to Haverhill town
>   By land or water so fair a bride.
> Glad as the glad autumnal weather,
>   The Indian summer so soft and warm,
> They walked through the golden woods together,
>   His arm the girdle about her form.
>
> " They passed the dam and the gray gristmill,
>   Whose walls with the jar of grinding shook,
> And crossed, for the moment awed and still,
>   The haunted bridge of the Country Brook.
> The great oaks seemed on Job's Hill crown
>   To wave in welcome their branches strong,
> And an upland streamlet came rippling down
>   Over root and rock, like a bridal song.
> And lo ! in the midst of a clearing stood
>   The rough-built farmhouse, low and lone,
> While all about it the unhewn wood
>   Seemed drawing closer to claim its own.
>
> " But the red apples dropped from orchard trees,
>   The red cock crowed on the low fence rail,
> From the garden hives came the sound of bees,
>   On the barn floor pealed the smiting flail."
>
>   . . . .

Greenleaf family, it is believed, were of Huguenot origin, and the name was probably translated from the French Feuillevert, as is suggested in Mr. Whittier's poem, "A Name." Edmund Greenleaf married Sarah Dole, and had several children born in England. He settled in Newbury, Mass. His son Stephen, born in 1630, married Elizabeth Coffin, daughter of Tristram Coffin, and their son Tristram, born in 1667, married Margaret Piper in 1689. Tristram's son Nathaniel, born in 1691, married Judith —— ; their daughter Sarah, born March 5, 1721, married Joseph Whittier, 2d, and her son John was the father of the poet. The Harvard professor, Simon Greenleaf, descended from John, an older brother of Tristram Greenleaf, above named. The name of Whittier was spelled in many ways by various members of the family with the license that prevailed not only in this country but in England in the seventeenth and eighteenth centuries. In the Essex County records may be found eighteen different ways of spelling this name. Thomas Whittier spelled it with one " t."

Mr. Whittier has himself sketched in prose, in " The Fish I did n't Catch," the old homestead in which his childhood and youth were spent. He speaks of the house as having been built about the time that the Prince of Orange drove out James the Second, and adds : —

" It was surrounded by woods in all directions save to the southeast, where a break in the leafy wall revealed a vista of low green meadows, picturesque with wooded islands and jutting capes of upland. Through these, a small brook, noisy enough as it foamed, rippled, and laughed down its rocky falls by our garden-side, wound, silently and scarcely visible, to a still larger stream, known as the Country Brook. This brook in its turn, after doing duty at two or three saw and grist mills, the clack of which we could hear in still days across the intervening woodlands, found its way to the great river, and the river took it up and bore it down to the great sea."

Great Hill, in the immediate vicinity, which was one of the poet's favorite resorts, is one of the highest elevations in the county, from which portions of more than thirty cities and towns may be seen, with Monadnock rising dome-like in the west, and Wachusett a little to the south, while the billowy Deerfield range edges the horizon in the north, and in the east the ocean, with its white sails, may be traced from Boar's Head to Cape Ann.

The great dome of Job's Hill, which took its name from an Indian chief of the neighborhood, though now almost bare of trees, was in Whittier's youth well covered with giant oaks, which must have added much to its apparent height. This hill rises so steeply from the right bank at the foot of the garden that it is difficult for many rods to get a foothold. Its height is so great that it materially shortens the winter afternoons for the dwellers in the valley. From the left bank of the noisy brook the garden lot sloped gently upward toward the front of the house, till it met a terrace, upon which were the flower garden and the well with its ancient sweep.

A little way up the brook may still be seen the remains of a series of dams constructed by some of the earlier Whittiers, perhaps by the pioneer himself, when the water was utilized for grinding grain or sawing lumber. It is possible that Thomas Whittier, when erecting his buildings, had this water power in view, as the brook in those days before the forests were cleared away was a much larger and more reliable stream than now. The house faces southeast, and just beyond the brook the main road from Amesbury to Haverhill climbs over a shoulder of the hill, while a cross-road bridges the brook, and passes the eastern end of the house.

Between the brook and the house was a row of butternuts, walnuts, and maples, and at the gateway stood picturesque Lombardy poplars, which have now disappeared, as from most New England landscapes. The bridle-post mentioned in " Snow-Bound " is a large boulder at the left of the gateway, with a projection in its inner face that served as a step. It can be readily imagined how this bridle-post with its step and mantle of snow might suggest an old man sitting

" With loose-flung coat and high cocked hat."

The doorstone of the porch is a small granite millstone, probably one of those used in the ancient gristmill upon the hillside brook. On the opposite side of the road were the barn, a granary, and an ancient shop once supplied with a forge. The barn was built by John and Moses Whittier, when the poet was thirteen years of age. The old

The Haverhill Homestead

barn, on the same side of the road with the house, stood for some years after the erection of the new one. Mr. Whittier once told the writer that the old barn had no doors, and the winter winds whistled through it, and snow drifted upon its floors, for more than a century. The horses and cattle were but slightly protected in their stalls and " tie-up." This was the early practice throughout New England. Our fathers, coming from the milder climate of England, had the traditional English slowness in adapting themselves to changed climatic conditions. The pioneers and their descendants for four or five generations adopted the policy of " toughening " themselves by exposure to cold, and they saw no reason for making their cattle more comfortable than themselves. Their boys were expected at an early age to take their part in the work of subduing the wilderness, and they housed and dressed themselves much as they had done in the milder climate of the mother country. Almost two centuries passed away before barns were made comfortable, and flannels and overcoats ceased to be regarded as extravagances.

Mr. Whittier was accustomed to attribute the delicacy of his health throughout life to the methods of toughening the constitution in vogue when he was a lad. No flannels were worn in the coldest weather, and the garments of homespun, though strong and serviceable, were of open texture compared with modern goods. Only a short spencer for overcoat, and mufflers and mittens were provided for extremely cold weather; and the drive to the Friends' meeting at Amesbury,

eight miles away, twice a week, on First and
Fifth days, with no buffalo robes or warm wraps,
was thoroughly chilling and uncomfortable, and
the meeting-houses of those days were seldom
provided with means of heating.   These were
among the hardships of the time and country,
common to all classes of the people, and were
endured as inevitable.   But, while lamenting this
needless exposure to cold, Whittier never complained of other hard youthful experiences, — the
unending contest with the rocky acres of his
father's farm, and the difficulties of obtaining an
education.

The new barn on the Whittier estate was
built in 1821, with most of our modern conven-
iences.   This was the barn to which that famous
path was cut through " a fenceless drift " that
" once was road."   Of late years this treasure-
house of the farm has been doubled in length, but
the end toward the road is nearly the same as on
that December day, when the boys reached it

"with merry din,
And roused the prisoned brutes within."

The house built by Thomas Whittier has a
heavy oaken frame, the principal beams being
hewed from timber that gave a width of fifteen
inches.   This building is about thirty - six feet
square, and built in the ancient fashion around
a massive central chimney.   At the northeastern
corner, which is nearest the road, is a porch
giving entrance to the kitchen.   This room is by
far the largest, as it is the most notable, room in

the house, being about thirty feet in length, and
of proportionate width. What other kitchen in
the world is more hallowed by associations that
touch the universal heart? Its first suggestion to
the imagination is the deep content and peace
of a happy, united family, gathered of a winter
evening around their blazing hearth-fire, while a
storm rages without. The great fireplace is of
itself almost as wide as the average kitchen of the
present day. The chimney is broad enough at its
base to allow a space of about eight feet between
the jambs. The oven is at the back of the fireplace on the right side, and if there were a large
fire upon the hearth, it would be difficult to manage the baking, as one must step into the fireplace to reach it. The old crane, swinging on its
stout hinges at the left, and the ancient trammels
and hooks remain, curious reminders of the clumsy
methods of cooking in olden times. When Mr.
Whittier last visited the place, the hearth was
worn and broken, and the Turk's head andirons
were gone. But a fire was readily kindled, and
" the great throat of the chimney " made to laugh
again, with its roaring draught, while in the gleam
of the crackling flames

> " the old, rude-furnished room
> Burst, flower-like, into rosy bloom."

On the opposite side of the kitchen is a cupboard,
at which the tramp mentioned by Whittier in his
" Yankee Gypsies," prospecting for brandy, filled
his mouth with whale oil, and spluttered inarticulate imprecations. A little bedroom, that was

known as " mother's room," opens at the north-west corner of the kitchen. The ancient sashes with their small panes remain in most of the windows. Perhaps some of these panes in the kitchen are the identical ones through which the painted savages wonderingly peered at the stout old pioneer and his family. It was certainly through these panes that the poet saw the mimic flames that appeared to glow in the sparkling drifts outside, and told its meaning in the old rhyme : —

"Under the tree,
When fire outdoors burns merrily,
There the witches are making tea."

The front rooms are the family sitting-room, in the southeast corner, and the spare room, some-times used as parlor and sometimes as bedroom, in the southwest corner. It was in the last-named room that the poet was born. Doors into each of these front rooms open directly from the kitchen on either side of the great fireplace. The front entry is small, and the front stairs turn in a cramped space against the back of the chim-ney. There is a straight and steep flight of back stairs leading up from the western porch. It was down these stairs that in his tenderest infancy the poet, wrapped in a blanket, was once rolled, as an experiment, by a little girl who had charge of him.

Originally, the roof sloped on the northern side down to the first story, but this was raised in 1801 to correspond with the front. In the second story is a large open and unfinished chamber, around which four more or less finished chambers are grouped. The boys' chamber was the little one over "mother's room," and above is a large attic, with its rafters studded with nails and pegs, from which five generations of careful Quakers have suspended braids of seed-corn, bunches of medicinal herbs, and all the articles to which the ancient New England attic is consecrate, and on the floor of which the boys of two centuries have spread butternuts, walnuts, and acorns, around the great chimney.

This was the home in which Whittier spent his childhood and youth, and where he dreamed the ambitious dreams of his young manhood. It afforded something more than the average comfort of farm life at that time. Whatever hardships he encountered were shared with the majority of farmers' families in New England. The meadows were boggy and undrained. The uplands that had been cleared of trees by the fathers were still incumbered with stumps, and strewn with boulders, large and small, which interfered with the easy working of the soil. Fair crops could be raised only at the expense of hard work. This was taken for granted, and as a rule was not shirked by the boys. Young Whittier did his share of the household chores, and as he gained strength worked with his father and uncle Moses in the fields and forests. When he last visited the homestead, in 1882, he pointed out a stone wall he helped to build, which is now standing between the brook and the gate. It is the garden wall referred to in "The Barefoot Boy:" —

"Laughed the brook for my delight
Through the day and through the night,
Whispering at the garden wall,
Talked with me from fall to fall."

He attained the full height of his mature years, five feet, ten and one half inches, when he was about fifteen years of age; but he was always slender, and never strong of muscle. At the age of seventeen he sustained injuries from over-exertion in farm work, from the effects of which he never fully recovered. Some phases of farm life he always enjoyed, such as watching the growth and development of the crops, the harvesting of such as did not overtax his strength, and the companionship of the domestic animals, especially the oxen. He had seven cows to milk, and this work he never relished. Beside the cows, there were kept on the farm a yoke of oxen, a few sheep, and one horse. His mother made butter and cheese which had such a reputation that it brought much better prices than the average. Their bread was supplied from grains raised on the farm. Rye was largely used instead of wheat, and much Indian corn. The only method of threshing grain, in his youth, was with the flail, the wielding of which required more strength than he possessed.

His brother, Matthew Franklin, nearly five years younger than himself, was his superior in strength, and led off in "breaking" the steers and colts, and in other enterprises requiring bodily vigor. Of a warm summer afternoon, when no work was pressing, the top of Job's Hill was the favorite resort of the boys, and of the cattle as well. The summit is a plateau of several acres, which was formerly dotted with large oaks. To this pasture came the cattle, to lie in the shade of the wide-spreading trees. All the winds found their way to this breezy height, and in the sultriest day the air was never stagnant. The varied charms of the fine outlook were not lost upon the young poet and his lively brother. Directly beneath them was the ancient homestead, and they could almost look down into the flues of the great chimney. A wide stretch of beautifully diversified country spreads away on all sides to a distant horizon. The dome-shaped hills peculiar to the lower valley of the Merrimac River were all about them. The southern ranges of the New Hampshire mountains could be seen at the north, and eastward rose Agamenticus, standing as a sentinel upon the coast of Maine. At the west, across the Great Pond (since christened Kenoza by the poet), were the spires of Haverhill. Southeast was a glimpse of the blue sea in Ipswich bay, with the rocks of Cape Ann beyond, and just across the Merrimac were the rolling hills of Newbury. Only five miles away, in Byfield, was the ancestral homestead of the Longfellows, where the grandfather of Henry Wadsworth Longfellow was born. A little to the left rose the spires of Newburyport, and the beautiful Po Hill in Amesbury, at the foot of which the poet was to find a home for more than fifty-six years, was another conspicuous feature in the wide landscape.

The boys delighted in petting the oxen, which were large ones, and seemed to appreciate all the kindness that was shown them. They were named "Buck" and "Old Butler." On the hill was one oak so much larger than all the rest that it was called "The Oak." As the oxen lay chewing their cuds under this tree the boys would often sit on their foreheads and lean on their horns as on an armchair. Although always disposed to tease his pets, Whittier secured the love of every living thing that came under his care. Old Butler once saved his life by a remarkable exhibition of strength, and by what would be called "presence of mind" if shown by a man. One side of Job's Hill is exceedingly steep, — too steep for such an unwieldy animal as an ox to descend rapidly in safety. Greenleaf went to the pasture one day with a bag of salt for the cattle, and Old Butler from the brow of the hill recognized him and knew his errand. As the boy was bent over, shaking the salt out of the bag, the ox came down the hill toward him with flying leaps, and his speed was so great that he could not check himself. He would have crushed his young master, but by a supreme effort, gathering himself together at the right moment, the noble creature leaped straight out into the air, over the head of the boy, and came to the ground far below with a tremendous concussion and without serious injury to himself.

Another incident of his childhood, in which Old Butler figured, was once related by Mr. Whittier. Quaker meetings were sometimes held in the large kitchen at his father's house. One summer day, on such an occasion, this ox had the curiosity to put his head in at the open window and take a survey of the assembly. While a sweet-voiced woman was speaking, Old Butler paid strict attention, but when she sat down and there arose a loud-voiced brother, the ox withdrew his head from the window, lifted his tail in air, and went off bellowing. This bovine criticism was greatly enjoyed by the younger members of the meeting.

Mr. Whittier could not remember incidents that happened before he was six years old. His first recollection was of the auction sale of a farm in the neighborhood, and he was surprised to find the next morning that the farm had not been taken away by the purchaser, and a large hole left in its place!

When he was nine years of age, President Monroe visited New England, and happened to be at Haverhill on the same day that a menagerie with a circus attachment was exhibited in that village. The Quaker boy was not allowed the privilege of seeing either the collection of wild beasts or the chief magistrate of the nation. He did not care much for the former, but he was anxious to see a President of the United States. The next day, he trudged all the way to Haverhill, determined to see at least some footsteps in the street that the great man had left behind him. He found at last an impression of an elephant's foot in the road, and supposing this to be Monroe's track, he followed it as far as he could distinguish it. Then he went home, satisfied he had seen the footsteps of the greatest man in the country.

When he was an old man, a little girl in Pennsylvania wrote to him inquiring about his childhood on the farm. These passages are from his reply : —

"I think at the age of which thy note inquires I found about equal satisfaction in an old rural home, with the shifting panorama of the seasons, in reading the few books within my reach, and dreaming of something wonderful and grand somewhere in the future. Neither change nor loss had then made me realize the uncertainty of all earthly things. I felt secure of my mother's love, and dreamed of losing nothing and gaining much. . . . I had at that time a great thirst for knowledge and little means to gratify it. The beauty of outward nature early impressed me, and the moral and spiritual beauty of the holy lives I read of in the Bible and other good books also affected me with a sense of my falling short and longing for a better state."

To illustrate the fact that children suffer intensely from causes which their elders regard as trivial, and which they themselves are inclined to laugh at in later life, Mr. Whittier once told this story of his boyhood to a friend who was passing with him the scene of the incident. It was at an ancient farmyard on a side-hill midway between East Haverhill and the village of Merrimac. In ascending this hill, his father was in the habit of relieving his horse by walking, and Greenleaf was expected to walk also. It was a terrible trial to him, and the sight of the place recalled vividly the terrors of his youth, though seventy years had passed. A gander would begin his warlike threats as soon as he saw the boy, and in later life Mr.

Whittier could have marched up a hill towards a
hostile battery without such a sinking of the heart
as he felt whenever he approached this harm-
less but noisy fowl. If he had dared to tell his
father of his agony of dread, he could have remained safely in the carriage. But the fear of
being laughed at prevailed over every other consideration. He thought this was the experience of
many children, and that parents should treat their
apparently petty troubles with more seriousness
than is their custom.

In "Snow-Bound" Mr. Whittier has sketched
each member of the family in which his early life
was moulded. John Whittier, his father, was a
tall, strongly-built man, who had been famous in
his youth for the strength and quickness he displayed in athletic games and exercises. He was a
man of few words, but prompt and decisive in his
utterances. He was several times elected a select-
man of Haverhill, and was often called upon to act
as arbitrator in settling neighborhood differences.
In speaking of his father's connection with town
affairs, Mr. Whittier once quoted this saying of
his, illustrating his opinion in regard to public
charities: "There are the Lord's poor, and the
Devil's poor; there ought to be a distinction made
between them by the overseers of the poor." Before his marriage he made several trips to Canada
through the wilds of New Hampshire, carrying on
a barter trade in various commodities. To these
excursions the poet refers in "Snow-Bound."

In repairing an old desk that is an heirloom in
the family, a few years ago, this memorandum was

found written by John Whittier upon the back of one of the drawers: " Last time Canada, I believe, 1799." It is probably a vow he then registered not to make another of those wilderness journeys.[1] The poet's comment upon his taciturnity,

" No breath our father wasted,"

is illustrated in this brief inscription meant for no eye but his own. He was a devout member of the Society of Friends, and carefully observant of Quaker traditions. He had little or no sympathy with the literary tastes and aspirations of the young poet, who, however, found in his mother, sisters, and brother all the appreciation and encouragement his nature demanded.

The poet's mother, Abigail Whittier, was esteemed by all who knew her as one of the loveliest and saintliest of women. She was a person of much native refinement of feeling and manners, with a dignity of bearing and benignity of expression that impressed and charmed all who knew her. Her face was full and very fair, her eye dark and expressive. For fifty years she was the guide,

---

[1] Mr. Whittier had from his father this anecdote of his visit to the Canadian frontier: " He joined a party of horsemen and they rode through the wilds up to the Lake Memphremagog. There they met a tribe of friendly Indians. The country was wild. No settlement had been made there by the whites. On the day of my father's arrival there these Indians had gone on a spree, and every man in camp was tipsy, with but one exception, and he was kept busy looking after his companions to prevent them from rolling into the lake, and getting into mischief. My father asked the sober Indian if he never got drunk. He replied, 'Oh, yes; me get drunk some time; not now; me keep watch this time; next time me get drunk.'"

counselor, and friend of her illustrious son, who
repaid her devotion with a love as deep and tender
as her own.   Her memory, as well as that of her
sister, Mercy Hussey, is cherished with affection
and respect not only in the family, and in the
religious sect to which they belonged, but among
all with whom they came in contact.

Of the poet's two sisters, Mary and Elizabeth,
the older possessed many of the characteristics
of her father, while the younger had the milder,
sweeter nature of her mother.   Mary, born September 3, 1806, married Jacob Caldwell of Haverhill, had two children, Louis Henry and Mary
Elizabeth, and died January 7, 1860.

Perhaps the tenderest touch in " Snow-Bound "
may be found in the lines referring to his sister,
Elizabeth Hussey, who spent her whole life with
the poet, sharing the enthusiasm and the dangers
of his labors in behalf of unpopular reforms, and
the cares and pleasures of his home life.   Eight
years younger than himself, she was from childhood his special pet and favorite, and as she grew
older, she responded to his love with all the wealth
of her warm affections and keen appreciation of his
gifts.   She became his most intimate and confidential literary friend, and with the same poetic temperament and tastes she possessed some qualifications in which he was deficient.   His shyness and
reticence found its complement in her easy social
intercourse, her affability, and facility of expression ; and with her quick sympathies and sparkling wit their frequent and various guests found
most charming entertainment.   Her conversation

abounded in happy phrases, not readily forgotten. Of a friend who had just returned from her wedding trip to western New York, she said: "She was very happy, — the glory of Niagara shone in her face." Like Dorothy Wordsworth, her life was one of unselfish devotion to her brother, and as a critic her assistance was highly prized by him, who, after she had passed away, thus touchingly recalls

> "the dear
> Memory of one who might have tuned my song
> To sweeter music by her delicate ear."

She, too, was a writer of no small merit, as indicated by her correspondence and published poems, which are included in all the complete editions of Whittier's poems. It was her brother's opinion that "had her health, sense of duty, and almost morbid dread of spiritual and intellectual egotism permitted, she might have taken a high place among lyrical singers." She was born December 7, 1815, and died September 3, 1864. "Snow-Bound" was written by her brother the year after her death, and while the grief for her loss, never outgrown, was still fresh.

Thomas Wentworth Higginson, during his pastorate in Newburyport, frequently visited Mr. Whittier, and he has in a recent sketch referred to three members of the family whom he regarded as "most typical Quaker women." The mother, placid, equable, elevating almost into religious rites the whiteness of her bread and the purity of her table linen, — a nature simple, noble, direct; and the gentle "Aunt Mercy" of "Snow-Bound,"

"The sweetest woman ever Fate
Perverse denied a household mate."

And above all " there was the gifted sister Lizzie,
the pet and pride of the household, one of the
rarest of women, her brother's complement, possessing all the readiness of speech and facility of
intercourse which he wanted; taking easily in his
presence the lead in conversation, which the poet
so gladly abandoned to her, while he sat rubbing
his hands, and laughing at her daring sallies. She
was as unlike him in person as in mind; for his
dignified erectness, she had endless motion and
vivacity; for his regular and handsome features,
she had a long Jewish nose, so full of expression
that it seemed to enhance, instead of injuring, the
effect of the large and liquid eyes that glowed with
merriment and sympathy behind it. . . . Her quick
thoughts came like javelins; a saucy triumph
gleamed in her great eyes; the head moved a little
from side to side with the quiver of a weapon, and lo!
you were transfixed. Her poems, tragic, sombre,
imaginative, give no impression of this side of her
nature. . . . She was a woman never to be forgotten; and no one can truly estimate the long
celibate life of the poet without bearing in mind
that he had for many years at his own fireside the
concentrated wit and sympathy of all womankind
in this one sister."

Whittier's only brother, Matthew Franklin, was
born July 4, 1812, and died January 7, 1883.
In middle life, during his residence in Portland,
Matthew Whittier took a deep interest in the anti-
slavery cause, and wrote a series of humorous

letters over the signature of "Ethan Spike of
Hornby," satirizing in a most caustic manner the
foibles of the pro-slavery politicians of the day.
The last thirteen years of his life were spent in
Boston, where he had a place in the custom-house.
He left three children: Charles Franklin, Eliza-
beth Hussey, and Alice Greenwood.

The family group, in Whittier's youth, was
completed by the presence of his bachelor uncle,
Moses Whittier, and of his maiden aunt, Mercy
Evans Hussey, both of whom their nephew has
sketched with loving touch. Moses, the youngest
brother of the poet's father, spent his whole life
at the homestead, in which he owned an equal
share with John. He delighted in hunting, fish-
ing, and story-telling. He had never read much
or traveled far, but he was wise in the traditions
of the family and neighborhood, an oracle to be
consulted about the weather, and a charming
companion for his nephews in their rambles.
In Greenleaf, especially, "Uncle Moses" had a
sympathetic listener. As they worked together
in the fields, or sat by the evening fireside, he
enjoyed the marvelous stories of the denizens of
the forest and stream, traditions of witchcraft,
and tales of strange happenings in his own times.
We can imagine the moods in which these stories
were received, and how they would be warmed
and colored in the kindling fancy of the youth.
As he stood at his uncle's knee at such times, he
fell into reveries from which the good man would
arouse him by the sharp exclamation, " Come,

M. F. Whittier

boy, get out of that *stood !*" Uncle Moses was
born in 1762, and died January 23, 1824. He
was fatally injured by the falling of a tree, which
he had cut down, and which, taking an unexpected direction, pinned him to the ground. His
faithful dog gave warning at the house, and he
was soon found and extricated; but he did not
long survive the accident.

"Aunt Mercy," a younger sister of the poet's
mother, lived in the family from his earliest
memory to the time of her death, in 1846.
With less of dignity and "presence" than her
sister, she had a singular sweetness of disposition,
and loving, helpful ways. Her gentle ministrations at the bedside of the sick and suffering gave
a peculiar significance to the name her parents
bestowed on this Quaker "sister of mercy."

Even the story of Aunt Mercy's quiet life was
not without a tinge of romance. In her youth,
according to the tradition of the family, she was
betrothed to a worthy young man. Late one
evening, as she sat musing by the fire in the old
kitchen, after the rest of the family had retired,
she felt impelled to go to the window, and, looking out, she recognized her lover on horseback
approaching the house. As she had reason to
suppose that he was then in New York, she was
surprised at his unexpected return, and his call at
so late an hour. Passing the porch window as
she hastened to open the door, she saw her lover
ride by it, and turn as if to dismount at the step.
The next instant the door was open, but no trace
of man or horse was to be seen. Bewildered and

terrified, she called her sister, who listened to her story, and tried to soothe her and efface the painful impression. "Thee had better go to bed, Mercy; thee has been asleep and dreaming by the fire," she said. But Mercy was quite sure she had not been asleep, and what she had seen was as real as any waking experience of her life. In recalling the circumstances of her vision, one by one, she at length took notice that she had heard no sound of hoofs! It may be imagined what was the effect of all this upon the sensitive girl, and she was not unprepared, after a weary waiting of many days, to learn through a letter from New York, written by a strange hand, that her lover had died on the very day, and at the hour, of her vision. In her grief she did not shut herself away from the world, but lived a life of cheerful charity. She did not forget her first love, and gave no encouragement to other suitors.

Among the characters mentioned in " Snow-Bound " is the " master of the district school," who

" Held at the fire his favored place."

Until near the end of Mr. Whittier's life, he could not recall the name of this teacher whose portrait is so carefully sketched, but he was sure he came from Maine. At length, he remembered that the name was Haskell, and from this clue it has been ascertained that he was George Haskell,[1] and that he came from Waterford, Me.

[1] George Haskell was born at Harvard, Mass., March 23, 1799. His father, Samuel Haskell, removed to Waterford, Me., in 1803. In 1821 he went to Phillips Exeter Academy, and entered

Mercy Hussey

The unwelcome guest, mentioned in "Snow-Bound," was Harriet Livermore,[1] an eccentric Dartmouth College in 1823; left his college class in the Sophomore year, and studied medicine until 1827, when he received the degree of M. D. from the college. While in college, he taught one term of district school in East Haverhill. He commenced practice at East Cambridge, Mass., in 1827; removed to Ashby, Mass., in 1828, and to Edwardsville, Ill., in 1831. Two years later he settled at Alton, Ill., where he was actively engaged in founding Shurtleff College, of which he was trustee and treasurer. In 1838, he removed to Rockford, Ill., where he practiced his profession until 1845, after which date he devoted his attention chiefly to raising of fruit. He gave to Rockford the land for its public park. In 1866, he removed to New Jersey, was engaged in founding an industrial school, and purchased with others a tract of 4000 acres, which was laid out for a model community. In 1857, Dartmouth College gave him the degree of A. B., as of the year 1827. He died in Vineland, N. J., in 1876. He does not appear to have been aware of the fact that his Haverhill pupil had immortalized him in the poem *Snow-Bound*. His nephew, Rev. Dr. Samuel Haskell, of Kalamazoo, Mich., says of him that "he was a man of scholarship and enthusiasm, a friend of struggling students, many of whom he befriended in his home and with his means."

[1] Harriet Livermore was born in Concord, N. H., April 24, 1788, and was a daughter of Hon. Edward St. Loe Livermore, who afterward resided in Newburyport, and represented the North Essex district in Congress from 1801 to 1811. Before he came to Massachusetts he sat upon the bench of the Supreme Court of New Hampshire, as did also his father, Samuel Livermore, and his brother Arthur before him. His Newburyport house, the early home of Harriet Livermore, was the same now owned and occupied by Joseph Cartland, where Mr. Whittier spent much time during the last years of his life. At the period referred to in *Snow-Bound*, Harriet Livermore had embraced the doctrine of the Second Advent, and went about proclaiming the Lord's speedy coming. She had but slight control over a violent temper, and quarreled with nearly every one with whom she associated. She spent many years in travel over Europe and the Holy Land. Harriet Livermore was at one time converted to Quakerism, and lived with a Friend at Amesbury; but she got into an argument on some doctrinal point with a young man in the

personage, whose wanderings occasionally brought her to East Haverhill, and her coming was dreaded by Whittier in his boyhood. In later years he did much to befriend 'her. She obtained opportunities to lecture in Philadelphia and in Washington through his influence.

The Whittier family had from the first held a leading social position in the East Parish. Their religious views were respected, although none of their immediate neighbors were of the same faith, and the pastor of the Congregational church in the same vicinity seldom passed them by, when making his pastoral calls. On First days, when the weather was suitable, the parents, or uncle and aunt, always drove to their meeting at Amesbury, taking with them, by turns, as many of the children as their one-horse carriage would accommodate.[1] A portion of the afternoon was generally spent by the assembled family in reading the Holy Scriptures, and such other religious books as their scanty library afforded.

These readings seem to have been characterized by much freedom of comment, in which the young poet sometimes expressed his doubts regarding the

family, and knocked him down with a stick of wood. That was the end of her connection with the Society. She went with her father, when he was a member of Congress, to Washington, attended parties, danced, and was fond of the gay society of the capital. Samuel Livermore, a brother of Harriet, was chaplain on board the Chesapeake when that frigate was captured by the British. When his ship was boarded, he wounded a British officer, and was himself wounded in that affair.

[1] Mr. Whittier's father had a chaise, the only one owned in the neighborhood. We find a receipt for an internal revenue tax of one dollar on this chaise for the year 1817.

morality of certain acts recorded in the Old Testament, on one occasion questioning whether King David, man of war as he was, could have been a member of the Society of Friends. In consequence of such criticisms, his parents deemed it best at one time to confine his study of the Bible mostly to the New Testament. To this faithful teaching in the home may be attributed in large measure Whittier's familiarity with the Scriptures and frequent quotations in his writings. As Stedman has truly said, "The Bible is rarely absent from his verse, and its spirit never."

While the home life was thus pure and elevating in its influence, the social privileges of the family were among the best in their vicinity. The father, holding offices of trust in the town, was associated with many of its notable citizens, and the proverbial hospitality and refinement of the mother and aunt drew around them a circle of more than usual cultivation. The visits of the itinerant ministers of the Friends were an element not to be overlooked in the religious development of the younger members of the family. These visits to the meetings and families of their fellow-members were more frequent seventy-five years ago than in later times, and often proved a source of much comfort and encouragement. One of these ministers from England, William Forster, the father of the Right Honorable William Edward Forster, who was entertained at the Whittier mansion, is referred to in the poem "William Forster."

Before the days of steam and electricity, the Eastern members of the Society, attending their

Yearly Meeting at Newport, R. I., generally performed the journey in their own carriages, depending largely upon their friends for entertainment
by the way, in which pleasant service the Whittiers had their full share, sometimes receiving
under their roof from ten to fifteen guests.

Among the incidents of his boyhood which made
a lasting impress upon his memory was a visit to
Salem with his parents to attend a Quarterly Meeting.   They passed a tree then standing on Gallows Hill, dead and leafless, but with the heart still
apparently alive, or left sound, and he was told that
this was the tree upon which the witches were
hanged.   He recollected having pointed out to him
on the Rocks Bridge, at East Haverhill, the place
where Mr. Davis, the draw-tender, died, in exact
fulfillment of a vision he had in which he saw the
manner of his death.   He never doubted the reality
of this prophetic vision.

These memories of the village nearest to his
birthplace we find in a letter written by Mr. Whittier in 1875 to a friend who was also a native of
East Haverhill : —

" Your note carries me back to my boyhood, to
the time when I used to know you at ' Rocks
Village.'   How well I remember the place and
the people ! Colonel Johnson and his tavern ;
Esquire Frost and his store ; Esquire Ladd and
his blacksmith shop ; Ephraim B. Orne and his
combs ; Poyen and his cigars ! How plainly rises
before me the figure of Dr. Weld in his drab coat
and breeches, — a true gentleman of the old school,
— a skillful physician, and benefactor of the peo-

ple! Colonel Poor, who used to search our woods for ship timber; widow Pettee, who used to make my homespun coats and trousers; old 'aunt Morse,' who was regarded by the average juvenile mind as a witch, — all these and many more are associated with my recollections of Rocks Village."

This fragment of an autobiography was found among Mr. Whittier's papers, and was evidently written in the days of "Union-saving" compromises: —

"In the order of Providence I was born within the pale of a society which had relieved itself of the wrong and inconsistency of slave-holding by voluntary emancipation on the part of its members. My father was an old-fashioned Democrat, and really believed in the Preamble of the Bill of Rights, which reaffirmed the Declaration of Independence. My mother used to tell us the sad story of the kidnapping and transportation of the negro children. At district school I learned the Decalogue without any hint on the part of my instructors that its every command might be piously violated for the sake of fulfilling prophecy, and insuring the curse of Canaan. The standard reading-book was the 'American Preceptor,' liberally sprinkled with anti-slavery prose and poetry. One of the pieces rings in my memory even now. It was the story of an insurgent slave, — a black John Bruce: —

'First of his race, he led his band
  Guardless of dangers hovering round,
 Till by his bold, avenging hand,
  Full many a despot stained the ground.'

His arrest, at last, and cruel death by torture were described, closing with an appeal to the reader's admiration and sympathy: —

> 'Does not the soul to Heaven allied
>   Feel the full heart as greatly swell
> As when the Roman Cato died,
>   Or when the Grecian victim fell?'

"In those days there was no Union-saving committee to do the work of expurgation, and prevent the young idea from shooting in the direction of Liberty. It was never my privilege to hear a proslavery sermon, and I grew up in blissful ignorance of the Gospel according to Parson Adams."

CHAPTER II.

1820–1828.

UNTIL he was nineteen years of age, the only schools young Whittier had attended were the meagre ones supplied during a small part of the year by the district. He was accustomed to say that only two of the teachers who were employed in that district during his schooldays were fit for the not very exacting position they occupied. Both of these were Dartmouth students : one of them George Haskell, to whom reference has already been made, and the other Joshua Coffin, who afterward became known as an antiquary and as the historian of Newbury. Coffin was associated with Garrison and Whittier in the beginning of their crusade against slavery, and enjoyed their friendship through life.

Whittier's first appearance in school was before he was of " school age," during a term when Joshua Coffin was teaching in the district. He accompanied his older sister, Mary, and was too young to be placed in any class except that in which the alphabet was taught. The schoolhouse was undergoing repairs at that time, and the school was held in the ell of a dwelling-house now standing. The other part of the house was occupied by a tipsy and quarrelsome couple, reference to which fact will be found in the poem "To My Old School-master." Some years afterward, in 1821, Coffin was again a teacher in that district, and he spent many of his evenings at the Whittier homestead, a most welcome guest.

There were few books in the house, and most of them not of a kind to satisfy the literary appetite of a boy in his teens, who found poor picking among the dry journals and religious disquisitions of the pioneers of Quakerism.[1] There were not more than thirty volumes in all. These and the Bible he had read and re-read until he knew them by heart. It may be readily imagined what a new life was opened to him when a lively student, fresh from college, sat at the fireside and spoke familiarly of other lit-eratures. His teacher brought with him books of travel and adventure, and read them to his mother and aunt, as they sat knitting by the fire. He little thought that the boy of fourteen was the most eager of his listeners. Coffin told wise and merry stories, and read from books such as otherwise would scarcely have entered this strictly Quaker household. One evening the teacher brought a vol-ume of Burns, and read many pages from it, explain-ing the Scottish dialect as he proceeded. Greenleaf listened spellbound in his corner. A fire was that evening kindled upon an altar that grew not cold for seventy years. Coffin had only thought of his older listeners as he read and explained. But as

---

[1] Speaking of the journals of Friends which made so large a part of his father's library, he said in later life that in his youth he read them so much that he had steeped his mind with their thoughts. He loved their authors because they were so saintly, and yet so humbly unconscious of it.

he shut the book he noticed that his tall, shy pupil
was in what Uncle Moses had quaintly called his
" stood." He recalled the lad to his ordinary senses
by offering to leave the book with him, if he was
interested in it. The offer was, of course, gladly
accepted. What this little volume thus loaned to
him was to young Whittier has since been told
in one of the finest tributes to Burns that have yet
been written. He soon began to try his own wings,
but at great disadvantage, hampered as he was by
his surroundings. He early developed a love for
books of biography and travel, and borrowed all
that were to be found in the neighborhood.

A story has been published to the effect that
young Whittier was punished at school for refusal
to learn the Westminster catechism. It had only
slight foundation in fact. The teacher required
the scholars to learn the catechism on Saturdays
from the New England Primer. Greenleaf had
no Primer, and was told by the teacher to get
one. His father told him he need not study the
catechism, as it contained errors. He reported this
to the teacher, and the study of the Primer was
not enforced in his case.

The room occupied by the boys during part of
their childhood was the chamber in the northwestern corner of the second story. The clapboards
were gone from some portion of the western gable
at that time, and the snow of winter sometimes
sifted through the cracks upon their bed. In this
room occurred the incident that has been made
the theme of a poem by J. T. Trowbridge. The
two little Quaker boys had found they could lift

each other, and one evening experimented upon
the proposition made by the elder, that by lifting
each other in turn they could rise to the ceiling,
and there was no knowing how much further, if
they were out of doors! To make it easy in case
of failure the prudent lads first tried the experi-
ment of standing upon the bed in this little room.
Trowbridge says : —

> " 'T was a shrewd notion none the less,
>   And still, in spite of ill success,
>   It somehow has succeeded.
> Kind Nature smiled on that wise child,
>   Nor could her love deny him
> The large fulfillment of his plan ;
> Since he who lifts his brother man
>   In turn is lifted by him."

Whittier's first visit to Boston was made while
he was yet in his teens, and he was accustomed to
tell with much amusement his adventures on that
occasion. He was the guest of his relative, Mrs.
Nathaniel Greene, wife of the postmaster of Boston, who was also editor of the " Statesman." Mrs.
Greene was a descendant of his own ancestor,
Rev. Stephen Bachiler, and she had visited the
Whittiers at their East Haverhill homestead. On
this occasion, he wore for the first time in his life
" boughten buttons " upon his homespun Quaker
coat, and it was a surprise to him that the bravery
of his apparel did not seem to impress those who
passed him in the street. He wore a broadbrim
Quaker hat made for him by his Aunt Mercy out
of pasteboard, covered with drab velvet. One
event which signalized this visit was his purchase
of a copy of Shakespeare. He had been strictly

cautioned by his mother to avoid the theatre, and
when he learned that a brilliant lady he met at
the table of Mrs. Greene, who had been very kind
in her attentions to the quaint, shy boy, and who
had quite won his heart by her simplicity and
grace, was an actress, it was a great shock to him ;
but he had the courage to refuse her invitation to
the play-house, and cut short his visit to the city
to avoid the terrible temptation to which he was
subjected. He had gone quite too far in buying
Shakespeare's plays, and fled homeward lest he
should bring disgrace upon his Quakerism. His
family were surprised to see him back so soon, but
he did not dare to tell them the startling episode
of his encounter with a live actress.

A copy of one of the Waverley novels, then fresh
from the hand of its unknown author, was somewhere obtained by young Whittier, but the fact
was kept from the knowledge of his parents, and
the book was read with surreptitious enthusiasm,
his sister enjoying with him the literary banquet.
He used to tell how they sat reading until late one
night, when just as they reached a critical part of
the story, their candle burned to its socket, and,
sadly disappointed, they were compelled to retire
in the dark.

Of the no doubt crude literary work undertaken
by Whittier during the next two years after he
made the acquaintance of Burns, from 1821 to
1823, scarcely any vestige remains. His schoolmates say he was in the habit of covering his
slate with rhymes, which were passed about from
desk to desk to the great amusement of the

school.[1]   When a small boy, it was noticed by
the family that after his "nightly chores" were
done, and they were gathered around their evening fire, instead of doing sums on his slate, like
many other boys, he was covering it with verses,
one of which was rescued from oblivion by the
memory of his older sister, and ran thus : —

> " And must I always swing the flail,
>   And help to fill the milking pail ?
>   I wish to go away to school ;
>   I do not wish to be a fool."

Another of his earliest effusions was an attempt
to make a rhymed catalogue of the books in his
father's library.   Here are a few of the verses : —

> " The Bible towering o'er the rest,
>   Of all other books the best.

> " William Penn's laborious writing
>   And a book 'gainst Christians fighting.

> " A book concerning John's Baptism,
>   Elias Smith's Universalism.

> " How Captain Riley and his crew
>   Were on Sahara's desert threw.

> " How Rollins, to obtain the cash,
>   Wrote a dull history of trash.

> " The Lives of Franklin and of Penn,
>   Of Fox and Scott, all worthy men.

> " The Life of Burroughs too I 've read,
>   As big a rogue as e'er was made.

> " And Tufts, too, though I will be civil,
>   Worse than an incarnate devil."

[1] It is a tradition that his first verses were written upon the
beam of his mother's loom.

Greenleaf began a diary when he was fourteen years old, his mother making a book for him by folding and stitching some foolscap paper. He could not think of anything to write in the diary, his life on the farm was so uneventful. His mother suggested that he write of some striking event in the past that had come under his observation. The only great event he could think of was the wind-storm of 1815, six years before; [1] so he wrote an account of that, and never afterward made an entry in this, or in any other diary.

The desk upon which young Whittier wrote his first rhymes was even at that time an ancient piece of furniture. It had stood by the eastern window of the kitchen in the old homestead at Haverhill ever since the days of his great-grandfather, the son of the pioneer, Thomas Whittier, more than a century before the birth of the poet. When the family removed to Amesbury, it was taken with them, but was soon after replaced by a new one, and the old desk went " out of commission." In the summer of 1891, Mr. Whittier's niece had this ancient desk repaired, and as her uncle was to spend the next fall and winter in Newburyport, it was sent to the house of his cousins, the Cartlands. Mr. Whittier was greatly pleased, upon his arrival, to find in his room the heirloom which was hallowed by so many associations connected not only with his ancestry, but

[1] This cyclone's path was a few miles away from the East Parish, but Greenleaf saw the whirling cloud and heard its roar. It took off the roof of the house of his Aunt Ruth Jones, in Amesbury, and this fact probably deepened the lines of his memory of it.

with his own early life. Nearly all the literary work of his last year was done upon this desk. To his niece he wrote : —

"I came here day before yesterday, and found it very homelike. I am writing at the old desk, which Gertrude has placed in my room, but it seems difficult to imagine myself the boy who used to sit by it and make rhymes. It is wonderfully rejuvenated and is a handsome piece of furniture. It was the desk of my great-grandfather [the first Joseph Whittier], and seemed to me a wretched old wreck when thee took it to Portland. I did not suppose it could be made either useful or ornamental. I wrote my first pamphlet on slavery, 'Justice and Expediency,' upon it, as well as a great many rhymes which might as well have never been written. I am glad that it has got a new lease of life." [1]

One of Whittier's earliest efforts at verse was a parody on "The Old Oaken Bucket," and was entitled "The Willows." It was never sent to the press by him, and exists only in manuscript, being now in the possession of Mr. Charles Aldrich, of the Iowa State Library. This is the first stanza :

---

[1] The old desk has been given by Mrs. Pickard, together with nearly all the family heirlooms which originally belonged at East Haverhill, and which came into her possession, to the trustees having the ancient homestead in charge, and it will have a permanent place in the same corner of the old kitchen in which it stood for more than a century. In renovating it, the memoranda of farm events, written upon the backs and bottoms of the drawers by his father and grandfather, have been preserved. Among the inscriptions upon the outside of the desk, at the back, are the letters "J. W." and the date "1786," written large in black paint, by his grandfather, the second Joseph Whittier.

Mary Whittier Caldwell

"Oh, dear to my heart are the scenes which delighted
   My fancy in moments I ne'er can recall,
When each happy hour new pleasures invited,
   And hope pictured visions more holy than all.
Then I gazed with light heart, transported and glowing,
   On the forest-crowned hill and the rivulet's tide,
O'ershadowed with tall grass and rapidly flowing
   Around the lone willow that stood by its side, —
The storm-battered willow, the ivy-bound willow, the water-
   washed willow that grew by its side."

It is written in small, neat, old-fashioned chiro-
graphy, on a foolscap sheet, on the back of which
is another poem never published, entitled "The
Emerald Isle." There is a clump of willows upon
Country Brook, near the Whittier homestead, and
close by the Country Bridge, which the young poet
probably had in mind when he wrote the first-
named poem.

While not shirking any of the tasks that fell to
him as the son of a farmer who expected him to
spend his life, as had several generations of his
ancestors, in tilling the soil, it became evident at
an early age that other thoughts and aspirations
were agitating the mind of the lad, although he
was himself hardly aware of any disloyalty to the
farm. His father discouraged what he thought a
foolish waste of time over his day-dreams, but his
mother "hid these things in her heart," a little
hope mingling with her apprehension of an unset-
tled life for her son. His sister Mary actively
encouraged him. He filled many foolscap pages
with neatly written verses on "Lafayette," "Contentment," "William Penn," "Benevolence," the
"Death of Alexander of Russia," and on other
themes, with no expectation of ever seeing them

in print.   Several of these pages are now extant,
but the verses written upon them he never wished
to have reproduced in any collection of his poems.
They are of interest chiefly as showing the steps
in which he groped, amid unpromising surroundings, toward literary culture.   These first poems
bear date from 1823 to 1826 inclusive.   They
were written before he had any advantage of the
academy or access to libraries.

His sister Mary, feeling confident that some of
his poems were as good as those she saw in the
poet's corner of the " Free Press," determined to
offer one of them to that paper without giving the
editor any hint of the source from whence it came.
William Lloyd Garrison had just started this
weekly paper, in Newburyport, and its humanita-
rian tone so pleased the Quaker John Whittier
that he subscribed for it.   Garrison was only two
years older than Whittier, but he began editorial
work at an early age, and was in literary experience
very much the senior of the young poet.   One day
he found under the door of his office a poem entitled " The Exile's Departure," and signed " W."
The piece was written during the previous year,
and Mary had selected it as in her opinion the
one most likely to be accepted.   She sent it without her brother's knowledge.   It was therefore a
great surprise to the young poet when he opened
the paper, and turned to the column in which
poetry was usually printed, to find his own verses
conspicuously displayed.   The paper came to him
when he was with his father mending a stone wall
by the roadside, picking up and placing the stones

in position. As they were thus engaged, the postman passed them on horseback, and tossed the paper to the young man. His heart stood still a moment when he saw his own verses. Such delight as his comes only once in the lifetime of any aspirant to literary fame. His father at last called to him to put up the paper, and keep at work. But he could not resist the temptation to take the paper again and again from his pocket to stare at his lines in print. He has said he was sure that he did not read a word of the poem all the time he looked at it.

The date of the " Free Press " that contained this poem was June 8, 1826. The date of composition was June 1, 1825. It did not appear in an early collection of his works, but may be found in the appendix of the Riverside edition of 1888. The success of this venture induced the sending of another poem, entitled " The Deity," an amplification of the sublime passage of Scripture to be found in the 11th and 12th verses of the 19th chapter of First Kings. This also was written in 1825, and was published in the " Free Press " of June 22, 1826. Mr. Garrison introduced it with the following eulogistic paragraph : —

" The author of the following graphic sketch, which would do credit to riper years, is a youth of only sixteen, who we think bids fair to prove another Bernard Barton, of whose persuasion he is. His poetry bears the stamp of true poetic genius, which, if carefully cultivated, will rank him among the bards of his country."

By inquiring of the postman, Mr. Garrison had

learned the locality from which the Haverhill poems emanated, and drove out to call upon his new and promising contributor, a distance of fourteen miles. The editor was a neatly dressed, handsome, and affable young gentleman, and his coming to the farmhouse accompanied by a lady friend caused quite a sensation. Whittier was at work in a field, clad with reference to comfort in a warm day, and was disposed to excuse himself, but his sister Mary persuaded him to make himself presentable and receive his city visitors. This was the beginning of the life-long acquaintance and friendship of those two remarkable men. It antedates by some years the anti-slavery agitation in which they were afterward intimately associated. Garrison, with the social tact that distinguished him, put the shy youth at his ease at once. He heartily commended his work, and assured him of his belief in his capacity for better things. He advised him to secure an education. Young Whittier's father came into the room, and Garrison urged upon him his duty to send his son to better schools than those kept in the district. The old gentleman was not pleased with the turn matters were taking, and told Garrison he did not wish him to put such notions into the boy's head.[1]

For a time the thought of sending Greenleaf to

---

[1] In a letter to Mr. Garrison, written in 1859, Mr. Whittier says of this incident : "My father did not oppose me ; he was proud of my pieces, but as he was in straitened circumstances he could do nothing to aid me. He was a man in advance of his times, remarkable for the soundness of his judgment, and freedom from popular errors of thinking. My mother always encouraged me, and sympathized with me."

an academy was given up ; Garrison had removed
to Boston, and the young poet offered his verses to
the Haverhill " Gazette," which had recently come
into the possession of Mr. Abijah W. Thayer, who
had previously edited a paper in Portland. Mr.
Thayer had such a high opinion of his young
contributor that in January, 1827, he went to his
father, as Mr. Garrison had done a few months
earlier, to urge him to give his son a classical education. A new academy was soon to be opened in
Haverhill, and he could attend it and spend a part
of each week at his home. The old gentleman
took into consideration the fact that two years
before Greenleaf had seriously injured himself by
attempting farm work that was too heavy for him,
and was at length inclined to yield, though pro-
testing it was contrary to Friends' custom to acquire the polish of literary culture. The mother
asked Mr. Thayer if he would take Greenleaf into
his family, and this was readily promised. The
only problem that now proved troublesome was
how to obtain the money needed to defray expenses. When John Whittier bought the interest
of the other heirs in his father's estate, he assumed
a debt that was not yet fully paid. There was a
mortgage of $600 upon the farm, and it was diffi-
cult to get ready money for their farm products,
beyond what was required to pay taxes and the
interest on the debt. The Whittier orchard at
that time had no grafted apples ; there were plenty
of cranberries in the meadow, and other berries in
the upland ; enough of ship-timber and firewood in
the forests, but there was then no market for any
of these things.

The young man had permission to attend the academy, but he must pay his own way. This task he set about with a glad heart. An opportunity soon appeared. A man who worked in the summer upon his father's farm made a cheap kind of slippers in the winter, and he offered to instruct young Whittier in the art. The offer was gladly accepted, and, as it was the simplest kind of sandal that was to be made, the mystery of the trade was soon acquired. The retail price of the slippers was only twenty-five cents a pair, and he received but eight cents a pair for his work; and yet during the winter of 1826–27 enough was earned to pay the expense of a term of six months at the academy. He calculated so closely every item of expense that he knew before the beginning of the term that he would have twenty-five cents to spare at its close, and he actually had this sum of money in his pocket when his half year of study was over. It was the rule of his whole life never to buy anything until he had the money in hand to pay for it, and although his income was small and uncertain until past middle life, he was never in debt.

James F. Otis, a nephew of Harrison Gray Otis, while reading law in the office of Hon. Nathan Crosby, in 1827, found in a newspaper a piece of poetry which he was told was written by a shoemaker in Haverhill, and he wished to go and find him. Upon his return, he told Mr. Crosby that he found a young man by the name of Whittier, at work in his shoe-shop, and making himself known to him, they spent the day together in wandering over the hills, and on the shores of the

Merrimac, in conversation on literary matters.
Otis, who was himself a poet, afterward became
an intimate friend of Whittier, and accompanied
him to Philadelphia, as a delegate to the anti-
slavery convention of 1833. Later, Otis went
South, and became an apologist for slavery.

On the first day of May, 1827, Whittier began
his "higher education" at the Haverhill Academy,
and the event was signalized in a way that gave
him a reputation at once. It was the first term
of a new academy, for which a fine brick building
had just been completed. The institution was
formally opened on the 30th of April, and the
dedicatory oration was delivered by the Hon.
Leverett Saltonstall, of Salem. The programme
announced that an ode was to be sung, "composed
for the occasion by John G. Whittier, of this
town." The principal of the new school was
Oliver Carlton. The fact that a young citizen of
the town, who was to be a student in the school,
had written the ode for an important public ceremony gave him a certain social and literary distinction at the start. He studied the ordinary
English branches, and also took lessons in French.
He took especial delight in the access he obtained
to the best private libraries in the village.[1]

One can imagine the surprise and pleasure of
such a mind as his when great fields of literature

---

[1] At the dedication of the Haverhill Library, in 1875, Mr.
Whittier wrote to Mayor Currier: "When my old friend James
Gale set up his circulating library, it was the opening of a new
world of enjoyment to me. I can still remember the feeling of
mingled awe and pleasure with which I gazed for the first time
on his crowded bookshelves."

hitherto closed to him were thrown open. He was
in the prime of his young manhood when he took
his first plunge into the glorious Shakespearian
flood. While reveling in the poetry of the great
masters, in the adventures of travelers, in the history of nations, and in the wit and satire of Sterne
and Swift, he neither neglected his studies, nor
omitted frequently to try his own wings in song.
These first six months of academy life were full
of intense activity. He had written in 1825
and 1826 about a dozen poems, which are extant,
although some of them were never printed. In
1827, there were published, in the Haverhill
" Gazette " alone, forty-seven of his poems, and
forty-nine in 1828. As he found these copied by
other papers, he occasionally sent his work to the
Boston " Statesman," edited by Nathaniel Greene,
a kinsman of his, and to the " National Philanthropist," edited by Garrison after he gave up the
" Free Press." He used a variety of signatures,
a favorite one being " Adrian ; " when he wrote
in the Scottish dialect he took the name of " Don-
ald ; " and still further to conceal his identity he
occasionally signed his poems " Timothy," " Mi-
cajah," and " Ichabod." All not signed with
either of these names had the letter " W." for signature. The first poem that appeared with his
full name was a long one, entitled " The Outlaw,"
printed in the " Gazette," October 28, 1828.
Nearly all have dates indicating the year and the
month of their composition. There were ten
poems written in the two months before he entered
the academy, besides the ode sung at the dedication. Of this ode no copy has been found.

On the 8th of November, 1828, the "Gazette" had a prose article by Whittier on Robert Burns. The next week he contributed an article on "Temperance." Mr. Thayer was one of the first editors in the country to publish regularly articles on this theme, and he secured the ill-will of the dealers in, and distillers of, intoxicants by his plain speaking. He was also justice of the peace, and had a hand in disciplining the "rummies." Mr. Whittier assisted him in this warfare upon the saloons, and after Mr. Thayer removed to Philadelphia, Whittier wrote to him February 16, 1836 : "Esquire Parker wishes me to remember him to thee. We have been lamenting over thy departure, and wishing it were possible for thee to sit once more in judgment over the rascals that are now ' unwhipped of justice.' Parker wishes me to tell thee, that as the only way of keeping the streets clear of the ' rum-'uns,' he has lately sent them off by the baker's dozen to Ipswich."

One year later he had the satisfaction of writing from Amesbury, whither he had meantime removed, " I have one item of good news from Haverhill. The old distillery has had its fires quenched at last. C. has sold out, and the building is to be converted into stores."

While attending the academy he boarded, according to promise, in the family of Mr. Thayer, who proved to be a valuable friend and adviser, not only at that time but in later years. In a letter to Mr. Thayer's son,[1] written in 1877, he says: " I never think of thy mother without feelings of

[1] Professor James B. Thayer, of the Harvard Law School.

love and gratitude. She and thy father were my
best friends in the hard struggle of my schooldays."   Every Friday night he walked to East
Haverhill, spent the Sabbath at the old homestead,
and delighted the hearts of his family with his
companionship and his reports of school life.
Mrs. Thayer, in her reminiscences of the poet[1] as
he appeared in those days, said she remembered
his handsome face and figure, and the appearance
of extreme neatness he always bore; but she had
more to say of the liveliness of his temper, his
ready wit, his perfect courtesy, and infallible sense
of truth and justice.   On account of his abilities
and his exemplary conduct, no less than on account
of his reputation as a rising poet, his society was
much sought after.   Whenever he came to Haverhill, in after years, he made his home with
the Thayers, until they removed to Philadelphia,
where Mr. Thayer set up a new paper.   When
Mr. Whittier went to Philadelphia, he again became an inmate of their house.

The late Mrs. Harriet Minot Pitman, a daughter
of Judge Minot, an intimate and lifelong friend
and correspondent of Mr. Whittier, wrote the following sketch of his personal appearance and manners in his youth : [2] —

" He was nearly nineteen years old when I first
saw him. He was a very handsome, distinguished-
looking young man. His eyes were remarkably
beautiful. He was tall, slight, and very erect; a
bashful youth, but *never awkward*, my mother

---

[1] Underwood's *Life*, p. 73.
[2] Underwood's *Life*, pp. 75–77.

said, who was a better judge than I of such matters. There were pupils at the academy of all
ages, from ten to twenty-five. My brother, George
Minot, then about ten years old, used to say that
Whittier was the best of all the big fellows, and
he was in the habit of calling him ' Uncle Toby.'
Whittier was always kind to children, and under
a very grave and quiet exterior there was a real
love of fun, and a keen sense of the ludicrous. In
society he was embarrassed, and his manners were,
in consequence, sometimes brusque and cold.
With intimate friends he talked a great deal, and
in a wonderfully interesting manner ; usually earnest, often analytical, and frequently playful. He
had a great deal of wit. It was a family characteristic. The study of human nature was very
interesting to him, and his insight was keen. He
liked to draw out his young friends, and to suggest
puzzling doubts and queries. When a wrong was
to be righted, or an evil to be remedied, he was
readier to act than any young man I ever knew,
and was very wise in his action, — shrewd, sensible, practical. The influence of his Quaker bring-
ing-up was manifest. I think it was always his
endeavor

> ' to render less
> The sum of human wretchedness.'

This, I say, was his steadfast endeavor, in spite
of an inborn love of teasing. He was very modest,
never conceited, never egotistic. One could never
flatter him. I never tried, but I have seen people
attempt it, and it was a signal failure. He did
not flatter, but told very wholesome and unpala-

table truths, yet in a way to spare one's self-love
by admitting a doubt whether he was in earnest or
in jest. The great questions of Calvinism were subjects of which he often talked in those early days.
He was exceedingly conscientious. He cared for
people, — quite as much for the plainest and most
uncultivated, if they were original and had something in them, as for the most polished. He was
much interested in politics, and thoroughly posted.
I remember, in one of his first calls at our house,
being surprised at his conversation with my father
upon Governor Gerry and the Gerrymandering of
the State, or the attempt to do it, of which I had
until then been wholly ignorant. He had a reten-
tive memory, and a marvelous store of information
on many subjects. I once saw a little commonplace book of his, — full of quaint things, and as
interesting as Southey's."

In a letter written a dozen years after this date,
Whittier refers to himself at this period in the
following terms : —

" For myself, I owe much to the kind encouragement of female friends. A bashful, ignorant
boy, I was favored by the kindness of a lady who
saw, or thought she saw, beneath the clownish
exterior something which gave promise of intellect and worth. The powers of my own mind, the
mysteries of my own spirit, were revealed to myself, only as they were called out by one of those
dangerous relations called cousins, who, with all
her boarding-school glories upon her, condescended
to smile upon my rustic simplicity. She was so
learned in the to me more than occult mysteries

of verbs and nouns, and philosophy, and botany, and mineralogy, and French, and all that, and then she had seen something of society, and could talk (an accomplishment at that time to which I could lay no claim), that on the whole I looked upon her as a being to obtain whose good opinion no effort could be too great. I smile at this sometimes, — this feeling of my unsophisticated boyhood, — yet to a great degree it is still with me."

In January, 1828, Mr. Thayer issued the prospectus of a book to be published by subscription, from which we make this extract : —

" THE POEMS OF ADRIAN. — Many of the poems now proposed to be published originally appeared in the 'Essex Gazette,' and were very favorably received by its readers. Some of them have been copied into the most respectable papers, in various sections of the Union, with strong expressions of approbation. When the circumstances under which these poems were written are known, they will be particularly interesting. The author (a native of this town) is a young man, about nineteen years of age, who has had, until very recently, no other means of education than are afforded in a common district school, and such as he improved in the *leisure hours* of an apprenticeship to a mechanical business. It is believed by his friends that these poems indicate genius of a high order, which deserves all possible culture. The design of thus offering his juvenile writings to the public is to raise money to assist him in obtaining a classical education. He is a worthy member of the

Society of Friends, and it is hoped that from them the volume will receive a liberal patronage."

The proposed volume was to be printed on superfine paper, to contain about two hundred pages, and be done up in boards, at the price of seventy-five cents. For some reason, this enterprise was not carried out by Mr. Thayer. During his second term in the academy, Mr. Whittier made considerable progress in compiling a history of the town of Haverhill, but when he was called away to Boston in the fall of 1828, he gave the materials he had collected to Mr. B. L. Mirick, who completed the work, and it was published by Mr. Thayer in 1831.

The Carrier's New Year's Address of the "Gazette," for 1828, was written by Mr. Whittier, as was also that for 1829, which he sent from Boston. The year's doings in the town are recounted in a lively way in each of these poems. There was a fire in the village in 1827, which called out several amusing stanzas, of which one is given below, and also one about the ghost that was troubling the East Parish. A note gives the information that many years previously a ghost was sent in "quest of wretches," and ordered to traverse the space between Country Bridge and the residence of Black Peter, and it was grimly added that "the ghost is still doing duty:" —

> " The old dumbetty engine poised on high
>   Wet all around, but kindly spared the fire ;
>   And strangers, dripping as they hurried by,
>   Cursed the old wreck, and bade them push it nigher ;
>   For, like the gun that honest Paddy bore,
>   It carried all behind it — and before !
>
> .   .   .   .

"Shad Parish still continues much the same ;
The unwearied ghost still watches Country Bridge,
Or walks with clattering teeth and eyes of flame
From his old station up to Peter's Ridge ;
Nay, smile not, reader, but as truth receive it. —
Shad Parish women to a man believe it ! "

Mr. Whittier wrote a series of prose articles on War, which were published in the "Gazette" in 1828. His poems began to be plagiarized in the same year. In February, 1828, the Philadelphia "Saturday Evening Post" apologized for an instance of this kind, by which it was hoaxed.

This anecdote, in which reference is made to the "Country Bridge ghost," is told by Rebecca I. Davis, author of "Reminiscences of Merrimac Valley," as part of a conversation she had with Whittier in 1884. She had told him of a recent visit to his birthplace, and spoke of "Peter's Ridge" (mentioned in "The Countess") and "Country Bridge," and his eye caught some of its youthful fire, she says, as he laughingly related an incident of his boyhood days in connection with the haunted bridge, where it is said the "unwearied ghost still watches."

"I remember," he said, "when a small boy, of being extremely startled by a woman coming to our house in the evening in great fright, saying she had seen a headless ghost as she came by Country Bridge, which fact caused several of us lads to go one moonlight night, myself promising to run upon the bridge, and call for the headless ghost. Never shall I forget how my courage failed when in sight, but true to my promise, I ran, and shouted for the ghost to come forth, and immediately ran from the scene with all my might."

A reminiscence of the same period, pertaining
to the witchcraft fancies of the time, occurs in a
letter by Mr. Whittier, in 1883, to his old school-
mate, Mr. C. C. Chase : —

"It was old Mrs. C——, wife of Moses C——,
of Rocks Village, a brother of Uncle Aaron's father,
who lived at Corliss Hill, whose relatives believed
her a witch, and one of her nieces knocked her
down in the shape of a persistent bug that troubled
her, and at the same time the old woman fell and
hurt her head!   Old Aunt Morse, on one occasion,
went before Squire Ladd, the old blacksmith and
justice of the peace at the Rocks, and took her
oath that she was not a witch!   I visited the site
of our old schoolhouse a year ago.   I thought of
Ossian's lament, ' I passed by the walls of Bal-
clutha and found them desolate ; the fox looked
out of the window.'   Not a fox, but a striped
squirrel sat on the wall, and watched me as I pon-
dered on old days."

Whittier's first and only experience as a school-
master was in the winter of 1827–28.   He took
a school in the Birch Meadow district, in West
Amesbury, now Merrimac, and earned enough to
pay for another term at the academy.   He went
to be examined as to his qualifications for teaching
with many misgivings ; but the committee asked
only for a specimen of his handwriting.   He had
no reason to be ashamed of this, for his penman-
ship, modeled upon the style prevailing during the
previous century, was neat and regular.   His principal trouble as a pedagogue was with the mathe-
matical puzzles the large boys would bring him for

solution. A failure to solve these was a disgrace to a teacher in those days. As a descendant of the Greenleafs he inherited some facility with figures; but the problems handed him by the mischievous young men among his scholars cost him many a sleepless night. He wrote several poems during this winter, one of which, never published, was a rhymed epistle to the editor of the Haverhill "Gazette." It has been preserved by his daughter, Sarah S. Thayer, and is here given: —

[WEST] AMESBURY, February 15, 1828.

FRIEND THAYER:

> The troubles of a pedagogue
> Nae mair my wanderin' muse shall clog;
> The management of fool and rogue
>   Is fairly done with,
> An' I can rhyme the same auld jog
>   My muse begun with.
>
> Last night the Rev. Mr. Eaton
> My Pandemonium took a seat in,
> With half a dozen mair completin'
>   The school committee,
> With questions hard my rabble treatin',
>   Devoid of pity.
>
> It turned out weel enough, however;
> My scholars answered pretty clever,
> And baffled somehow each endeavor
>   To prove them fools,
> And for the full time really never
>   Transgressed my rules.
>
> I thank'd them for 't. I wish you could
> Have heard my speech — 't was really good.
> I said they had the gratitude
>   Of friends an' tutor,
> And then advised them how they should
>   Behave in future.

No parson's sermon e'er was graver,
It had the very pulpit flavor,
Yet with the unction and the savor
    Of my entreating
Was doubtless something of the quaver
    Of Monthly Meeting.

This scrawl by Nathan Chase I send it,
In haste as thou may see I penned it ;
To write a lengthy song or mend it,
    I have no leisure.
To see thee soon I sure intend it,
    With greatest pleasure.

.   .   .   .

If you have got the " Rustics " done,
By Nathan please to sen' me one,
And I will try my hand upon
    A short review,[1]
Before the critics have begun
    To search it through.

But Nathan on his old gray mare
Sits waiting — I've no time to spare —
My best respects to Mrs. Thayer,
    An' all who trouble you
With any question, how may fare
    Their young friend,
                        " W."

In the edition of the poems of Robert Dinsmoor, there is a poem addressed to the author by John G. Whittier which is not included in his complete works. It was the first poem of his to appear in any book. This stanza of it sounds like the premonitory call of the " Voices of Freedom : " —

---

[1] This review of a volume of poems by Robert Dinsmoor, of Windham, N. H., known as the "Rustic Bard," may be found, with some additions, in Mr. Whittier's Prose Works, vol. ii. pp. 245–260. The poems were printed at the office of the Haverhill *Gazette,* during the winter of 1827-28.

"Shall vice an' crime that taint the nation,
        Pass on unheeded ?
No ! let the muse her trumpet take
'Til auld offenders learn to shake,
An' tremble when they hear her wake
        Her tones of thunder ;
'Til pride an' bloated ignorance quake,
        An' gawkies wonder."

Mr. Whittier returned to the academy in the spring of 1828, and after six months of study his schooldays were ended. He had partially defrayed the expenses of his last term at the academy by posting the ledgers of a Haverhill merchant.

It was during his schooldays that Whittier wrote " The Song of the Vermonters, 1779," and some years after sent it anonymously to J. T. Buckingham, who published it in the " New England Magazine " in 1833. As it was not a " Quakerly " poem, its author never claimed it as his, and it was a surprise to him when, nearly sixty years after it was written, it appeared with his name attached to it. In the long meantime it had been extensively copied, and in some cases credited to Ethan Allen. In March, 1887, there was controversy about the authorship, and Mr. Whittier wrote this letter to the Boston " Transcript : " —

" ' The Song of the Vermonters, by Ethan Allen,' was a piece of boyish mystification, written sixty years ago and printed anonymously. The only person who knew its authorship was my old friend Joseph T. Buckingham, and I supposed the secret died with him. We were both amused to find it regarded by antiquarian authorities as a

genuine relic of the old time.   How the secret was
discovered, a few years ago, I have never known.
I have never intentionally written anything in
favor of war, but a great deal against it."

THE SONG OF THE VERMONTERS, 1779.

Ho — all to the borders!   Vermonters, come down,
With your breeches of deerskin and jackets of brown;
With your red woolen caps, and your moccasins, come,
To the gathering summons of trumpet and drum.

Come down with your rifles!   Let gray wolf and fox
Howl on in the shade of their primitive rocks;
Let the bear feed securely from pig-pen and stall;
Here's two-legged game for your powder and ball.

On our south come the Dutchmen, enveloped in grease;
And arming for battle while canting of peace ;
On our east, crafty Meshech has gathered his band
To hang up our leaders and eat up our land.

Ho — all to the rescue!   For Satan shall work
No gain for his legions of Hampshire and York!
They claim our possessions — the pitiful knaves —
The tribute we pay shall be prisons and graves !

Let Clinton and Ten Broek, with bribes in their hands,
Still seek to divide and parcel our lands ;
We've coats for our traitors, whoever they are ;
The warp is of feathers — the filling of tar :

Does the " old Bay State " threaten ?   Does Congress com-
    plain ?
Swarms Hampshire in arms on our borders again ?
Bark the war-dogs of Britain aloud on the lake —
Let 'em come ; what they can they are welcome to take.

What seek they among us ?   The pride of our wealth
Is comfort, contentment, and labor, and health,
And lands which, as Freemen, we only have trod,
Independent of all, save the mercies of God.

Yet we owe no allegiance, we bow to no throne,
Our ruler is law, and the law is our own;
Our leaders themselves are our own fellow-men,
Who can handle the sword, or the scythe, or the pen.

Our wives are all true, and our daughters are fair,
With their blue eyes of smiles and their light flowing hair,
All brisk at their wheels till the dark even-fall,
Then blithe at the sleigh-ride, the husking, and ball!

We 've sheep on the hillsides, we 've cows on the plain,
And gay-tasseled corn-fields and rank-growing grain;
There are deer on the mountains, and wood-pigeons fly
From the crack of our muskets, like clouds on the sky.

And there 's fish in our streamlets and rivers which take
Their course from the hills to our broad-bosomed lake;
Through rock-arched Winooski the salmon leaps free,
And the portly shad follows all fresh from the sea.

Like a sunbeam the pickerel glides through the pool,
And the spotted trout sleeps where the water is cool,
Or darts from his shelter of rock and of root
At the beaver's quick plunge, or the angler's pursuit.

And ours are the mountains, which awfully rise,
Till they rest their green heads on the blue of the skies;
And ours are the forests unwasted, unshorn,
Save where the wild path of the tempest is torn.

And though savage and wild be this climate of ours,
And brief be our season of fruits and of flowers,
Far dearer the blast round our mountains which raves
Than the sweet summer zephyr which breathes over slaves!

Hurrah for Vermont! For the land which we till
Must have sons to defend her from valley and hill;
Leave the harvest to rot on the fields where it grows,
And the reaping of wheat for the reaping of foes.

From far Michiscom's wild valley, to where
Poosoonsuck steals down from his wood-circled lair,
From Shocticook River to Lutterlock town —
Ho — all to the rescue! Vermonters, come down!

Come York or come Hampshire, come traitors or knaves,
If ye rule o'er our land, ye shall rule o'er our graves;
Our vow is recorded — our banner unfurled,
In the name of Vermont we defy all the world!

While Whittier was at the academy, his friend
Garrison was in Boston, editing the "Philanthropist," a weekly paper devoted mainly to the cause
of temperance, and published by William and
William R. Collier. It was the first temperance
paper ever published. The young agitator did not
find in this occupation so wide a field of usefulness
as he wished; there were other reforms he desired
to advocate that his publishers did not favor. He
thought of his Haverhill friend, and procured for
him the offer of the editorship of the "Philanthropist." This offer came to Whittier while he
was anxiously considering the question of a profession. In the following letter he asked the advice of a friend he had learned to trust : —

SHAD PARISH, 28th of 11th mo., 1828.

FRIEND A. W. THAYER, — I have been in a quan-
dary ever since I left thee, whether I had better
accept the offer of Friend Collier, or *nail* myself
down to my seat, — for, verily, I could not be kept
there otherwise, — and toil for the honorable and
truly gratifying distinction of being considered " a
good cobbler." . . . No — no — friend, it won't
do. Thee might as well catch a weasel asleep, or
the Old Enemy of Mankind in a parsonage-house,
as find me contented with that distinction.

I have renounced college for the good reason
that I have no disposition to humble myself to
meanness for an education — crowding myself

through college upon the charities of others, and leaving it with a debt or an obligation to weigh down my spirit like an incubus, and paralyze every exertion. The professions are already crowded full to overflowing; and I, forsooth, because I have a miserable knack of rhyming, must swell the already enormous number, struggle awhile with debt and difficulties, and then, weary of life, go down to my original insignificance, where the tinsel of classical honors will but aggravate my misfortune. Verily, friend Thayer, the picture is a dark one — but from my heart I believe it to be true. What, then, remains for me? School-keeping — out upon it! The memory of last year's experience comes up before me like a horrible dream. No, I had rather be a tin-peddler, and drive around the country with a bunch of sheepskins hanging to my wagon. I had rather hawk essences from dwelling to dwelling, or practice physic between Colly Hill[1] and Country Bridge [the most sparsely settled portion of the East Parish].

Seriously — the situation of editor of the "Philanthropist" is not only respectable, but it is peculiarly pleasant to one who takes so deep an interest, as I really do, in the great cause it is laboring to promote. I would enter upon my task with a heart free from misanthropy, and glowing with that feeling that wishes well to all. I would rather have the memory of a Howard, a Wilberforce, and a Clarkson than the undying fame of Byron.

I may be wrong, but I confess I cannot see the

---

[1] " Corliss Hill " was usually called " Colly Hill " by those living in the neighborhood.

why and wherefore. I have written to friend Collier, but have entered into no engagement. Will
you be kind enough to send by Chase the " Philanthropist " of to-day ? I prepared the piece on card-
playing for the " Gazette," but I own I was afraid
of having my wig pulled, and so sent it to Boston.[1]
I should like to see or hear from Mr. Carlton [the
principal of the academy] before I do anything.
He is one of the best men — to use a phrase of *my
craft* — " that ever trod shoe leather."

If I had not written something about him, I
would wish you to let Mr. Carlton see this. He
will see my reasons — some of them, I mean — for
they are " plenty as blackberries."

A poem entitled " To the Merrimack," written
by Whittier, was published in the " Philanthropist "
of June 6, 1828. A few lines of introduction by
Garrison commend these verses, and call for original poems from other sources, with the proviso,
" This invitation is meant for poets only."

Thus ended his schooldays, but this was only
the beginning of his student life. By wide and
well-chosen reading, he was constantly adding to
his stores of information. While reveling in the
fields of English literature, he became familiar
through translations with ancient and current literature of other nations, and kept abreast of all
political and reformatory movements.

[1] A short prose sketch, entitled " The Gamester," which was
published in the *Philanthropist*, November 28, 1828, is here referred to.

CHAPTER III.

1828–1832.

MR. WHITTIER decided to enter the printing-office of the Colliers, and in December, 1828, we find him in Boston, a member of the household of Rev. Mr. Collier, a Baptist clergyman, the senior partner of the publishing firm. The Colliers, father and son, published two weekly papers and a monthly magazine. One of the weeklies was the "American Manufacturer," a political journal, friendly to Henry Clay. The monthly was the "Baptist Preacher." The partisan politics of the "Manufacturer" suited Mr. Whittier as well as did the cause represented by the "Philanthropist," and it was the Henry Clay paper that bore his name at the head of its editorial columns, on the 1st of January, 1829. The new editor began a spirited discussion of the tariff question, favoring duties to protect American industries, and also wrote sketches and poems for each number of his paper. It was a temperance poem with which he led off, entitled "Take Back the Bowl." This is the first stanza : —

> "Take back the bowl! I will not seal
> The hallowed memories of the past;
> They add no pangs to those I feel,
> Nor shadows on the future cast.

Aye, take it back! let others bring
    Oblivion o'er the haunted soul;
My memory is a blessed thing —
    Away! away! take back the bowl."

Nearly every number of the "Manufacturer" contained a poem by its editor, but scarcely any of them were considered by him worth preserving, even when he made his first collection of poems; and yet they were widely copied and gave him a constantly increasing reputation as a poet. In April, 1829, he began a series of satirical political poems, under the title of "Tariffiana." It was soon after this he wrote the poetical tribute to Henry Clay, which was recited by the partisans of that statesman throughout the country in each campaign when the gallant "Harry of the West" was a candidate.[1] About ten years ago, the editor of a literary journal asked permission to republish this poem as a literary curiosity. Mr. Whittier's reply was: "I have looked over the Henry Clay ballad, and have come to the conclusion that the least said about it the better. . . . It strikes me as grandiloquent and highfalutin." He was not ashamed in his later years of his youthful enthusiasm for Clay, but thought that he was in his day

---

[1] This poem was written for the Cincinnati *American*, and the date of its composition was 4th mo. 17, 1830, while he was at his home in Haverhill. In a note to the editor he says: "The perusal of an article from your paper has prompted the following feeble tribute to the services and merits of the Western statesman." It was copied into nearly all the papers of the party in the Union. The enemies of Clay had made vigorous assertion that he had been guilty of "bargain and corruption" in taking a place in the cabinet of J. Q. Adams, whose election he had secured by his influence in the House of Representatives.

much overrated. His influence was not so permanent as that of Calhoun, whom he considered the most powerful intellect of his period.

While Whittier was editing the "Manufacturer," the question of the tariff was complicated with that of the personal fitness of General Jackson for the Presidency. It is not surprising that the young Quaker non-resistant should fall in with the general feeling of his State, at that time, that it was unsafe to intrust to a warrior the destinies of a country that more than anything else needed years of peace for its growth and development. The mills of Massachusetts, from which much — and as it has proved not too much — was expected, were just beginning to be anxious for the success of the policy of the brilliant Kentuckian. Previous to 1828, all New England opposed the plan of developing American industries, to which Clay had converted the West and a part of the South. Webster opposed it for a while with all his massive strength, fearing it might put restraint upon the commerce of New England. Of the great men of that period, Clay alone had favored this policy from first to last, so that his name was thoroughly identified with it. When Clay was a candidate for the Presidency against Jackson, in 1832, Massachusetts was one of the few States that supported him, and by his earnest advocacy Whittier won political popularity, which was then as pleasing to him as literary reputation.

In a letter to Mr. A. W. Thayer, Mr. Whittier says under date 2d mo. 6, 1829: "The 'Manufacturer' goes down well, thanks to the gullibility of the public, and we are doing well, very well. Have had one or two rubs from other papers, but I have had some compliments which were quite as much as my vanity could swallow. Have tolerable good society, Mrs. Hale and her literary club, etc. I am coming out for the tariff by and by — have done something at it already — but the *astonisher* is yet to come! Shall blow Cambreling and McDuffie sky-high."

When Garrison gave up his paper at Bennington, Vt., and went to Baltimore in company with Benjamin Lundy, Whittier said of him : " A bolder pen never portrayed the evils of slavery, and a better or kinder heart never throbbed with sympathy for the sufferings of humanity." At another time he wrote to Garrison : " I admire your plan of directing your efforts against those fearful evils, slavery, intemperance, and war. Heart and hand I unite with you in denouncing them. It shall be my endeavor to merit that name which I consider of all others the most worthy of our ambition, — the friend of man."

The following anecdote, as told by Mr. Whittier, illustrates this part of his career : Rev. Mr. Collier used to travel through the State canvassing for subscribers to his " Baptist Preacher," leaving his son William in charge of the office. Each number of the magazine contained a sermon by some eminent Baptist divine. On one occasion, when the old clergyman was away, no sermon was left for copy, and the day of publication of the " Preacher " was perilously near. William proposed to young Whittier to write a sermon in place of the one that had failed to arrive. At this period of his life, Mr. Whittier said he felt more confident than he ever had since that he could do anything, from the writing of a sermon to the conducting of a political campaign. So the young Quaker readily undertook to fill the columns set apart for the great divines of that day, young Collier promising to lend his valuable assistance. The sermon was actually written and partly in type when the old gentleman returned, and a discourse under which a congregation had actually slept took the place of Mr. Whittier's effort. It is easy to believe that this first and only sermon of the young poet was more than worthy of the space it came so near occupying, for it was a serious essay, and no burlesque.

It was during his employment in this office that he first met Charles Sumner. An anti-Masonic journal, in which Sheriff Sumner was interested, was for a time printed in the office of the "Manufacturer." One day the sheriff's son, Charles, came in with the copy. He was then a student at Harvard, seventeen years of age, a tall, slender, graceful youth. Whether the copy he brought was written by himself, or sent by his father, Mr. Whittier did not recall, but he had a vivid remembrance of the young man who in twenty years was to become one of his most intimate friends.

He remained in this Boston printing-office until August, 1829, when he was called home by the failing health of his father, and the necessity of caring for the farm. Of his meagre salary of nine dollars a week he saved about one half, and this went toward freeing the farm from the incumbrance of the mortgage. His residence in Boston had given him access to large libraries, an opportunity he improved to the utmost. He wrote several poems during these few months that were widely copied. "The Sicilian Vespers," "The Earthquake," and "The Spirit of the North" belong to this period.

Soon after he gave up the editorship of the "Manufacturer," he wrote from Haverhill to a friend in New York, who had been a fellow-boarder at the Colliers', and who had expressed surprise at his giving up the paper: "Why should you be surprised? You know what kind of a concern it was ; you know, if I mistake not, my dissatisfaction." From this it would appear that he had other reasons beside the illness of his father for resigning his first editorship.[1] We find hints in

---

[1] In the same letter, he makes this reference to his former room-mate, Garrison: "Have you seen Garrison's Baltimore paper, the *Genius of Universal Emancipation?* I had a letter from him the other day; he says he has been in low spirits ever since he left Boston ; says he is home-sick, and what is worse, *love-sick*, which last sickness he justly supposes will be immortal. . . . I have become a notable fellow in gallantry of late; I mean old-fashioned gallantry, however. I have given my whiskers a more ferocious appearance, and take the liberty of frightening into good nature those who will not be complaisant of their own accord." His correspondent, more than thirty years after, sent him this old letter, and received the following comment upon it, dated Amesbury, 1st mo. 2, 1860: "I was about as much surprised to read that old letter of my boyhood as if I had seen the ghost of my former self. It was a very absurd and ridiculous epistle, — and the utter folly of it is more striking from the fact that at that very time I was in reality a shy, timid

other letters of this period that he had to contend with jealousy and detraction in the office of his employers.

Whittier remained in Haverhill until his father's death, in June, 1830, spending all his spare hours in study, and in preparing contributions in prose and verse for various periodicals. For the first six months of 1830 he edited the Haverhill " Gazette," doing most of his work upon this paper at home, three miles away from the office of publication. He also contributed poems and political essays to the " New England Review," of Hartford, Conn., a political paper then edited by George D. Prentice. Mr. Whittier's ambition at this time had taken a political turn, and his studies were in that direction. Mr. Prentice was much pleased with the contributions he received from the young Quaker on the Haverhill farm, and a friendly correspondence sprang up between them. The only letter that is preserved of this correspondence is one from Prentice, written January 2, 1830. He was at a hotel in Providence, enjoying a short respite from his editorial work. The letter, which is a long one, is frolicsome in its tone, and gives the impression that he and his correspondent were intimate friends. And yet they had never met. If Prentice had been better acquainted with the Quaker lad he was addressing, he would hardly have written the first paragraph here quoted : —

recluse, afraid of a shadow, especially the shadow of a woman. There is a period in life — a sort of tadpole state, between the boy and the man — when any sort of pretense, egotism, and self-conceit may be expected."

" Whittier, I wish you were seated by my side, for I assure you that my situation, just now, is very much to my particular satisfaction. Here am I in my hotel, with a good-natured fire in front of me, and a bottle of champagne at my left hand. Can you imagine a situation more to a good fellow's mind? . . . Then you have more imagination than judgment. . . . The gods be praised that I am not a member of the temperance society!

" Would to fortune I could come to Haverhill, before my return to Hartford — but the thing is impossible. I am running short both of time and money. Well, we can live on and love, as we have done. Once or twice I have even thought that my feelings towards you had more of romance in them than they possibly could have if we were acquainted with each other. I never yet met for the first time with a person whose name I had learned to revere, without feeling on the instant that the beautiful veil with which my imagination had robed him was partially rent away. If you cannot explain this matter, you are no philosopher."

It would be easy to quote a great many complimentary newspaper comments on Whittier's poetry appearing from week to week, as when the " New England Review" copied some lines from " The Minstrel Girl," a poem not thought worthy of being published in any, not even in the first, of Whittier's collections of verse, with the sweeping statement, " We do not know that we have ever seen the following description of sunset equaled." The wonder is that such a reputation as he was certainly acquiring should have grown out of a

series of poems that so soon sank into oblivion.
For about five years, say from 1827 to 1832, Whittier was writing and publishing a poem almost
every week, scarcely twenty of which are now extant. They are to be found only in the files of the
several papers in which they first appeared, or into
which they were copied. The literary fame so
freely promised for him has indeed crowned his
work, but it is not based on anything then accomplished.

As the elder Whittier's failing health had called
the young editor away from his office, so now the
death of his father left him free to resume his
occupation, and the acquaintance which he had
formed with Prentice led to a new opening. Prentice had been asked by Henry Clay to come to
Lexington, Ky., and write his biography, in antici-
pation of a nomination for the Presidency in 1832.
The "New England Review," which Prentice
edited, was owned by leading politicians of Connecticut, of the party favorable to Clay. When they
learned they were to lose Prentice for a time, they
asked him to recommend some one to fill his place.
His advice to send for Whittier was acted upon.
This call to edit the leading party paper of a State,
with the local politics of which he had no acquaintance, was a great surprise to the young poet;
but it was in the line of his principal ambition,
and he did not hesitate to accept the position.
While connected with the "Manufacturer," he
had come into personal communication with the
principal men of his party in Massachusetts, and
had been making a study of political economy, in

the expectation of taking up political journalism as his life work. He had never received pay for his verses, and had not thought of depending upon poetry for his bread. The salary offered him as editor of the "Review" was about $500 a year. Small as it was, he now saw a prospect, by the practice of strict economy, of wiping out the debt that had incumbered the Haverhill farm. This part of his ambition was soon gratified.

If he was surprised by the offer of this editorship, he was accustomed to say he thought the Connecticut statesmen, who came into the office of the "Review" to see the new editor, were equally surprised to find at the desk that had been occupied by the genteel and spirited Prentice a shy lad, in homespun clothes of Quaker cut, straight from a Massachusetts farm. He must at first glance have appeared out of place in the editorial chair of their State paper, in the midst of a fierce political campaign, and as the successor of one of the most trenchant and dashing editors America had produced. Among his intimates, Whittier was always a ready and sprightly talker, but among strangers he held his peace. His bright eyes, and the quick intelligence of his handsome face, must have speedily reassured those interested in the paper he was to edit. They saw that his homely Quaker clothes covered a youth of good parts, honest, earnest, intelligent, and ambitious. By listening to the talk of the party leaders who made his office their rendezvous, he soon mastered the shibboleth of local politics, and gave good satisfaction.

It would be difficult to find two men more entirely

unlike than were Prentice and Whittier. Prentice delighted in giving pain with his caustic pen, and he used his great power of satire with reckless disregard of the feelings of his opponents. Whittier was a man of the sweetest nature, kind and courteous, but of the truest courage. He was content to disarm an antagonist without drawing a drop of his blood. They had each achieved some distinction as writers of both prose and verse. Prentice was five years the senior, and is now best remembered as the witty and slashing editor of the Louisville, Ky., "Journal." He did not come back to Connecticut as he had expected. In his editorial of farewell Prentice said of his successor : —

" I cannot do less than congratulate my readers on the prospect of their more familiar acquaintance with a gentleman of such powerful energies, and such exalted purity and sweetness of character. I have made some enemies among those whose good opinion I value, but no rational man can ever be the enemy of Mr. Whittier."

An intimate friend of the poet contributes to this memoir the following report of a conversation she once had with Mr. Whittier about his acceptance of the editorship of the Hartford paper : —

George D. Prentice, he said, had been writing letters to his own paper, purporting to come from the " Man in the Moon." After a while they were discontinued for several weeks, and then one appeared which Whittier thought was from a different hand ; so he tried one himself and sent it on, hardly expecting ever to hear from it again ;

but in course of time back it came to him in print,
with a letter from Prentice saying he would like
to hear from him again.   It was upon this letter
that he first saw himself called " Mr."   After a
while there came another letter — he did not have
many letters then — saying Mr. Prentice was to
be gone six months and would like to have him
take charge of the paper during his absence.   He
told his mother, but no one else, thinking they
would laugh at him.   His father had recently
died, and he felt he was needed at home.   He lay
awake all night, and finally concluded he would
go.   Being asked how he could know in the least
what to do, he said he did not — he knew nothing
about it — but took care to conceal his ignorance.
When he was going to write on any subject he
read up on it.   After he had been in Hartford a
few weeks, he opened one of the exchanges, — the
" Catskill Recorder," he believed, — and there
was a long article headed " John G. Whittier,"
filled with abuse and ridicule of him and his editorship.   It was a terrible blow to him.   He hid the
paper so that his publishers and the people about
the office should not see it, and every once in a while
he would take it out and read it over.   He went
home to his boarding-house, and some of the young
ladies, seeing marks of trouble in his face, asked
him what was the matter; but he did not tell them.
Every paper he opened, he expected to see this copied at full length.   He did not dare say much about
it in his paper, because he did not want his readers
to know what had been said of him.   Finally, he
wrote a letter to the Catskill man, remonstrating

with him; to which an answer came worse than the
original offense, saying that if he was so thin-
skinned as that he would better quit the newspaper business, for it was not a circumstance to
what would happen as time went on. A few days
afterward, the New York " Courier and Enquirer,"
then edited by the Noahs, he thought, and Mr.
James Brooks, came to the office with a flattering
notice, and marked " Please exchange; " this com-
forted him. He thought if a great paper like this
praised him, it was not so much matter about the
little Catskiller. Bryant's paper, the " Evening
Post," followed suit, and some editors asked him
to call on them if he ever came to New York.
Prentice did not return, and he stayed in Hartford eighteen months. There was much dissipation
there. He had been in town but a little while
before they made him a member of a club composed of the young men of the first families, who
did little but drink and carouse. He only went
one night; did not care about such things. He
would not drink with them. During his residence
in Hartford, he once visited New York, and, as
requested, called upon the editors of the " Courier
and Enquirer." Major Noah was in, a large,
portly Jew. " Is this Mr. Whittier ? " " Yes."
" Of the Hartford ' Review ' ? " " Yes." " Ah!
yes, yes, a younger man than I supposed." Mr.
Brooks was ill, so he called at his house and was
very courteously entreated, and went to the club
in the evening — where he saw oysters for the first
time. Did he enjoy it? No, not very much; he was
rather shy and knew scarcely any one. While go-

ing by a theatre one night, he saw a man, too drunk
to stand alone, holding on by the railings of the
steps. As he turned to look at him, the man said,
" Don't thee come in here, Quaker, this is no place
for thee. I will report thee to Friend Jenkins, and
he will turn thee out of the Monthly Meeting."

If he had been disposed to attend places of vain
amusement, his Quaker dress, he found, would have
been a constant protection. He entered heartily
into social life in Hartford, and left a pleasant
memory in many families. In a reminiscent letter
that is published in the " History of Hartford
County," he says : —

"I boarded first at the old Lunt tavern, and
afterward at Jonathan Law's, formerly postmaster
of Hartford. I knew well some of the best people
in the little city, Judge Russ, Hon. Mr. Trumbull,
Hon. Martin Welles, Dr. Todd, Mrs. Sigourney ;
Isaac E. Crary — afterward General Crary, member of Congress from Michigan — and Charles
Emerson, then young lawyers there, wrote for my
paper, as did also F. A. P. Barnard, now president of Columbia College, New York."

The intimacy with Barnard, who was at that
time a teacher in the asylum for the deaf and
dumb, sprang from the fact that both of them
were especially interested in Eastern history and
romance. It was for this reason that " Miriam,"
an Eastern poem, was dedicated to him ; its opening lines refer to the old days at Hartford : —

> " The years are many since, in youth and hope,
> Under the Charter Oak, our horoscope
> We drew thick-studded with all favoring stars."

Mrs. Sigourney was in the height of her popularity as a writer, when Whittier was in Hartford, and of her he says in a letter written long after her death: " I knew Mrs. Sigourney well, when as a boy I came to Hartford. Her kindness to the young rustic stranger I shall never forget." Late in life he wrote these lines for the tablet placed near her pew in Christ Church : —

> " She sang alone, ere womanhood had known
> The gift of song which fills the air to-day:
> Tender and sweet, a music all her own
> May fitly linger where she knelt to pray."

The first two or three weeks of the month of January, 1831, were spent by Mr. Whittier in the city of New York. He was at this time editing the " Review," but there is not a word in his paper referring to this visit, and only an indirect reference after his return to his editorial desk to the fact that he had been absent. All that we know of this episode is found in his correspondence with his friend, Jonathan Law,[1] of Hartford, in whose family he resided for some months while editing the " Review." It was a two days' journey from Hartford to New York, by stage to New Haven, and by steamboat thence to New York. The steamboat was caught in the severest storm known for many years, and the first letter to Mr. Law, written in mid-passage, gives a graphic description of the miseries of the voyage, enlivened with humorous

---

[1] Mr. Law was an educated and scholarly man, familiar with the poets, and Mr. Whittier had occasion to acknowledge great indebtedness to him for his aid. He had a large house and a good library. He was postmaster at Hartford from 1800 to 1829.

comment upon many distressing situations. The letter closes with the enigmatical remark, " Tomorrow I shall be busy; whether for good or ill, I know not. All that men in our situation *can* do shall be done." He was accompanied and assisted by a young lawyer, Mr. Isaac E. Crary.[1] They arrived Saturday, January 1, and on the next day he wrote: —

"I have reached New York at last, and am already surrounded with papers and musty documents. I find not so much difficulty as I anticipated. *The Ghent treaty is safe.* It was not among the missing. My first letter was dated on board the steamboat — that floating pandemonium — that pestilential hospital ship. I shudder even now at the bare thought of it. We spent Friday night on the boat, a few miles below the city. It was almost a sleepless one. We are now sitting in our room, Crary and myself; there is a noble fire in the grate, and we are working away for dear life. We are, in fact, perfect hermits, and we abide by our room as Diogenes did in his tub. . . . We have no news to relate, none in the world; and yet, as I promised to write, I fulfill my engagement. I have seen no one as yet. The editor of the ' Mercantile Advertiser ' has just called on me, in the name of Forrest, the tragedian, of Halleck, Wetmore, and Leggett, of

[1] Crary went to Michigan soon after, and became delegate from the Territory in Congress. He was also member of Congress from Michigan when it became a State, and was largely instrumental in developing the plans by which the grant of the general government for educational purposes became a fund of great and permanent value.

New York, and of Hill, of Boston, to attend a convivial meeting of the *Literati*, this evening. I have declined. I have no idea of soaking my brains in champagne or Madeira, when I have so much use for them. At present I must have a clear lookout, or all may go for the 'Old Harry' instead of our own Harry."

This last sentence and the reference to the Treaty of Ghent indicate that the search was for some part of the record of Henry Clay; and that the results of the search were not encouraging appears in a reference to it, in a passage not here quoted, as an "ugly affair" he would be glad to have off his hands. After a fortnight's work upon this mysterious business, he writes to his Hartford friend, under date of Seventh day evening, 1st mo. 15th : —

" I am yet in the land of the living, and would give half a kingdom to be in your goodly city of Hartford. We have had a wearisome time of it, and the end has not yet come. We have been sick, and given over to the buffeting of the 'Indigo Demons.' Verily, we have seen enough of vexation, enough of agony, spiritual and bodily, to make our very hairs as white as those of Methuselah when a thousand winters had gone over his venerable head. We have ransacked every street; we have turned over the huge folios of every library; we have read, inquired, cogitated, and written and rewritten, until our brains are in a worse state than Ovid's chaos."

The files of the "Review," from July, 1830, to March, 1831, show a large amount of work from

Whittier's own hand, not only in political leaders, but in poems and sketches. There are twenty-three poems signed with his initials, beside several that are probably his, not signed; also, several legends and short stories. In the first number of the paper after he took charge of it, July 19, 1830, appears a poem, "To L. E. L., Author of the Improvisatrice," which was copied in other periodicals during the lifetime of Letitia E. Landon, but which Mr. Whittier never placed in any collection of his works. Another poem, "Christ in the Tempest," was published August 16, 1830. This became familiar to the public in Emerson's "First Class Reader." Of this he wrote to Rev. R. H. Howard, in 1888 : —

"It was for some reason omitted by my publishers; I think because it was not thought valuable in a merely literary point of view. I had not seen it for a long time; but I have just hunted it up, and find it better than many things in my collected poems. The storm on the little lake may have been exaggerated; but as a whole the piece is not altogether unworthy, certainly, so far as the sentiment is concerned."

Here are the first and last stanzas of the poem:

> "Storm on the midnight waters. The vast sky
>   Is stooping with the thunder. Cloud on cloud
>   Reels heavily in the darkness, like a shroud
> Shook by some warning spirit from the high
> And terrible wall of heaven. The mighty wave
>   Tosses beneath its shadow, like the bold
> Upheavings of a giant from the grave
>   Which bound him prematurely to its cold
> And desolate bosom. Lo, they mingle now —

Tempest and heaving wave, along whose brow
　Trembles the lightning from its thick fold.

．　．　．　．　．　．　．　．　．

"Dread Ruler of the tempest! Thou before
　Whose presence boweth the uprisen storm,
To whom the waves do homage round the shore
　Of many an island empire! If the form
Of the frail dust beneath Thine eye may claim
　Thine infinite regard, oh, breathe upon
The storm and darkness of man's soul the same
Quiet and peace and humbleness which came
　O'er the roused waters, where Thy voice had gone,
A minister of peace — to conquer in Thy name."

The other poems of this period which appear in his collected works are: "Isabella of Austria," "The Frost Spirit," "The Fair Quakeress," "The Cities of the Plain," and "Bolivar." This last-named poem was written one month after the death of the South American patriot. In the "Review" for October 18, 1830, three of his poems appear, and the best of the three, "New England," was unsigned, but to the copy found among his papers he has appended his initials. This poem, with the exception of the last stanza, appears in "Moll Pitcher." The self-assertion in this last stanza probably seemed to him too strong at the time of its publication. But it reveals the high spirit of his youth, and now that its speculation may be looked upon as fulfilled prophecy, it properly belongs in these pages: —

"Land of my fathers! — if my name,
Now humble and unwed to fame,
Hereafter burn upon the lip,
　As one of those which may not die,
Linked in eternal fellowship
　With visions pure and strong and high —

> If the wild dreams, which quicken now
> The throbbing pulse of heart and brow,
> Hereafter take a real form
> Like spectres changed to being warm;
> And over temples worn and gray
> The star-like crown of glory shine, —
> Thine be the bard's undying lay,
> The murmur of his praise be thine!"

He busied himself also at this time in the preparation of his first book, " Legends of New England,
in Prose and Verse." No advertisement of this
book appeared in the paper he was conducting until
the week before it was issued.[1] It was printed in the
office of the " Review." There are now but few
copies of this earliest venture of his in existence.
Whenever, in later life, Mr. Whittier obtained possession of a copy, he destroyed it. On one occasion
he paid five dollars for a copy, and burned it. He
said he looked it through, and " it seemed like somebody else."

When his " Legends of New England " ap-

---

[1] This book was published February 23, 1831, by Havener &
Phelps, Hartford. The first announcement of it contained the name
of the author, but the advertisements that appeared after it was
issued do not mention the author's name. The table of contents
was as follows : " The Midnight Attack ; The Weird Gathering ;
The Rattlesnake Hunter ; Metacom ; The Murdered Lady ; The
Unquiet Sleeper : The Haunted House ; The Spectre Warriors ;
The Powow ; The Spectre Ship ; The Human Sacrifice ; The Indian's Tale ; A Night among the Wolves ; The White Mountains ;
The Black Fox : The Mother's Revenge ; The Aerial Omens ; The
Last Norridgewock." Nine of these pieces are poems, and of
these only two are to be found in his complete works, published
in 1888, viz., "Metacom" and "Mount Agiochook," which last
title has been substituted for "The White Mountains." Not one
of the prose sketches has been deemed worthy of preservation.

peared, he had been five years before the public as a writer. At this time more than one hundred poems of his had been printed in various periodicals. Only twenty of these are to be found in any extant edition of his works. It must be acknowledged that his judgment in suppressing them was correct. The few specimens of his early work that he allowed to appear in the latest and fullest collection of his poems are sufficient to show the first steps of his literary progress.

It may be said that some of the discarded early poems are devoted to phases of "the tender passion." There is no reason to suppose that he was not possessed of at least the average susceptibility of young people, and yet the verses to which reference is here made must not be taken as the measure of that susceptibility. His youthful letters to intimate friends abound in passages like this to Edwin Harriman, written from Boston, in 1829, while editing the "Manufacturer:" —

"Here I have been all day trying to write something for my paper, but what with habitual laziness, and a lounge or two in the Athenæum Gallery, I am altogether unfitted for composition. . . . There are a great many pretty girls at the Athenæum, and I like to sit there and remark upon the different figures that go flitting by me, like aerial creatures just stooping down to our dull earth, to take a view of the beautiful creations of the painter's genius. I love to watch their airy motions, notice the dark brilliancy of their fine eyes, and observe the delicate flush stealing over their cheeks, but, trust me, my heart is untouched, — cold

and motionless as a Jutland lake lighted up by
the moonshine.   I always did love a pretty girl.
Heaven grant there is no harm in it! . . . Mr.
Garrison will deliver an address on the Fourth of
July.   He goes to see his Dulcinea every other
night almost, but is fearful of being ' shipped off,'
after all, by her.   Lord help the poor fellow, if it
happens so.   I like my business very well; but
hang me if I like the people here.   I am acquainted with a few girls, and have no wish to be
so with many."

In March, 1831, he was called home to assist his
mother in the settlement of his father's estate, and
he remained until June of that year.   From Haverhill he sent several letters to the " Review."
One of these gives a lively account of his stage-
ride homeward, and another is devoted to politics.
Gideon Welles, afterward Abraham Lincoln's Secretary of the Navy, was then a leader in the Democratic party of Connecticut, and edited the Hartford " Times."   Mr. Whittier's political discussions
during his stay in Hartford were mainly with this
champion of the Democracy.   While at Haverhill
he continued his work upon the " Review," his articles being sent by mail.   In one of his letters he
says : " A little sister of mine, a girl of sixteen
summers, has, like her luckless brother, a disposition to make rhymes.   The following, which I
have somewhat feloniously and of malice afore-
thought abstracted from her writing-desk, is a specimen of her versifying."   The poem is a description
of an autumn sunset, of which this is the first
stanza : —

"Oh, there is beauty in the sky — a widening of gold
Upon each light and breezy cloud, and on each vapory fold!
The autumn wind has died away, and the air has not a sound,
Save the sighing of the withered leaves as they fall upon the
ground."

Then follows a familiar political talk, of which
this is a specimen : —

"How goes on the politics of the State? In
supporting the ticket nominated by the convention
I act not from personal feeling. I might even
have preferred other men to those now nominated,
but I conceive it to be the duty of every man who
would maintain a consistent support of the great
principles for which we are exerting ourselves at
the present time, to lay aside everything local and
unimportant, and act for the general good. In opposing the corruption and misrule of the administration we must move on unitedly, if we hope for
success. Without union we may fail, even where
five eighths of our citizens are enemies of Jacksonism. The Calhoun business looks encouraging.
Crawford is to all intents 'nullified,' and the
friends of 'the greatest and best of men' are leaving him, as his political horoscope seems at the
present time so very ill-boding. This place [Essex
North Congressional District] has been the theatre
of a warm political warfare. Mr. Cushing is the
most popular candidate for Congress, and I trust
he will be elected."

On the 14th of July, 1831, he wrote to his
friend, Jonathan Law : —

"I have been driving about 'from pillar to post'
ever since I left Hartford. The worst of it is, that

all this locomotion has not improved my health, which is still in a rather suspicious state. I have been away 'Down East,' and have just returned. I have not received a line from Hartford since I left; I do wish to hear from you, as I shall probably remain in this section two or three weeks longer. I want some information about political matters in Connecticut. . . . My sister Elizabeth has been obliged to leave the academy on account of her health. What a poor miserable thing is human nature, after all! —

> 'The slightest breath can shake it,
> And the light zephyr easily can break it.' "

Before definitely giving up his editorial work on the "Review," he made another trip to his home in Haverhill, and was accompanied by Dr. Crane, as in the condition of his health it was not thought prudent for him to travel alone. But he sent the physician home with this note to Mr. Law, dated October 27, 1831: "You have got Dr. Crane; but for me, I am off for Salem, notwithstanding the doctor's pledge to return me 'hale and breathing,' or with my bones neatly done up in his traveling trunk. I shall probably see Hartford in the course of a week or ten days."

His expectation of returning to Hartford was not realized, although early in December he started from Haverhill with that intention. In his absence he had been appointed a delegate from Connecticut, to attend a convention of the National Republican party, that was to meet in Baltimore on the 12th of December, to nominate

Elizabeth Hussey Whittier

a President and Vice-President of the United States. As a friend of Henry Clay, he desired to attend this convention, and to visit Hartford on his way. He made the attempt, but upon reaching Boston found he had not the strength to proceed farther; indeed, he was too ill to return at once to Haverhill.

It became necessary now definitely to resign his editorship of the "New England Review," and to give up his Hartford life, which he did the first of January, 1832. He left behind, apparently, the copy for the "Literary Remains of J. G. C. Brainard," a Connecticut poet, who died in 1828. He edited the volume and wrote a biographical sketch, but in a letter to a Hartford friend, written in the autumn of 1832, he says: "I have not seen a copy of it; the proof was not sent, and from an extract or two which I have seen, it is pretty well spiced with mistakes." Meanwhile he was living at home in Haverhill, with more leisure indeed, and with many plans, but with that consciousness of physical weakness which thereafter was seldom absent.

The following letter to his friend, Jonathan Law, dated Haverhill, January 5, 1832, shows how hard it was for him to give up his political and literary work, at the demand of a persistent disease : —

"Well, I have *at last* written, — or am going to, — being the third time in which I have actually written to you since I left Hartford, and delayed because I expected to be the bearer of my own epistle. I have been at home — that is to say, in this vicinity — all the time, — half sick, half mad. For the last fortnight I have been kept close. Mr. Barnard has doubtless told you that I started for Hartford about three or four weeks since, and was obliged to return. Now you may suppose that I have got the 'hypo.' No such thing. It is all as real as the nose on my face, this illness of mine, — alas, too real. Nor am I under the cerulean influence of the blue devils *now*. The last blue-visaged imp has departed with my exorcism ringing in his ears — ' Conjuro te, sceleratissime, abire ad tuum locum.' But nonsense apart, my dear sir, what shadows we are, and what shadows we pursue! We start vigorously forward with something for our object — up, up, among the very clouds; we toil on, we sacrifice *present* ease and *present* happiness; we turn from *real* blessings to picture *future* ones — unsubstantial as the fabric of the summer cloud or the morning mist. We press on for a time, the overtaxed nerves relax from their first strong tension, until the mysterious machinery of our existence is shattered and impeded, until the mind realizes that, chained down to material grossness, and clogged with a distempered and decaying mortality, it cannot rise to heaven. Perhaps it is well — indeed we know it is — that this should be the end of human ambition. But, oh, how humiliating to the vanity of our nature!

"Now, don't imagine for one moment that I have become morose and melancholy. Far from it. I am among anxious friends. I have a thousand sources of enjoyment, even in the midst of

corporeal suffering. I have an excellent society
here to visit and receive visits from, — my early
companions and those who have grown up with
me, who have known me long and well. I have
spent some time in Boston, Salem, Marblehead,
Andover, etc., among 'brave men and fair women;' have dabbled somewhat in local politics,
and am extensively popular just now on that account. The girls here are nice specimens of what
girls should be. You will find a description of
one or two of them in a poem which I shall send
you in a few weeks, perhaps in less time, — a
poem partly written at your house, and which is
being published. It lay around in fragments,
staring me everywhere in the face, and at last, to
get rid of it, I have given it over to the book-
makers. They will have a hard bargain of it.

"Decency forgive me! I 've filled up two pages
with that most aristocratic little pronoun which
represents the writer of this epistle. Misery
makes a man an egotist, the world over."

In a letter to Mrs. Sigourney, a month later,
February 2, 1832, he repeats this information
about his work, but adds intimation of another
literary scheme not elsewhere noted.[1]

"A thousand thanks for your kind letter, which
is now before me! It has acted upon my melancholy feelings like a spell of exorcism.

> ' Welcome as the odor fanned
> Around the weary seaman's keel
> From some unseen and flowery land.'

---

[1] This and a subsequent letter to Mrs. Sigourney have been
kindly furnished by Hon. Charles T. Hoadley, of Hartford.

I say *melancholy* feelings — they are so only in consequence of ill health, and visit me only at long intervals. In this vicinity I have everything to make me happy, — quiet, contentment, and a large circle of warm and kind-hearted friends. And yet, I long to visit Hartford; it has for me a thousand pleasant associations; and the opportunity which my residence there afforded me of a personal acquaintance with yourself is to me a constant source of self-congratulation. When your letter arrived, I had just been reading for the second time your admirable story in the 'Amaranth.' I know not what others may say, — indeed I care not, — but I do honestly think that the short story of Jehiel Wigglesworth, aside from the laudable object which the author evidently had in view, contains more *nature*, a better delineation of New England character, and a closer imitation of the real Yankee dialect, than all the tales and novels which have heretofore filled the circulating libraries or the newspapers of this country.

"I intended when I left Hartford to proceed immediately to the West. But a continuance of ill health has kept me at home. I have scarcely done anything this winter. There have been few days in which I have been able to write with any degree of comfort. I have indeed thrown together a poem of some length, the title of which ('Moll Pitcher') has very little connection with the subject. This poem I handed to a friend of mine, and he has threatened to publish it. It will not have the advantage or disadvantage of my name, however.

I have also written, or rather begun to write, a
work of fiction, which shall have for its object the
reconciliation of the North and the South, — being
simply an endeavor to do away with some of the
prejudices which have produced enmity between
the Southron and the Yankee. The style which I
have adopted is about half-way between the abruptness of Laurence Sterne and the smooth graceful-
ness of W. Irving. I may fail, — indeed I suspect
I shall, — but I have more philosophy than poetry
in my composition, and if I am disappointed in
one project, I have only to lay it aside and take
another up. If I thought I deserved half the
compliments you have been pleased to bestow upon
my humble exertions, I should certainly be in
danger of becoming obnoxious to the charge of
vanity. The truth is, I love poetry, with a love
as warm, as fervent, as sincere, as any of the more
gifted worshipers at the temple of the Muses.
I consider its gift as something holy and above the
fashion of the world. In the language of Francis
Bacon, 'The Muses are in league with Time,'
— which spares their productions in its work of
universal desolation. But I *feel* and know that

> 'To other chords than mine belong
> The breathing of immortal song.'

And in consequence, I have been compelled to
trust to other and less pleasant pursuits for distinction and profit. Politics is the only field now
open for me, and there is something inconsistent
in the character of a poet and modern politician.
People of the present day seem to have ideas

similar to those of that old churl of a Plato, who
was for banishing all poets from his perfect republic.

"Did you ever read these lines from Halleck? —

> 'But when the grass grows green above me,
>   And those who know me now and love me
>   Are sleeping by my side,
>   Will it avail me aught that men
>   Tell to the world with lip and pen
>   That I have lived and died ? —
>   *No ;* if a garland for my brow
>   Is growing, let me have it *now,*
>   While I 'm alive to wear it ;
>   And if in whispering my name
>   There 's music in the voice of fame,
>   Like Garcia's, *let me hear it !* '

Now I feel precisely so. I would have fame with
me *now,* — or not at all. I would not choose between a nettle or a rose to grow over my grave.
If I am worthy of fame, I would ask it now, — now
in the springtime of my years ; when I might
share its smile with the friends whom I love, and
by whom I am loved in return. But who would
ask a niche in that temple where the *dead* alone
are crowned ; where the green and living garland
waves in ghastly contrast over the pale, cold brow
and the visionless eye ; and where the chant of
praise and the voice of adulation fall only on the
deafened ear of Death?

"I have written to my friend B. on the subject
of the 'Amaranth,' and will take care to do your
other errand in Boston. I have a book in my possession — the poems of Alonzo Lewis, who wished
me to hand it to you. I shall be in Hartford as

soon in the spring as the traveling will admit.
Will you remember me kindly to my friend Sta-
miatiades? I am happy to see that the people of
Hartford are alive on the subject of education in
Greece. My friend Mr. Law will hand you this.
Excuse this hasty, and I fear incoherent, letter,
and believe me that nothing would afford me
greater pleasure than a speedy return to Hartford."

The poem to which he refers in the above letters
was being printed in Newburyport. It was published by Carter & Hendee, Boston, in a pamphlet
of twenty-eight octavo pages. It was dedicated to
Dr. Eli Todd, of Hartford, and the name of the
author does not appear on its title-page. The
following note is given by way of preface: —

" The following pages, dear reader, are published
neither for a poetical reputation nor for money.
The former is unfortunately a most indefinite, and
too often ' stale, flat, and unprofitable,' commodity,
inasmuch as it could puzzle the French cook, who
made fifty different dishes of a parsnip, to make
either meat or drink of it. As for the latter, I
have not enough of the poetical mania in my disposition to dream of converting, by an alchemy
more potent than that of the old philosophers, a
limping couplet into a brace of doubloons; or a
rickety stanza into a note of hand. 'Moll Pitcher'
(there 's music in the name) is the offspring of a
few weeks of such leisure as is afforded by indisposition, and is given to the world in all its original negligence, — the thoughts fresh as when first
conceived."

The story of the poem is of a maiden consulting

the witch in regard to her lover, who is at sea. The witch has some cause of grievance against the maiden, and frightens her into a mild insanity by predictions of dire calamity. The lover returns safely, and, finding his betrothed in this demented condition, gradually, by love's ministrations, recalls her to her right mind, and at length " the thousand fancies which were nursed in madness vanish one by one." The concluding scene is at the death-bed of the witch, whose last hours are soothed by the gentle care of a daughter of the woman she so cruelly wronged, and to whom in dying she gives her blessing.

In 1840, a revised edition of " Moll Pitcher " was published by Joseph Healy, of Philadelphia, this edition for the first time connecting Mr. Whittier's name with the poem, and with it was printed " The Minstrel Girl," which was originally published in John Neal's " Yankee," in 1829. This last-named poem as a whole is unworthy of re-production, but contains some stanzas of merit. It makes eight pages of the 12mo pamphlet.

Mr. Whittier was more successful in suppressing " Moll Pitcher " than he was with his later poem, " Mogg Megone." It has never been published in any collection of his works, and as a whole does not deserve to be perpetuated.

Mr. Whittier sent several contributions of prose and verse to the " Pearl," published by Isaac C. Pray, first in Hartford and afterward in Boston.

" The Prisoner for Debt " was originally published in the " Pearl " for December 12, 1835, and the date, 1849, given to it in the edition of 1888 is

an error. It had when first published these lines
of Pierpont as a preface : —

> " Cast down, great God, the fanes
> That to unhallowed gains
> Round us have risen ;
> Temples whose priesthood pore
> Moses and Jesus o'er,
> Then bolt the poor man's prison."

Among the periodicals to which Mr. Whittier
contributed from 1829 to 1832, beside those already
named, were the " Columbian Star," the " Connecticut Mirror," and the " Ladies' Magazine." Mrs.
Sarah J. Hale was then editing the magazine
last named. When the publication of the " Yankee " was suspended, its subscription list was trans-
ferred to Mrs. Hale's magazine, and John Neal
for a short time assisted in editing it. To illustrate the personal style of journalism in those days,
N. P. Willis's editorial comment upon this arrange-
ment may be cited. He mentioned the union of
the two totally dissimilar periodicals, and added,
" The mustard-pot is upset in the milk-pan."

The Haverhill " Iris," of September 29, 1832,
contains a poem entitled " To a Poetical Trio in the
City of Gotham," which was signed by no name,
and was not known to be Whittier's until since his
death. But among his papers was found a letter,
written many years after the publication of this
poem, by one of the " Trio " satirized in it, which
fixes its authorship, even if the internal evidence
were not convincing. It is an appeal to Bryant,
Leggett, and Lawson, well-known poets of that
day, and at the same time editors of leading Jack-

son papers in New York city, to give up their partisan work, and come out for Freedom, as Moore,
Campbell, and Bulwer were doing in Great Britain.
Here is the poem in full, with the notes that accompanied it : —

TO A POETICAL TRIO IN THE CITY OF GOTHAM.

> Three wise men of Gotham
> Went to sea in a bowl.

BARDS of the island city ! — where of old
　　The Dutchman smoked beneath his favorite tree,
And the wild eyes of Indian hunters rolled
　　On Hudson plunging in the Tappaan Zee,
Scene of Stuyvesant's might and chivalry,
　　And Knickerbocker's fame, — I have made bold
To come before ye, at the present time,
And *reason* with ye in the way of *rhyme*.

Time was when poets kept the quiet tenor
　　Of their green pathway through th' Arcadian vale, —
Chiming their music in the low sweet manner
　　Of song-birds warbling to the " Soft South " gale ;
Wooing the Muse where gentle zephyrs fan her,
　　Where all is peace and earth may not assail ;
Telling of lutes and flowers, of love and fear,
Of shepherds, sheep and lambs, and " such small deer."

But ye ! lost recreants — straying from the green
　　And pleasant vista of your early time,
With broken lutes and crownless skulls — are seen
Spattering your neighbors with abhorrent slime
Of the low world's pollution ! [1]　Ye have been
　　So long apostates from the Heaven of rhyme,
That of the Muses, every mother's daughter
Blushes to own such graceless bards e'er sought her.

" *Hurrah for Jackson !* " is the music now
　　Which your cracked lutes have learned alone to utter,

---

[1] Editors of the *Mercantile Advertiser* and the *Evening Post*
in New York, — the present organs of Jacksonism.

As, crouching in Corruption's shadow low,
   Ye daily sweep them for your bread and butter,[1]
Cheered by the applauses of the friends who show
   Their heads above the offal of the gutter,
And, like the trees which Orpheus moved at will,
Reel, as in token of your matchless skill !

Thou son of Scotia ! [2] — nursed beside the grave
   Of the proud peasant-minstrel, and to whom
The wild muse of thy mountain-dwelling gave
   A portion of its spirit, — if the tomb
Could burst its silence, o'er the Atlantic's wave,
   To thee his voice of stern rebuke would come,
Who dared to waken with a master's hand
The lyre of freedom in a fettered land.

And thou ! — once treading firmly the proud deck
   O'er which thy country's honored flag was sleeping,
Calmly in peace, or to the hostile beck
   Of coming foes in starry splendor sweeping, —
Thy graphic tales of battle or of wreck,
   Or lone night-watch in middle ocean keeping,
Have made thy " Leisure Hours " more prized by far
Than those now spent in Party's wordy war.[3]

And last, not least, thou ! — now nurtured in the land
   Where thy bold-hearted fathers long ago
Rocked Freedom's cradle, till its infant hand
   Strangled the serpent fierceness of its foe, —

---

[1] Perhaps, after all, they get something better ; inasmuch as the Heroites have for some time had exclusive possession of the Hall of St. Tammany, and we have the authority of Halleck that

> " There 's a barrel of porter in Tammany Hall,
> And the Bucktails are swigging it all the night long."

[2] James Lawson, Esq., of the *Mercantile*. A fine, warm-hearted Scotchman, who, having unfortunately blundered into Jacksonism, is wondering " how i' the Deil's name " he got there. He is the author of a volume entitled *Tales and Sketches*, and of the tragedy of *Giordano*.

[3] William Leggett, Esq., of the *Post*, a gentleman of good talents, favorably known as the editor of the *New York Critic*, etc.

Thou, whose clear brow in early time was fanned
  By the soft airs which from Castalia flow ! [1] —
Where art thou now ? feeding with hickory ladle
The curs of Faction with thy daily twaddle !

Men have looked up to thee, as one to be
  A portion of our glory ; and the light
And fairy hands of woman beckoned thee
  On to thy laurel guerdon ; and those bright
And gifted spirits, whom the broad blue sea
  Hath shut from thy communion, bid thee, " *Write,*"
Like John of Patmos.   Is all this forgotten,
For Yankee brawls and Carolina cotton ?

Are autumn's rainbow hues no longer seen ?
  Flows the " Green River " through its vale no more ?
Steals not thy " Rivulet " by its banks of green ?
  Wheels upward from its dark and sedgy shore
Thy " Water Fowl " no longer ? — that the mean
  And vulgar strife, the ranting and the *roar*
Extempore, like Bottom's, should be thine, —
Thou feeblest truck-horse in the Hero's line !

Lost trio ! — turn ye to the minstrel pride
  Of classic Britain.   Even effeminate Moore
Has cast the wine-cup and the lute aside
  For Erin and O'Connell ; and before
His country's altar, Bulwer breasts the tide
  Of old oppression.   Sadly brooding o'er
The fate of heroes struggling to be free,
Even Campbell speaks for Poland.   *Where are ye ?*

Hirelings of traitors ! — know ye not that men
  Are rousing up around ye to retrieve
Our country's honor, which too long has been
  Debased by those for whom ye daily weave
Your web of fustian ; that from tongue and pen
  Of those who o'er our tarnished honor grieve,
Of the pure-hearted and the gifted, come
Hourly the tokens of your master's doom ?

[1] William C. Bryant, Esq., well known to the public at large
as a poet of acknowledged excellence ; and as a very dull editor
to the people of New York.

Turn from their ruin! Dash your chains aside!
  Stand up like men for Liberty and Law,
And free opinion. Check Corruption's pride,
  Soothe the loud storm of fratricidal war, —
And the bright honors of your eventide
  Shall share the glory which your morning saw;
The patriot's heart shall gladden at your name,
Ye shall be blessed with, and not "damned to fame"!

Both Bryant and Leggett, in a few years, became champions of freedom, to the great delight of Whittier, who wrote not only a spirited poetical tribute to Leggett, when "St. Tammany" proposed to build a monument to the man whom living they persecuted, but a brilliant eulogy in prose of one who gave up a splendid prospect of political preferment rather than forswear his allegiance to the despised cause of abolitionism. The poem, "Bryant on his Birthday," gives Whittier's later estimate of his older brother in poetry. Lawson [1] was the only one of the "Poetical Trio" who did not take part in anti-slavery work; but that the Scotchman retained his personal friendship for Whittier is shown by a letter written by him thirty-six years after the publication of the sharp satire given above. But for this letter, found among the papers of Mr. Whittier, no one would have guessed that it was the Haverhill poet who had taken these three stalwart New Yorkers over his knee. The

[1] James Lawson, born in Glasgow, Scotland, in 1799. Resided in New York city and in Yonkers, after 1815. Published *Tales and Sketches, by a Cosmopolite*, in 1830, and, at various times, *Giordano*, a tragedy, and many fugitive prose and poetical articles in periodicals. Allibone says he was one of the first to introduce American letters to the notice of British readers. He retired from active literary work in 1833.

poem does not appear to have been copied in the papers of the day, and is now reproduced for the first time.

Other articles, both in prose and verse, from the pen of Whittier, may be found in files of the Haverhill " Iris " for 1832. In the number for April 12 is a prose sketch entitled " The Stormed Fort," a tale of the East Indies in the year 1766. A drunken Irish sailor captures a well-garrisoned fort, single-handed and against orders, and when threatened with punishment for his foolhardy act, vows he will never take another fort so long as he lives, which so amuses the admiral that he is let off.

From 1831 to 1835 Mr. Whittier contributed prose and verse to the " New England Magazine," edited by Joseph T. Buckingham, afterwards editor of the " Boston Courier." It was in this magazine that " Mogg Megone " first appeared, and eight shorter poems, including " Toussaint L'Ouverture," " The French Martyr," " A Lament," " Song of the Vermonters," and " The Demon of the Study." His prose contributions to this monthly included " The Opium Eater," " Passaconaway," and " Powow Hill." This last named hill is now known as Po Hill, an abbreviation of its original name; the river which flows at its base is still called the Powow. The legend opens with the following description of the hill, and account of the origin of its name : —

" On the border of the Merrimac, some eight or ten miles from the ocean, there rises a steep eminence called Powow Hill. It is a landmark to the skippers of the coasting craft that sail up Newburyport harbor, and strikes the eye by its abrupt elevation and orbicular shape, the outlines being as regular as if struck off by the sweep of a compass. It obtained its name from that pagan ceremonial of the aborigines; for in ancient times, ere our worthy and pious ancestors routed these heathen from the land, the hill in question was the grand high place of Indian worship, and the nocturnal powows upon its summit were the terror and abomination of the whole neighborhood. While the savages lingered in these parts they never failed annually to assemble on this consecrated mount and practice their mysterious orgies, greatly to the scandal and annoyance of all the Christian folk that dwelt round about, they having a pious horror of the practice of powowing, deemed by Cotton Mather as damnable and demoniacal. Even when the last of the red men had disappeared from the country, the scene of their mystic incantations continued to be regarded with profound awe. A spirit of the pagan mysteries dwelt about the spot. Strange sights were seen. A marvelous legend was current."

The legend as told by Whittier is of a bewitched Yankee who was taken by his runaway horse to the top of the hill, into the midst of a spectral powow of savage ghosts. It is one of a large number of sketches written by Whittier between the years 1829 and 1833, which he did not care to have reproduced in any collection of his works.

As intimated, and as the letters already printed plainly show, Whittier's interest was divided between literature and politics; and how strongly the latter absorbed his attention may be most clearly

seen by the manner in which it forces itself into
a letter to Mrs. Sigourney, who naturally would be
his literary rather than his political confidante.
The letter was written in January, 1833.

"I have often feared, and perhaps not without
reason, that those whom I most truly love and
esteem, and whose good opinion I value above all
other human considerations, are sometimes inclined
to doubt the sincerity of my friendship and the
warmth of my heart. In my personal intercourse
with them a boyish diffidence, which manhood
has not been able to forget, and a most unpardon-
able lack of *words*, — a want of the ready coin, —
the circulating medium of conversation, — have, I
am well aware, too often made me appear cold, distant, and as incapable of appreciating the delicate
attentions and generous sympathies of friendship
as of returning them. And, in my epistolary correspondence, my habit of procrastination — per-
petually resolving to do *to-morrow* what should be
done *to-day* — has made me liable to the charge
of neglecting my friends. But if I know my own
heart (and I have long been in the habit of turning a severe eye upon myself, and closely analyz-
ing my own feelings), I am *incapable* of will-
fully neglecting any one who feels an interest in
my welfare, and, however unfortunate I may be
in their expression, however ambiguous and con-
tradictory may seem their revelation to others, I
have warm and deep and kind feelings. I believe
there is not a particle of misanthropy in my disposition ; and I am more at peace with the whole
world than with myself, not *that I and myself* are

much in the habit of quarreling. But, I believe
in the holy realities of friendship, — pure, lofty,
intellectual; a communion of kindred affinities,
of mental similitudes, — a redemption from the
miserable fetters of human selfishness; a practical obedience to the beautiful injunction of our
Common Friend, 'Love thy neighbor as thyself.'
I believe, too, that the pure love which we feel
for our friends is a part and portion of that love
which we owe and offer to our Creator, and is
acceptable to Him, inasmuch as it is offered not
to the decaying elements of humanity, but to
those brighter and holier attributes which are of
themselves the emanations of the Divinity, — to
those pure emotions of the heart and those high
capacities of the soul in which that Divinity is
most clearly manifested; and that, in proportion
as we draw near to each other in the holy communion and unforbidden love of earthly friendship, we
lessen the distance between our spirits and their
Original Source, — just as the radii of a circle in
approaching each other approach also their common
centre.

"I hope, my dear Mrs. S., you will not attribute
my neglect to answer your letter, and to acknowledge my obligations for the beautiful notice of
Brainard, to anything like disregard on my part.
All my friends are complaining of me for not
answering their letters. Continued ill health
and natural indolence, and the daily duties of
a large farm, *must* be my excuse. Of poetry I
have nearly taken my leave, and a pen is getting
to be something of a stranger to me. I have been

compelled again to plunge into the political whirl-
pool; for I have found that my political reputation is more influential than my poetical: so I try
to make myself a man of the world — and the public
are deceived, but *I* am not.   They do not see that
I have thrown the rough armor of rude and tur-
bulent controversy over a keenly sensitive bosom,
— a heart of softer and gentler emotions than I
dare expose.   Accordingly, as Governor Hamilton,
of South Carolina, says, I have 'put on athletic
habits for the occasion.'

   "And speaking of South Carolina, what think
you of the prospect in the political heavens?   To
me, all is dark and fearful.   If the Protecting
System is abolished, New England must suffer
deeply and wrongfully; and if, on the other
hand, the bloodthirsty old man at the head of our
government shall undertake to put down South
Carolina with the bayonet, from that moment our
Union will be broken up — never to unite again.
Blood cannot cement it.   For one, I thank God
that He has given me a deep and invincible horror
of human butchery, — that I am not one of those
who 'look on blood and carnage with composure.'
When Paine put forth his strong, and at that
time, at least, well-directed, energies in favor of
sparing the life of Louis XVI. before the French
Convention, Marat fiercely denounced him as 'a
Quaker, destitute of that philosophic liberality
requisite for putting men to death.'   I meet with
a great many Marats at the present day.

   " I have occasionally seen an article of your poetry
during the last year.   I wish you would take the

trouble to send me, if convenient, such new pieces as you may publish. I have written two or three prose articles for 'Buckingham's Magazine.' Have you seen the 'Knickerbocker,' published by Peabody & Cole, of New York? I don't think much of No. 1. There is not an article of poetry in it which *you* would think paid the trouble of reading. Halleck, Irving, Paulding, Hoffman, and Bryant are engaged in it, I understand. I have been requested to write for it, but don't know as I shall be able to. I am glad to see that the 'Bouquet' still continues; 't is the last light in your benighted literary horizon. Hartford is by no means a literary place, and it has been remarked that were it not for yourself it would be only known as the place where a certain Convention once assembled. Have you seen Garrison's 'Thoughts on Colonization'? I wish you would read that book. I know your predilection for the Colonization Society, but I regret it.

"This letter will be handed you by Mr. Law, with whom I occasionally correspond. Is Mr. Stamiatiades with you now? If so, remember me kindly to him, and assure him of my best wishes; and, for yourself, let me assure you that your letters, whether frequent or far between, are to me as *angel visits*."

The following letter to Jonathan Law, written on the 13th of September, 1832, gives a further glimpse of his life on the farm, while relieved of editorial work, and shows how the Asiatic cholera, which was then spreading over New England, affected the public mind: —

" I have not forgotten my kind friends at Hartford. Whatever may be my faults, I trust ingratitude is not among their number. I already owe you and your family more than I shall ever suitably repay. But if my life and health are spared me, you may always rely upon me as a firm, and I hope not altogether useless, friend. My health has been bad, nay, is so at this moment, but I have still tolerable courage, and I am able to see to the affairs of the farm. I am happy to find that your city continues healthy. We have had only one case [of cholera] in our village, and the patient is now nearly recovered. The disease has at last broken out in Boston; five fatal cases have occurred within the last day or two. For my own part, I felt extremely nervous about the cholera when it broke out in Montreal and Quebec; but it has now come to our doors, and familiarity softens its terrors. It is a singular fact in the philosophy of the human mind that in proportion as the dangers which we most fear at a distance gather closer around us, we become reckless, hardened, and secure. I have vainly tried to analyze my own feelings in this matter. . . . I send you a copy or two of the ' Essex Gazette,' containing two numbers of a series of articles upon that scandalous veto of Amos Kendall's. I have written nothing of late save local political paragraphs, with the single exception of a piece published in the Haverhill ' Iris,' which you probably noticed, headed ' Stanzas,' and prefaced by two extracts from the speeches of Henry Clay. . . . Do you often see our mutual friend, Mrs. Sigourney? I think highly of that woman, — she has fine talents, and they are all devoted to the best of causes.

" If I recollect aright, in your last letter you spoke despairingly of a matter connected with the elevation of Mr. Clay to the Presidency. [Mr. Law had been postmaster of Hartford, but was displaced by Jackson. Probably he had expressed the opinion that Clay, if elected, would not replace him.] I do not view the matter as you do. I believe that justice will be done if that desirable event takes place. I see no reason now for despairing of Mr. Clay's election. New York is lost, and so is Kentucky, and so is Pennsylvania to the Jackson cause. If Henry Clay is elected, all will be well. Restoration must follow as a necessary consequence of our abhorrence of proscription for opinion's sake. . . . I know not when I shall be in Hartford again; even if my health was restored I should not leave this place. I have too many friends around me, and my prospects are too good to be sacrificed for any uncertainty. I have done with poetry and literature. I can *live* as a farmer, and that is all I ask at present. I wish you could make me a visit, you and Mrs. Law; our situation is romantic enough, — out of the din and bustle of the village, with a long range of green hills stretching away to the river; a brook goes brawling at their foot, overshadowed with trees, through which the white walls of our house are just visible. In truth, I am as comfortable as one can well be, always excepting ill health."

There are other letters of this period which show that it was political and not literary ambition that was animating him in the years immediately preceding his consecration to the cause of the oppressed. When he speaks of his prospects being "too good to be sacrificed for any uncertainty," his meaning is that he is aware of his political popularity in his district. At about the time when this letter was written, he was considering a proposition made by his friends that he should become a candidate for Congress. All that prevented his doing so was the fact that he was not yet quite twenty-five years old, and therefore, as he supposed, barred out by a provision of the Constitution.

CHAPTER IV.

1832–1837.

UP to 1832, when he returned from Hartford to his home in Haverhill, Mr. Whittier's highest ambition, as we have seen, had been to make his mark in politics. To be sure, he had written, in about three years, more than a hundred poems, counting only those that were published. He must have taken some pride in seeing his verses widely copied, and in the reputation as a rising poet that was accorded him by some of the best writers of his time. But poetry was praised and not paid for in those days, and literature offered no alluring prizes to American youth. The academies and colleges were turning out a mob of amateur rhymesters. Theological students were intent upon giving a new twist to the Psalms of David. Young doctors and lawyers were translating the Odes of Horace while waiting for patients and clients. Even Daniel Webster, in his ponderous way, dallied with the Muses, and John Quincy Adams, the busiest man of his day, spent hours in fashioning rhymed lines for albums. Scarcely a professional man of that generation was so utterly prosaic as to escape the infection. The field was certainly not an encouraging one for a poet who should de-

pend upon his verses for a living. Mr. Whittier
had tried his wings in the gusty air of politics and
found they would bear him, and it was in this
direction that he was looking for his life work.
While managing his farm, he kept up his contributions to political papers, and took an active part
in the politics of his native town, and of Essex
County.

Caleb Cushing, of Newburyport, had just returned from Europe, and was beginning to feel
the stirrings of political ambition. Young Whittier helped him to secure a seat in Congress, and
Cushing, who was seven years his senior, encouraged his aspirations to political preferment. For
a time, all his impulses were in that direction.
His work as a political editor had brought him in
contact with the leaders of his party, and his
marked ability as a writer and his honesty and
sagacity in the party councils were appreciated.
He was becoming known as an anti-slavery man,
it is true, but that did not then disqualify one for
leadership in either party, in New England.
Besides, his Quakerism was a good excuse for his
conscience. Our orthodox fathers in that generation were taking more kindly to Quakers than to
heretics in other sects, like Unitarians and Uni-
versalists, and were ready to humor what were
regarded as their whims. So that up to 1833,
when Whittier was in the twenty-sixth year of his
age, whatever thought he had for the future, outside of his work as a farmer, was in the direction
of politics. In 1833, his attention had been called
by Garrison, of whom he had seen little for the

past three years,[1] to the importance of arousing
the nation to a sense of its guilt in the matter of
slavery. He did not need any change of heart to
become an abolitionist. As a birthright Quaker
he inherited the traditions of his sect against the
institution of slavery. But he had been hoping
by moral means, and by efforts within the lines of
the old parties, to secure the gradual extinction of
a system so out of harmony with our otherwise
free institutions. A word from Garrison caused
him thoroughly to study the situation. All the
literature of the subject within his reach was
examined carefully. Among the Southern newspapers to which he had access he found evidence
that whatever thought of extinguishing slavery
had animated the fathers of the republic, and
prompted the anti-slavery utterances of Washington
and Jefferson, no such idea was now entertained
by any of the Southern people. The demand for
slave labor in the rice swamps and cotton fields of
the extreme South had made the raising of slaves
profitable in Virginia, and in other States in which
hitherto the " institution " had seemed doomed to
extinction as an economic mistake. He found, too,
that both the great parties of the North were
beginning to discipline their members who were
too urgent in pressing measures that might lose to
them the support of the Southern States. He had
learned something of this change in the popular

---

[1] It is to be noted that in November, 1831, he published in the
Haverhill *Gazette* his poem, " To William Lloyd Garrison," which
now introduces the section *Anti-Slavery Poems* in his collected
works.

feeling from the experience of his friend Garrison, who had been imprisoned at Baltimore for his free utterance of anti-slavery sentiments. This incident occurred at about the time when Whittier took the editorship of the " New England Review," in 1830. In January, 1831, Garrison began the publication of the " Liberator," in Boston. He uttered his memorable ultimatum : " I am in earnest, I will not equivocate, I will not excuse, I will not retreat a single inch, and I will be heard." Whittier counted the cost with Quaker coolness of judgment before taking a step that closed to him the gates of both political and literary preferment. He realized more fully than did most of the early abolitionists that the institution of slavery would not fall at the first blast of their horns. When he decided to enter upon this contest, he understood that his cherished ambitions must be laid aside, and that an entire change in his plans was involved. He took the step deliberately and after serious consideration.

In later life, in giving counsel to a boy of fifteen, Mr. Whittier said that his own early ambition had been to become a prominent politician, and from this ideal he was persuaded only by the earnest appeals of his friends. Taking their advice, he united with the persecuted and obscure band of abolitionists, and to this course he attributed all his after success in life. Then, turning to the boy, he placed his hand on his head, and said in his gentle voice : "My lad, if thou wouldst win success, join thyself to some unpopular but noble cause."

In the spring of 1833, while caring for his farm, and doing some literary work for the Haverhill " Gazette " and other journals, he wrote the pamphlet entitled "Justice and Expediency," and published it at his own expense. It must have cost him a good part of his year's earnings, beside the time spent in examining the many authorities he cites. It is an argument to prove the expediency of being just. The injustice of slavery is shown with much warm rhetoric. The entire literature of the subject had evidently been carefully studied. Every statement is backed up by quotations from unquestioned authority, and by references in footnotes. Probably no single anti-slavery paper ever published covered the ground so completely as this. It is thorough in statement, carefully reasoned, and enforced by direct appeals to the conscience and the heart of the nation. Many good men, both at the North and at the South, had satisfied their consciences by promoting the scheme of the African Colonization Society. A few slaveholders had freed their slaves, and many thousands of dollars had been spent in colonizing them in Liberia. With these freed slaves had been sent a large number of negroes who had never been slaves. Henry Clay was the President of the Colonization Society, a position he had held for twenty years, and thereafter until his death. The political party with which Whittier had acted numbered among its leaders many active promoters of the colonization scheme. Collections for it were taken up regularly in the churches. To denounce this society,

as not a help, but a great hindrance to the cause
of the blacks, was therefore a bold act for a young
man who had been looking forward to a life in
politics. The pamphlet gives six reasons why the
Colonization Society was unworthy of support,
and fortifies them by citations from the official
papers of the society. It points out the ludicrous inconsistency of the advocates of colonization, who in one breath say with Henry Clay,
" Each emigrant is a missionary, carrying with
him the holy cause of civilization, religion, and
free institutions ; " and in the next breath say,
with the official organ of the society, " Free
blacks are a greater nuisance than even slaves
themselves." It shows that the only adequate
remedy for slavery is abolition. The pamphlet is
published in full in the prose works of Mr. Whittier.[1]

It attracted immediate attention, and the edition he had issued was soon exhausted. Lewis
Tappan, of New York, caused it to be printed in
the monthly organ of the American Anti-Slavery
Society, and paid for issuing an extra edition of
5000 copies. Moses Brown, of Providence, an
aged and wealthy Quaker philanthropist, had influence enough to procure its publication in the Providence " Journal," although the conductor of that
paper had no sympathy with its tone. Some idea
of the temper with which this pamphlet was received at the South is shown by the fact that, for
lending to a brother doctor this pamphlet of Mr.
Whittier's, Dr. Reuben Crandall, of Washington,

[1] Riverside edition, vol. vii.

was in 1834 arrested, and confined in the old city prison, until his health was destroyed, and he was liberated only to die. This incident is referred to in the poem " Astræa at the Capitol: " —

> " Beside me gloomed the prison cell
> Where wasted one in slow decline
> For uttering simple words of mine,
> And loving freedom all too well."

At the time when Mr. Whittier was writing this pamphlet, he was not calculating upon the far-reaching effect it might have upon his own fortunes. It did not occur to him until his manuscript was ready for publication that it would seriously interfere with his political ambitions. He was all that summer actively helping the canvass of Caleb Cushing, writing spirited communications to the " Iris " over various signatures, and sending them with private notes of political advice to Editor Harriman.[1]

His letters to Cushing and other political associates at this time are also full of enthusiasm for his party. But as he was about to issue his pamphlet, a prophetic glimpse of its real effect came to him, and it caused him sleepless nights. A decision to follow the path of duty at all hazards ended the struggle, and the decision was never regretted,

---

[1] As a specimen of the style of these notes, take this, dated at his farm, "5th mo. 15, 1833 :" " Fullington, at the Rocks, says there is no chance for Cushing, and thinks it would be better to take a Cushing man from Lowell. I don't see the use of this ; you can do nothing with the Lowell folk ; choose a man there for *this* Congress, and he will stand for the *next*. If Osgood [the Jackson candidate] is elected, National Republicanism in this district will go to its long home."

although it crowded his life with hardships for many years, and ended all his dreams of political preferment. He announced to Caleb Cushing his intention to publish "Justice and Expediency," in the following letter, dated "5th mo., 1833." After urging his friend not to decline the candidacy, even if the next ballot should go against him, and prophesying ultimate election, he says : —

"About a fortnight ago, I took up a pamphlet containing your remarks at the colonization meeting in Boston. In that frankness which accords with my ideas of doing to others as I would be done by, I cannot but say that I deeply regret this publication. So far as literary merit is concerned the speech is worthy of you, but I dissent from your opinions most radically, and so do a great majority of the people in this vicinity. I shall probably send you in a week or two a pamphlet on the subject of slavery, written hastily and under many disadvantages. Most of the facts it contains you are probably already acquainted with. There may be some, however, which have escaped your observation. I beg of you to lend your mind to the investigation of this most momentous question, believing as I do that you can do a great deal for the cause of suffering humanity. I should like to have you make this pamphlet and others recently published on the subject the basis of an article in some of our reviews or magazines. That you will differ from me I know, and shall therefore expect to be handled without gloves, but credit me, my dear sir, I had much rather fall under the *stoccado* of a gentlemanly and scientific swordsman than be bunglingly hewed in pieces like Agag of old under the broadaxe of the Prophet. I have only time again to beg you, whatever may be the result of this trial, to allow yourself to be a candidate still. Sooner or later we must triumph.

" I am almost sorry that I troubled you in a former letter with my own private matters. But that letter was written under an exciting sense of unprovoked injury. With all my Quakerism, I cannot but sometimes give way to indignant feeling, when my best motives are tortured into evil ones."

Both Garrison and Whittier had been actively friendly to the Colonization Society up to 1830. The papers conducted by them set forth its claims, and in his Fourth of July address, delivered in Park Street Church, Boston, in 1829, Mr. Garrison made an earnest appeal for the cause. Even after his pamphlet was issued, in 1833, Whittier continued for a year working for the cause of Henry Clay, in the hope that eventually he would assume the role of the champion of freedom. But in 1834 he wrote: " We regret that truth and the cause of humanity, which he has betrayed, compel us to speak of Henry Clay as the enemy of Freedom." His last tribute to the Kentucky statesman, written in 1833, began with this stanza: —

> " The Grecian as he feeds his flocks,
>   In Tempe's vale, on Morea's rocks,
>   Or where the gleam of bright blue waters
>   Is caught by Scio's white-armed daughters,
>   While dwelling on the dubious strife
>   Which ushered in his nation's life,
>   Shall mingle in his grateful lay
>   Bozzaris with the name of Clay."

In 1830, when Garrison was imprisoned at Baltimore, Whittier appealed to Clay for his release, and Clay, who recognized the value of Whittier's friendship, promptly responded to the appeal. But Arthur Tappan, of New York, had even more promptly paid Garrison's fine, else the young agitator would have owed his release to the Kentucky slave-owner.[1]

Among the Southern papers that took notice of Whittier's pamphlet was the Richmond " Jeffersonian," which complained that no sooner had the accursed tariff ceased to be the stone of stumbling and the rock of offense, than Northern enthusiasts began to interfere with the domestic institutions of the South. Whittier, well primed with anti-slavery quotations from Jefferson and other Virginian statesmen, made a ringing reply to the " Jeffersonian " in the " Essex Gazette," published at Haverhill. He showed that the doctrines of the men for whom their paper was named were every whit as anti-slavery as those of the enthusiasts who were accused of furnishing a sufficient reason for " poising the Ancient Dominion on its sovereignty," and rousing every slave-owner to military preparation. This reply to the " Jeffersonian " is a far more pointed paper than the original pamphlet. Like that, it is full of quotations, and abounds in footnotes, showing great research, and a special familiarity with Virginia politics, not only of that

[1] Mr. W. H. Smith, who has possession of Clay's papers, and is preparing his biography, has found a letter of Whittier's, written in 1837, earnestly urging the Kentuckian to come out as the champion of freedom ; so strong still was the personal attraction which his early political idol had for him.

time but of former generations. He quotes at every
turn from Jefferson, Madison, and Monroe; from
Blackstone, Lafayette, and O'Connell; from the
statute-books of South Carolina, and from the statistics of the census. He acknowledges they have
under the Constitution the power to hold their slave
property, but denies they have any moral right to
take advantage of the power. New England, he
says, will abide unto the death by the Constitution
of the land, but she asks to be relieved of the duty
of hunting down fellow-men like wild beasts, when
they are struggling desperately for liberty. In
attacking slavery, the abolitionists recommend no
measure conflicting with the Constitution. They
would not excite or encourage a rebellion among
slaves. They hold such attempts in utter abhorrence, by whomsoever made. They are opposed to
any political interposition of the government in
regard to slavery, as it exists in the States. He
goes on at some length to reiterate and emphasize
this disclaimer. He says slavery has made desolate and sterile one of the loveliest regions of the
whole earth, and points to the hillsides gullied and
naked, the fields run over with brier and fern.
Then he shows how the rocky soil of New England
lies green and luxuriant beneath the sun of our
brief summer. Free labor has changed a landscape
wild and savage as the night scenery of Salvator
Rosa into one of pastoral beauty, the abode of independence and happiness. One of the concluding
paragraphs of the paper makes this reference to
John Randolph, then recently deceased : —

" The late noble example of the eloquent statesman of Roanoke, the manumission of his slaves, speaks volumes to his political friends. In the last hour of his existence, when his soul was struggling from its broken tenement, his latest effort was the confirmation of this generous act of a former period. Light rest the turf upon him, beneath his patrimonial oaks! The prayers of many hearts made happy by his benevolence shall linger over his grave, and bless it."

These letters in reply to the Richmond paper were written in July, 1833, less than one month after the death of Randolph, and published in the " Essex Gazette." The passage last quoted, as he wrote it in prose, probably awakened the inspiration of his noble poem, " Randolph of Roanoke," which was first published in the " National Era," in January, 1847, it being one of his earliest contributions to that paper when he assumed the position of corresponding editor. It had probably been lying in his portfolio for more than thirteen years. Several lines in the poem indicate that it was written not long after Randolph's death,[1] which occurred June 24, 1833.

The die was now cast. Whittier had com-

---

[1] The manumitted slaves of John Randolph, three hundred in number, could not be allowed to remain free in Virginia. Randolph's executor bought land, erected buildings, and made other preparations for them in Bremen, Mercer County, Ohio, at an expense of over $30,000. But when it came to settling them on the new purchase, the people of the vicinity, including the very men who sold the land and had the money in their pockets, raised a mob, and insisted on driving them back into Virginia. A bond had to be given that the negroes should not become paupers, before they were allowed to remain upon the land purchased for them.

mitted himself to a cause he was sagacious enough
to see was not to be a winning one for a long
series of years. He had sacrificed to it the ambitions of his young manhood, and knew as a poet
and editor he had lost all chance of gaining the
position to which he had been aspiring. Now
came years in which he felt the pinch of poverty,
as he had not before experienced it. The poems
that were arousing the conscience of the nation
brought him no income. His mother and sister
heartily approved his course, and aided him in
maintaining it. Strict economy enabled him to
keep out of debt, meagre as were the supplies
from such editorial and book-keeping work as he
found to do. His pen was kept busy in advocating the cause he had espoused, and the poems
known as the " Voices of Freedom " came rapidly
one after another, — hammer strokes against flinty
prejudice. Sparks followed each blow. Those
who are old enough remember how these spirited
verses stirred and warmed the young hearts of the
North, and prepared the soil from which sprang
the great political party which took from him the
watchword, " Justice the highest expediency."

There was a sudden, even startling change in
the character of Whittier's poetry, when he made
up his mind to champion the cause of the slave.
The hundreds of poems he had written previous to
1833 were mere exercises in rhetoric and versifi-
cation ; they had none of the vivifying spirit which
breathes in all he wrote after he consecrated himself to the holy cause of liberty. Whittier himself
was always ashamed of his early literary work,

both prose and verse, and little of it was with
his consent saved from oblivion. And yet, as we
have seen, these early writings gave him a literary reputation which would have been highly
valued by any other author of that time. They
were widely copied in the newspapers of the land.
It is in accordance with the wish of Mr. Whittier
that his biographer, who has before him great numbers of these early and forgotten poems, decides to
bring to light only the few verses to be found in
preceding pages, to show their quality, and to indicate the remarkable change to which reference
has been made. When this change came, as has
been said of him by another, " he became the Voice
for which a few had been wearily waiting, yet
which exasperated and terrified the whole country.
To these few, therefore, Whittier at once became a
prophet; to the many, an object of detestation."
His first years of literary work had given him
a reputation at once general and flattering, which
was thrown aside without regret when the voice
which called him to higher duty was heard.

Early in November, 1833, Mr. Garrison wrote
to Whittier, asking him to go as one of the delegates from Massachusetts to the National Anti-
Slavery Convention, to be held in Philadelphia
in December. In answer to this call, he wrote to
Garrison from Haverhill, November 11, 1833 : —

"I long to go to Philadelphia, to urge upon the
members of my religious Society the duty of
putting their shoulders to the work, to make their
solemn testimony against slavery visible over the
whole land; to urge them by the holy memories

of Woolman, and Benezet, and Tyson, to come up as of old to the standard of Divine Truth, though even the fires of another persecution should blaze around them. But the expenses of the journey will, I fear, be too much for me, as thee knows our farming business does not put much cash in our pockets. I am, however, greatly obliged to the Boston Young Men's Association for selecting me as one of their delegates. I do not know how it may be, — but whether I go or not, my best wishes and my warmest sympathies are with the friends of emancipation. Some of my political friends are opposed to my anti-slavery sentiments, and perhaps it was in some degree owing to this that, at the late convention for the nomination of Senators for Essex, my nomination was lost by one vote. I should have rejoiced to have had an opportunity to coöperate personally with the abolitionists of Boston. . . . Can thee not find time for a visit to Haverhill before thee goes on to Philadelphia? I wish I was certain of going with thee. At all events, *do* write immediately on receiving this, and tell me when thee shall start for the Quaker City."

The pecuniary difficulty was removed by the generosity of Samuel E. Sewall, one of the earliest and most efficient supporters of the cause of emancipation. The journey to Philadelphia was mostly by stagecoach. Mr. Whittier, the youngest delegate to the convention, was accompanied by other members from New England, including William Lloyd Garrison, Joshua Coffin, Arnold Buffum, and eight others from Massachusetts, and Rev.

David Thurston, of Winthrop, Maine, the oldest
delegate in the convention. Mr. Whittier was
appointed one of the secretaries, and he was also
on the committee, of which Garrison was chairman, that drafted the memorable " Declaration of
Sentiments."

In an article published in the " Atlantic
Monthly," February, 1874,[1] Mr. Whittier gives
reminiscences of this convention, with pen-portraits
of some of his associates. He makes in this connection an interesting remark in regard to the division that had recently taken place in the Society
of Friends. This division was regarded as unfortunate for the interests of the convention, as the
coöperation of the Society had been counted upon
when Philadelphia was selected as the place of
meeting. He says : —

" The Society of Friends had but recently been
rent asunder by one of those unhappy controversies which so often mark the decline of practical righteousness. The martyr age of the society had passed, wealth and luxury had taken the
place of the old simplicity, there was a growing
conformity to the maxims of the world in trade
and fashion, and with it a corresponding unwilling-
ness to hazard respectability by the advocacy of
unpopular reforms. Unprofitable speculation and
disputation on the one hand, and a vain attempt on
the other to enforce uniformity of opinion, had
measurably lost sight of the fact that the end of
the gospel is love, and that charity is the crown-

---

[1] Reprinted in vol. vii. of the Riverside edition of Whittier's
writings.

ing virtue. After a long and painful struggle the disruption had taken place, the shattered fragments under name of Orthodox and Hicksite, so like, and yet so separate in feeling, confronted each other as hostile sects."

In these words he describes the closing scenes of the convention : —

" On the evening of the last day of our session, the Declaration, with its few verbal amendments, carefully engrossed on parchment, was brought before the convention. Samuel J. May rose to read it for the last time. His sweet, persuasive voice faltered with the intensity of his emotions as he repeated the solemn pledges of the concluding paragraphs. After a season of silence, David Thurston, of Maine, rose as his name was called by one of the secretaries, and affixed his name to the document. One after another passed up to the platform, signed, and retired in silence. All felt the deep responsibility of the occasion; the shadow and forecast of a life-long struggle rested upon every countenance."

Mr. Whittier's own appearance at this convention is sketched by J. Miller McKim : —

" He wore a dark frock-coat, with standing collar, which, with his thin hair, dark and sometimes flashing eyes, and black whiskers, not large, but noticeable in those unhirsute days, gave him, to my then unpracticed eye, quite as much of a military as a Quaker aspect. His broad square forehead and well-cut features, aided by his incipient reputation as a poet, made him quite a noticeable feature of the convention."

Of the sixty-two members of the convention, twenty-one were Quakers. There were twelve delegates from Massachusetts. The Declaration of Sentiments, drafted by Garrison, urged immediate emancipation as a moral duty, to be accomplished by peaceful measures only, and conceded the right of the States to manage their domestic institutions, without interference from the general government. But the duty of suppressing the slave-trade between the several States, and of abolishing slavery altogether in the District of Columbia and in the Territories, was set forth with much force. This declaration was engrossed on parchment, and signed by all the delegates. Of his own signature to this declaration Mr. Whittier said: "I set a higher value on my name as appended to the Anti-Slavery Declaration of 1833, than on the title-page of any book." A facsimile of this document, framed in oak from the ruins of Pennsylvania Hall, destroyed by the mob of 1838, was always given a conspicuous place in his home at Amesbury.[1]

In January, 1834, the New England Anti-Slavery Society held its annual meeting in Boston. Mr. Whittier was not able to attend, but sent a letter the reading of which is said to have had a thrilling effect upon the audience.

In March, 1834, Mr. Whittier wrote the following letter to Rev. Dr. William Ellery Channing,

---

[1] Since his death it has been given to the youngest son of William Lloyd Garrison, who has also the table upon which the document was signed and the inkstand which was used on this historic occasion.

hoping to induce this eminent divine to lend the
cause of immediate emancipation the weight of his
great influence. Channing had already been considering the subject of slavery, and had begun to
write his clear, logical, dispassionate, but incisive
essay against the institution. His letter to Dr.
Follen upon this theme was soon after made public,
and later, in the same year, a sermon was delivered
by him against the mobs which had then begun to
disgrace New England cities. His great work on
slavery was published the next year. He took
his own way, as was his wont in all matters, in
dealing with this reform, and this led to severe
criticism upon him from one wing of the anti-
slavery reformers; but from the first, Whittier
recognized the great value of his service to the
cause, and did not join in the detraction. His
letter to Channing was written from Haverhill, on
the 24th of 3d month, 1834. He said : —

"A recent perusal of thy sermons published in
1832, by Bowen, has induced me, although a
stranger, to address thee. From all that I have
seen of thy writings, it has seemed to me that it was
thy aim to make Christianity a practical matter ;
a living, a beneficent reality, such as its Founder
intended ; a real bond of holy brotherhood which
should unite all the human family, unshackle
mind and body, and bless all the children of our
Heavenly Father with that liberty wherewith He
has made them free. My attention has been particularly directed to the sentiment expressed in
the sermons above mentioned in pages 153, 162,
165, 166. To my mind the elevated sentiment of

these passages has a direct bearing upon a great question now agitating the community, — I allude to the slavery question, — the doctrine of immediate emancipation. I am but an humble individual, and were my subject less important I should not seek with my feeble voice the ear of one whose name and fame have no narrower limits than those of Christianity itself; but I cannot forbear expressing to thee my heartfelt desire, my earnest hope, that these great powers of intellect with which a merciful God has favored thee may be exerted at this crisis in the great cause of emancipation. I cannot doubt thy sentiments on this subject; may I beg of thee to openly coöperate with that great and deserved influence which Providence has allotted to thy profession, with those who are now striving in this cause, 'to break every chain of selfishness, to enlarge and invigorate the kind affections, to identify themselves with other beings, to sympathize not with a few, but with all the living and rational creatures of God.' [An extract from Channing's writings.] So shall the blessings of many who are ready to perish come upon thee. The deep interest which I feel in this great point of Christian duty must be my apology for this abrupt epistle."

We now come to the period when Mr. Whittier was to experience some of the difficulties attending the warm advocacy of an unpopular cause. Mr. Garrison began the publication of the "Liberator" in January, 1831. He had previously, at Baltimore and Bennington, Vt., shown his strong purpose to fight the institution of slavery to the death.

At first, he had sympathy and help from all classes of people at the North. The colonization scheme had for some time been looked upon with favor by philanthropists, at the South as well as at the North; but, as it afterward appeared, for widely different reasons. At the North it was looked upon as a means of gradually extinguishing slavery, by removing the negroes to Africa. At the South, there was less and less purpose to do away with the institution, either gradually or at all. It was just beginning to be profitable. Colonization meant to the slaveholders a way of disposing of the free people of color, who made the slaves uneasy, and occasionally helped them to escape, while at the North, the Colonization Society was generally regarded as engaged in a worthy mission of Christian philanthropy — indeed as a branch of the foreign mission work. For would not the Christianized negroes carry to benighted Africa the religion and the civilization they had acquired during their stay with us?

It was when Garrison began to denounce the Colonization Society as " the handmaid of slavery " that he stirred up a tempest among the churches. For a long series of years they had been taking up collections for this handmaid of the missions, as they had regarded it. The call for immediate emancipation had not given much offense among the churches outside the commercial cities, as slavery was universally considered at the North an evil to be done away with at some time, and the general feeling was, the sooner the better.

All over the North, it was for a time an easy

matter to organize an anti-slavery society. Hundreds of them were at work upon public sentiment in New England, and every town in some parts of Ohio had such societies, and they were approved by all the churches. There was comparatively little objection (except in the cities) to the word "immediate," which was insisted upon by Garrison. But many prominent clergymen, statesmen, and merchants, who were identified with the colonization movement, were angered at once when their pet philanthropy was denounced as a bulwark of slavery. Whittier's pamphlet and his replies to the Virginia editors had strongly reinforced the position taken by Garrison.

The mobs that for a series of years disgraced the cities of New England had their origin partly in the feeling that the abolitionists were in conflict with the churches, and partly in the fear of business men that our commercial relations with the South were imperiled by the agitation. The dirty work of these riots was done by men who had no care about the principle involved, but who saw that they had license for rough sport and even violence, and that they would not be interfered with by the classes which usually insisted upon order.

When Garrison was in England, in 1833, he invited George Thompson to visit this country, and deliver anti-slavery addresses. Thompson was one of the most eloquent of the English reformers who had secured the abolition of slavery in all the British colonies. He came to America in September, 1834, and wherever he appeared

was at first well received. Garrison says of him
that he was a young man of thirty, tall, graceful,
and with a sweet voice. " As an orator," he adds,
" he surpasses any speaker I have ever heard."
He was prudent enough at the start not to attempt
addressing audiences in New York or Boston.
He spoke at several small places in Massachusetts, where his eloquence was greatly admired.
He went to Maine, and was well received in Portland and Brunswick, but met his first demonstra-
tion of violence at Augusta, where his windows
were broken.

At length, the word seems to have been passed
over the whole country that he was a " British
emissary," who had come to make trouble between
North and South, and cause a disruption of our
Union, for the benefit of the manufacturers and
merchants of England. The jealousy of our mother country was intense at that time, and it was
easy to stir the passions of the populace against
an Englishman. Thompson's life was thereafter
often endangered, but when driven out of one city
he appeared in another, with the unwelcome message he was bravely determined to deliver.

This was the condition of things when Mr.
Whittier was entering upon his work as an opponent of slavery and of the Colonization Society.
In 1835, his native town sent him to represent her
in the General Court. He had already written
and published in the " Liberator " of September
13, 1834, the " Stanzas " [1] beginning with the line :

[1] This poem, originally called *Stanzas*, was afterward entitled *Follen*, and in the latest edition of Whittier's collected

" Our fellow-countrymen in chains! "

It happened to be first printed just one week before the arrival of Thompson in this country. It was a passionate outburst of indignation against the system of slavery, and it rang at once through the North. It was recited by anti-slavery orators with great effect in their meetings, and the schoolboys found it a piece suitable for declamation. The number of the " Liberator " in which this poem originally appeared has this appreciative comment upon it from the hand of Garrison : —

" Our gifted brother Whittier has again seized the great trumpet of Liberty, and blown a blast that shall ring from Maine to the Rocky Mountains."

As a member of the legislature of Massachusetts, Mr. Whittier was active and influential, though not a debater. He took especial interest in a movement to abolish the death penalty, and secured a petition of sixty-seven citizens of Haverhill, headed by his own name, for this object. He was reëlected as representative from Haverhill for the year 1836, but his physician assured him it would be unsafe for him again to undertake the work that had seriously injured him in 1835. Hon. Robert Rantoul, Jr., represented Gloucester in the Massachusetts legislature at the time when Mr. Whittier represented Haverhill. They had rooms together for a time at a boarding place in Franklin Street, by the Bulfinch urn. Their rela-

works is named *Expostulation*. Neither of these names can be regarded as adequate for such a noble outburst of hot indignation.

tions were intimate so long as Rantoul lived, and
how his memory was cherished after his death is
shown in several poems in which he is directly or
indirectly mentioned.

It was while he was in attendance upon a special session of the legislature, October 21, 1835,
that Whittier witnessed the Boston mob, led by
" men of property and standing," which broke up a
meeting of the Female Anti-Slavery Society, and
dragged Garrison in the street, with a rope about
his body. Hearing of the disturbance, while in
his seat in the State House, and knowing that his
sister Elizabeth was at the meeting, he hurried to
the spot. In a letter written on the occasion of
the semi-centennial commemoration of the affair,
in 1885, he says : —

" I found the street thronged and noisy with tur-
bulent respectability and unwashed rascality. I
was anxious for my young sister, who I knew was
in the women's anti-slavery meeting ; but I heard
that the ladies had all left and were safe. The
fury of the mob seemed to be directed against
George Thompson, but failing to find him, they
seized upon Garrison. I heard their shout of ex-
ultation and caught a glimpse of their victim just
as he was rescued and driven off to Leverett Street
jail. Thither Samuel J. May and myself followed,
and visited him in prison. I could sympathize
with him, for only a short time before, the Concord
mob, which could not get hold of Thompson, fell
upon me with stones and missiles, and my escape
with nothing worse than a few bruises was something to be thankful for. The rioters had just

roughly used a poor traveling Quaker preacher, quietly passing through the town, who had the misfortune of being mistaken for myself. It seemed to be a case of suffering by proxy all around. From our present standpoint we can pity and forgive the actors in those scenes."

The Concord riot, referred to by Mr. Whittier in this letter, happened September 4, 1835, and the circumstances that led to it will now be traced. An anti-slavery society was organized in Haverhill in the spring of 1834, and Mr. Whittier acted as its corresponding secretary. The speakers from other places who lectured before this society were welcome guests at the Whittier homestead in East Haverhill. On the 21st of August, 1835, George Thompson came to Haverhill to rest from the exertions incident to a series of mobs through which he had passed, and made his home with Whittier. He delivered a lecture in Haverhill which was well received. In a diary kept by Elizabeth Whittier, under date 24th of 8th month, 1835, is this entry:

" The three past days have been full of incident and excitement. Oh, we have been too proud of our country; we have been flattered, inordinately flattered, till like the self-glorying Pharisee we have thanked God we were not like other nations. America is working everlasting disgrace for her future name. The shameful record must be written down, that in this land of Bibles and law and learning and *freedom*, a minister of Christ, — a Paul in his zeal for the promotion of every cause of righteousness and truth, — a stranger, led by the holiest impulses of humanity, coming among us to

proclaim in his own wonderful and fervid eloquence
the eternal principles of justice to mankind, — that
such a man, with such purposes, was slandered by
Americans, hated by Americans, and *mobbed* by
Americans; that in Massachusetts thousands of
dollars were offered for his assassination! Oh, I
am sure I shall never be proud of my country. I
shall much sooner be ashamed of my fatherland,
while it is thus unchristianized."

Three days afterward there is a record in the
diary that George Thompson had left for his home
" day before yesterday." It appears that he went
to Salem, and that Mr. Whittier and his mother
also went to Salem, to attend a Quarterly Meeting
of the Society of Friends. Among Elizabeth's
papers is found a note hurriedly written by her
brother, which reads as follows: —

SALEM, 5*th day afternoon,*
8th mo. 27.

I write by our good friend, Thomas Spencer, to
request thee to welcome brother Thompson to our
house, as his friends are somewhat fearful for his
personal safety at this time. Mother and myself
will be at home on Seventh day, if nothing happens. In great haste,

J. G. WHITTIER.

Thompson will remain with us some days at
Haverhill.

But Thompson did not arrive at East Haverhill
on Friday, as was expected, and this record is found
in Elizabeth's diary: —

" *7th day eve.* Never have I felt so deeply the necessity of Christian forbearance and long suffering on the part of the abolitionists as at present. . . . George Thompson was to have been in Haverhill, on his way to New Hampshire, yesterday afternoon; but he has not come. What can have detained him? I have watched very anxiously for his coming, and have been fearful that all was not well. Heaven grant it may be, and I trust it is. Sickness or something of less importance may have kept him. I wish I was good enough to pray acceptably for his and all our dear friends' safety."

Her prayers were answered promptly, for Thompson arrived safely on the evening the above entry was made in her diary. On Monday, August 31, she writes: —

" Our friends, George Thompson and Samuel J. May, came late on Seventh day eve, and their coming relieved us of much anxiety. Yesterday morning, Greenleaf left here in company with George Thompson on a short tour to New Hampshire. Yesterday afternoon S. J. May occupied the pulpit of N. Gage. He had come to Haverhill with the expectation of addressing the people on the subject of American slavery, on last evening, in the First Parish meeting-house. But for reasons best known to themselves the gentlemen comprising the committee saw fit to refuse the house, and the Christian church was obtained; the house was filled to overflowing; at half past seven the lecturer arose, and in his peculiarly winning tones commenced an appeal in behalf of the two and a half millions of our countrymen who are in slavery in our land.

He was listened to with almost breathless attention ;
the interest of the audience was so intense that the
noise outside the house had not been noticed. Most
of the people did not believe — how could they ? —
that there were those among us sufficiently misled
to do what has scarcely ever been done in our
country, — violate the sanctity of the Sabbath by
a reckless and outrageous assault upon a peaceable
assemblage. But we were made to believe it when
a stone was thrown, breaking the window, and scat-
tering the glass among the startled audience. But
all were soon still, and listening to the calm tones
of the speaker. I only felt fear for the speaker,
as his figure was visible on the outside, and I was
not mistaken, for the next moment a heavy missile
was thrown forcibly against the window of the
pulpit. The speaker paused an instant, and then
endeavored to proceed. But another heavy stone
thrown among the crowd drove most of the audience
from their seats, and a fourth and heavier stone
from without completed the scene of confusion.
The lecturer was anxious to proceed, but expressed
his willingness to be guided by the advice of his
friends. Rev. E. N. Harris arose, and remarked
that the unlawful proceedings had so disturbed the
meeting that it would be useless for his brother
May to attempt to go on with his remarks. Yielding to the advice of his friend, and to the dictate
of prudence, the speaker closed his notes, and the
crowd who were hurrying towards the door paused
as the blessing of the God of all peace was invoked
by the outraged advocate of human rights."

Elizabeth Whittier does not tell to her diary

how she and her friend, Harriet Minot, daughter
of Judge Minot, took the hands of Mr. May, one
on each side, and pushed their way through the
mob of their townsmen, and, though rudely
treated, were not injured. Neither does she tell
the most shameful part of the story. A heavily
loaded cannon had been dragged near the
church, and at the same time the wooden steps
at the doors had been pulled away. The plan
of the miscreants was to break the windows and
discharge the cannon, thus causing a rush to the
doors, and, the steps being removed, the audience would have been precipitated several feet;
limbs would have been broken, and perhaps
lives lost in the panic. For some reason, the gun
was not fired, and the brief pause for the benedic-
tion gave time to discover that the steps were removed and to replace them. Miss Whittier and
Miss Minot were well known to the citizens of
Haverhill, and that Mr. May was not roughly
handled when he came out of the church was due
to their protection. The mob was composed of
about two hundred men and boys. It was probably known in the town that Thompson arrived on
Saturday, and it was supposed he was at this
meeting. Perhaps the disturbance grew out of
this misunderstanding, for there was a bitter feeling against the famous English orator, which was
just then working like leaven throughout New
England.

Whittier and Thompson, entirely unconscious
of the disturbance they left behind them, were
on their way to meet a more violent mob. The

object of their journey was to visit Nathaniel P. Rogers, at Plymouth, N. H. They arrived on Monday, and Thompson delivered three lectures in the place, which were well received. On their way to Plymouth, they had stopped for the night at Concord, at the house of George Kent, who was a brother-in-law of Rogers. Kent made preparations during their absence for an anti-slavery meeting, to be held in Concord upon their return. He caused handbills to be circulated, announcing a meeting at the court house, Friday evening, September 4, at which "the principles, views, and operations of the abolitionists would be explained, and questions answered, by George Thompson and John G. Whittier." Nearly all his life Mr. Whittier avoided public speaking, but in those days he occasionally addressed anti-slavery meetings. Kent's handbill made a great stir. At a political meeting held Thursday evening, a protest was made against allowing the abolitionists a hearing in Concord. The selectmen warned those who were active in the matter that it would be unsafe to hold the proposed meeting, but they persisted. As the hour set for the meeting approached, a crowd, evidently bent on mischief, filled the street in front of the court house, and the selectmen ordered that the doors should not be opened. Thereupon the multitude, determined that "the incendiary Thompson" should not escape them, began the search for him, and the cry was raised, "To George Kent's, and the wine in his cellar." On their way they met Whittier, who was with J. H. Kimball, editor of the "Herald."

His Quaker coat did not prevent the mob from supposing he was Thompson. They began to pelt him with rotten eggs,[1] with mud and stones, although Kimball assured them he was not the man they sought. He received only slight injuries, for though the missiles fell around them and upon them, no stone happened to touch their heads. They were somewhat lamed by those which struck them elsewhere, and were covered with the dirt of the street which had been cast at them. In speaking of it in later years, Mr. Whittier said he could remember the sound of the stones that missed their aim and struck the wooden fences by their side, and that it made him realize how St. Paul felt when he was thrice stoned. Mr. William A. Kent, a brother of George Kent, saw them passing his house, while thus beset, and though not an abolitionist, he opened his door to them, and they thankfully sprang up the steps three at a time. As soon as they were safely inside, the crowd, who were disposed to enter and pull them out, were bravely met by Mr. Kent, who told them that if they came in it would be over his dead body. The crowd were soon after convinced, by Rev. Mr. Thomas, a Unitarian clergyman (whose wife was a niece of N. P. Rogers), that they had mistaken their man, and passed on

---

[1] The coat Mr. Whittier wore on this occasion was so soiled by rotten eggs that it could never be cleansed. It was kept as a relic until after the war, when boxes of clothing were sent from Amesbury to the needy freedmen. Mr. Whittier contributed the old coat, among other things, and at least one Southern negro derived a benefit from the little affair that happened in New Hampshire thirty years earlier.

to George Kent's, where a small company of anti-
slavery people had assembled to pay their respects
to the famous English orator, and to the poet, his
companion. Among these were two nieces of
Daniel Webster, daughters of his brother Eze-
kiel. When the mob reached the house, Thompson had left it by a back street, accompanied by
Mr. Kent. A demand was made that Thompson
be sent out to them, which was answered with the
assurance that he had gone, and that there were
only ladies in the house. General Davis then addressed the crowd, and told them they had done
all they came for ; they had prevented Thompson
from speaking, and he advised them to go home.
They went away, but not homeward. After visiting the liquor saloons, they constructed an effigy,
labeled it " George Thompson," and burned it in
the State House park. Then they indulged in
fireworks, and brought out a cannon to celebrate
their victory.

In the mean time, Mr. Whittier, hearing the
guns, and being anxious for the safety of his
friends, changed his Quaker hat for that of Rev.
Mr. Thomas, and, thus disguised, ventured again
into the street, passed through the mob, which was
frenzied with drink, and soon found Mr. Thompson,
who had also returned to George Kent's. The mob
came back from the State House to Mr. George
Kent's, and kept up a disturbance from two o'clock
to daybreak, having a suspicion that Thompson
had returned. In the early morning, while the
noisy multitude were shouting and firing guns
about the house, an escape was effected. Their

horse was harnessed and brought to a side door. When Whittier, Thompson, and Rev. Mr. Putnam, of Dunbarton, were in the carriage, the gate was suddenly opened, and the horse was driven at a gallop through a mob too surprised to stop the carriage. They were soon out of hearing of the yells and gunshots of the maddened crowd. They left Concord by the way of the Hookset bridge, all other avenues being guarded, and hastened back towards Haverhill. Stopping at an inn, for breakfast, they found a little knot of rough men to whom the landlord was telling extravagant stories of the brave times at Haverhill, the last Sunday night, when George Thompson, the English incendiary, and a fanatical Quaker named Whittier, were so roughly handled that they could not soon address another abolition meeting. They had escaped into New Hampshire, and he showed a printed notice asking all good citizens to aid in securing Thompson, and giving him his just deserts. Whittier inquired how the rascal was to be recognized, and was answered, " Easily enough, he is a tonguey fellow." As they were about to leave, being already in the carriage, Whittier said to the landlord, "This is George Thompson, and my name is Whittier." The man stared with open mouth until they were out of sight. Brief accounts of the Concord mob were given to the press by both Whittier and Thompson, soon after the occurrence. They both make light of the affair, and mention but few of the incidents that have since been gathered from conversations with Mr. Whittier and from other sources. Thompson was so many times in jeopardy

in 1835, and had escaped unhurt so often from the
hands of previous mobs, that the Concord violence
made little impression upon him. Nearly fifty
years after the event, Mr. Whittier met in Portland
a man who confessed that he was one of the mob.
Whittier asked what would have been done to
Thompson and himself, if they had fallen into the
hands of the crowd, and the man replied that preparations had been made to blacken their faces so
that it would have been difficult to remove the
coloring matter. Tar and feathers were also in
readiness. Thompson returned with Whittier to
East Haverhill, and spent a week at the old homestead. Elizabeth's talks with her diary are sus
pended during these days, but after their guest has
gone she has time to write again, and says : —

" It must have been a noble sight ! Five hundred
patriotic citizens of New Hampshire, marching
with cursing and shouting to the rescue of the
Constitution ! Even the Quaker coat of J. G. W.
does not quite defend him from the chivalry of the
brave band ! It was a manifestation of extraordinary courage on the part of the belligerents to
venture an attack on two Quaker gentlemen, walking soberly and peaceably under their broadbrims.
Was there not a manifestation of Satanic influence
in the rush of the crowd to George Kent's with the
evident purpose of destruction to the beautiful mansion of an intelligent Christian, and kind-hearted
fellow-citizen ? . . . On First day evening, a
prayer meeting was holden in our little schoolhouse, and George Thompson, the man who passed
triumphant and applauded through all the great

cities of England and Scotland, as the eloquent pleader for the poor down-trodden slaves of the British colonies, whose appeals have been listened to and admired by immense audiences, was present, and at the earnest request of Rev. J. R. Cushing briefly addressed the meeting, before closing it with a truly fervid and Christian prayer. . . . George Thompson left us on Second day morning, and I was very, very sorry to have him go. I had begun to think of him not with the reverence and awe I used to connect with the name of George Thompson, the eloquent English orator, but quite as a dear friend. It is altogether too high, too happy a station. I am not worthy to be *his* friend, but I am proud that I am privileged to think of him as *my* friend. . . . As an appendix to our loss of Second day, Greenleaf left us on Third day, to recommence his legislative duties at Boston."

One other mob Mr. Whittier encountered in these times, and the story of it is as follows: An Essex County anti-slavery convention was to be held in Newburyport, in 1837, but no hall or church could be obtained, and so the meeting was held in the garden of Mrs. Charles Butler, on Brown Square. A rough crowd from the wharves, led by citizens who considered themselves respectable, broke up the meeting by beating upon tin pans, blowing fish-horns, and howling. They also assaulted some of the speakers, causing little injury, however, except to clothing. Henry B. Stanton, who was one of the speakers, had the buttons cut from his coat. Mr. Whittier relates this incident of the affair : —

"As we were being assailed with decayed eggs, sticks, and light missiles, I thought discretion the better part of valor, and hurried away at what my friend N. P. Rogers called 'an undignified trot,' in company with an aged Orthodox minister, one of the few who had the moral courage to attend an anti-slavery meeting in those days, and who was settled in a neighboring town. As soon as we stopped to recover breath, I said to him: 'I am surprised that we should be disturbed in a quiet, Puritan city like Newburyport. I 've lived near it for years, and thought it was a pious city.' Laying his hand on my shoulder the clergyman said, 'Young man, when you are as old as I am you will understand that it is easier to be pious than it is to be good.'"

In these New England mobs Mr. Whittier has said he never apprehended serious danger to life or limb, and indeed he was better prepared for such danger than for anything like personal indignity. The thought of such indignities affected him more than even the dread of death. In an article published in the "Atlantic Monthly," February, 1874, he says: —

"I had read John Trumbull's description of the tarring and feathering of his hero, McFingal, when, after the application of the melted tar, the feather-bed was ripped open and shaken over him, until

'Not Maia's son, with wings for ears,
Such plumes about his visage wears,
Nor Milton's six-winged angel gathers
Such superfluity of feathers;'

and I confess I was quite unwilling to undergo a martyrdom which my best friends could scarcely refrain from laughing at."

In a letter to his friend Thayer, who was then editing the " Commercial Herald " in Philadelphia, under date Haverhill, 29th of 11th mo., 1835, Mr. Whittier writes that he is busy with farm work, and adds : " Anti-slavery is going on well in spite of mobs, Andover Seminary, and *rum*. This town has gone for Jackson, and our senators have got in (four of them) with the skin of their teeth. The State is almost Van Burenized."

Early in 1836, Mr. Thayer urged him to come to Philadelphia, to engage in a newspaper enterprise with him. He replied from the old homestead in Haverhill (where he appears to have been snowbound again), under date of 16th of 2d mo., 1836 : —

" Blocked up by a four-feet snow I have had no means of sending to the village. . . . I must decline thy proposal ; my health recently has been uncertain, and I am just getting over an attack of my old complaint, — palpitation of the heart. I should not dare to engage in such an undertaking at present. I nevertheless have wished a hundred times that we could be together as formerly, as we used to agree so perfectly on most points."

During part of the year 1836, Mr. Whittier was editing the Haverhill " Gazette," while managing his farm. Early in 1837, he had again a call to Philadelphia, this time to edit an anti-slavery paper. At about the same time he had a call to Portland. The following paragraphs from a letter to Mr. Thayer were written while undecided. He writes from Amesbury, 31st of 3d mo., 1837 : —

" I have a wish on many accounts to live in your city ; but the Portland folks are very desirous of getting me to go 'Down East.' They have offered me $1200 per annum. The climate would not, however, suit me so well as yours, and, to tell the truth, there is hardly field enough for doing a great deal of good in Maine, at present. Our friends in Boston are fully persuaded that the grand battle is now to be fought in Pennsylvania, between mobocracy (excited by the slaveholding influence of Virginia and Maryland, and by the President's outrageous and abominable sentiments expressed in his inaugural message) and the friends of liberty. One word, *sub rosa :* If Ritner can be sustained in his own State, the entire North, save New Hampshire and Maine, would go for him for the Presidency. I have not felt at liberty to go to Portland until I have heard from Philadelphia. On the receipt of a letter I shall be able to decide immediately."

The decision arrived at, some months later, was in favor of Philadelphia.

CHAPTER V.

1836–1838.

In April, 1836, the Haverhill farm, of one hundred and forty-eight acres, was sold to Aaron Chase, and a cottage in the village of Amesbury was bought a few weeks afterward. This one-story cottage, which was enlarged and remodeled at various times, was the poet's home until his death, a period of a little more than fifty-six years. The farm was sold for $3000, and the house and lot in Amesbury cost $1200. Two reasons induced the selling of the farm and the removal to Amesbury. Mr. Whittier was so fully occupied with his literary and reform work, and at the same time so broken in health, that it became necessary for him to give up the care of a difficult farm; moreover, there was no Friends' meeting nearer than Amesbury, and his mother and sister found it beyond their strength to attend meetings regularly at such a distance. When the farm was sold, the horse was given up, and the poet never afterward owned one. The new home was located nearly opposite the Friends' meeting-house. The present meeting-house, built more than forty years ago, upon plans made by Mr. Whittier, is not far distant on the same street.

The Home at
Amesbury.
S.L.S. Sc.
1894

The Amesbury Home

Three successive meeting-houses have been built
by the Friends in Amesbury during the past two
hundred years, all of them on Friend Street, upon
which Mr. Whittier's house stands. In the oldest
one, Thomas Story, one of William Penn's councilors of state, held forth in 1704, when he defended his faith in a notable debate. He was the
first man to express a doubt about the world being
made in six literal days, and the first to suggest
that the days alluded to in the Scripture account
of the creation were ages in length. The present
edifice was erected in 1851, and the details of its
construction were left by the society to the care
of Mr. Whittier. But as the poet had at that
time mixed with the world's people more than most
of his brethren, there was some fear among the
more conservative that he would provide too many
modern comforts for the worshipers — perhaps
even give them a steeple! Mistrusting this, and
to set their hearts at rest, he wisely employed as
builders three venerable carpenters, one of whom
was a Quaker minister, and the other two elders
of the society. The result of their joint labors
was, as might have been expected, a perfectly
orthodox Quaker meeting-house, without steeple or
filigree work of any kind,[1] but very neat and comfortable.

[1] Several years ago a worthy missionary, anxious to reform a
pagan neighborhood in a town just over the New Hampshire
border, called upon Mr. Whittier for a subscription. "Does thee
propose to put a steeple on thy church?" he inquired. "Yes,
sir." "Well, I am glad thee has undertaken to christianize that
neighborhood, and am willing to help thee. But I am sorry
about the steeple. I will subscribe, however, on condition that
no part of *my* money goes into that extravagance."

The lot upon which the Amesbury cottage was built afforded a garden that every year produced a great variety of fruits and vegetables. Mr. Whittier gave much attention to it, enjoying the work as he could not enjoy the heavier labor on his ancestral acres. About forty years ago, the eastern end of the cottage was made two stories in height, and at the southeastern corner an addition was made of the same height. The lower room in the addition was fitted up for a study, and the upper room, after the death of his sister Elizabeth, in 1864, became Mr. Whittier's chamber. The study was always known as the "garden room." Mr. Whittier objected to the use of the word "study," or "library," for such an unpretentious literary workshop. It was warmed by a Franklin stove. In the recess on one side of the chimney were book-shelves, and in the corresponding recess on the other side was placed his writing-desk.

The book-shelves held only a small part of Mr. Whittier's constantly increasing library, which overflowed into nearly all the rooms. The northern window, next the desk, was in a door opening upon a little veranda, and gave a view of the street and the southern slope of Po Hill, which is close at hand. This pleasant little room naturally became the sitting-room of the family. For Mr. Whittier loved domesticity, and could read and write without disturbance in the midst of household affairs. It is the room held in most loving remembrance by the friends and visitors of the poet. In it he did his best work. Here "Snow-Bound" was written, and many of his most popular poems. The western end of the house remained one story in height until the year 1884, when another story was added, giving the house its present appearance. In the midst of all the alterations here described, the little parlor, at the northwestern corner of the original cottage, has remained unchanged. This room also has its open fireplace.

The ancient towns of Amesbury and Salisbury, until within a few years, when they were consolidated, were divided by the Powow River, and the principal village of each town was located at the falls in this rapid stream. To a stranger they seemed but a single village, the river for most of its course being entirely hidden by the wide arches which span it to bear up the main street, and by the factories on each side of the stream. The part which is thus concealed is a fall of about eighty feet over jagged ledges, and here the power for the mills is obtained. In a letter to a friend who suggested that he celebrate Po Hill, the picturesque eminence overlooking his Amesbury residence (as Job's Hill overlooks his birthplace), he says: "I quite agree with thee that Po Hill is well worthy of being celebrated in song. I have mentioned it in my poem, 'Abram Morrison,' and in the prelude to 'Miriam.' It is also referred to in 'Cobbler Keezar's Vision,' in which the swift Powow stream is described as it appeared to the early settlers, coming down from the south side of the hill in a series of cascades, the finest of which are now hidden by the mills, or arched over by the main street of busy Amesbury : —

"Woodsy and wild and lonesome,
    The swift stream wound away,
Through birches and scarlet maples,
    Flashing in foam and spray, —

"Down on the sharp-horned ledges
    Plunging in steep cascade,
Tossing its white-maned waters
    Against the hemlock's shade."

The family removed from Haverhill to Amesbury on the 6th of July, 1836. Seven weeks after, Elizabeth writes in her diary : —

"So now we are here at Amesbury, and must henceforth call it *home*. How strange! The evening I left our home at [East] Haverhill there was quite too much confusion to allow us to think. I spent a fortnight with sister Mary at Haverhill, and on our way to Amesbury we rode up to the old gateway which always before had worn the cheerful look of home. There was nothing there to welcome us, save my own poor cat — and she was right glad. . . . I have been here now five weeks, and save my brothers and sister have seen but five of my Haverhill friends, and certainly these few seemed dearer than ever. I wonder if I shall ever love Amesbury or its people! I shall when I forget the dear ones and things at Haverhill, perhaps. I know scarce any of the abolition people here, but expect to like them all — or at least their abolition."

She was soon after elected president of the Women's Anti-Slavery Society of Amesbury.

In bringing into one chapter the introduction of Whittier to the work which was so strongly to affect his nature and his occupation we have anticipated the narrative, and now we partially re-trace our steps to speak of his relations to political parties after leaving Hartford. Mr. Whittier's editorship of political papers in Boston and Hartford gave him a taste for political life which he enjoyed, and woke an ambition to be serviceable to his State and the nation, not only in moulding the policy of his party so as to aid the reforms he favored, but in selecting the men who were to carry its principles into effect. The following notes to Mr. Harriman, editor of the Haverhill " Iris," indicate how eagerly he followed public events from the seclusion of his farm.

East Parish, 1831.

I have been embargoed for the past three weeks, unable to stir; and for a week past unable to *see*, the same persistent influenza having finally taken possession of my eyes. I send you something which I scrawled yesterday with a bandaged eye. Try to set it up correctly, for 't is horribly written. If you could notice my leaving the paper at Hartford, and mention at the same time that I was for some time editor of the " Essex Gazette," and that had I remained so I should have warmly advocated the cause of Mr. Cushing, it might do good at this time. But say nothing disparagingly of Mr. Thayer. He is on the wrong side, but he does pretty well with a bad cause. Did you ever read Burke's speeches and writings? If not, read them attentively. They will prove valuable to you, as they have to me.

EAST PARISH, 2d of 2d mo., 1832.

I am starving for newspapers; I now and then get one from Boston and Washington, but not until they are gray-headed with age. Could you send me a lot of papers of any kind? Cushing's speech is excellent, admirably calculated for the *Lowell* meridian. If he should be nominated, he would get it next trial. I don't like, however, what he says of General Jackson.

Have you Mr. Choate's speech on the tariff, made last session? I have never seen it. I see that he has lately made a speech on Verplanck's bill, in which he unequivocally admits the necessity of *reducing the revenue to fifteen millions.* You mention a *rumor* about Clay and Webster. I trust that Mr. Webster will beware how he lends himself to Jacksonism, and that Mr. Clay will hold aloof from Nullification. The one is Scylla, the other Charybdis. But I *do* hope that Mr. Clay will oppose the placing of the whole military force of the United States in the hands of General Jackson. I would as soon trust it in the hands of the devil. To be consistent he *must* do so. Both Mr. Clay and Mr. Calhoun denounced the lawless conduct of the military chieftain in Pensacola, and in the Seminole war.

1832.

There is no other way but to go right ahead with Cushing. The other party hold a sort of convention to-day, I understand. But whatever they may offer, *beware of them.*

I have got the rheumatism to pay for riding in the teeth of the northwest wind from Newburyport.

To the end of his life he cherished all the privileges of citizenship, and, believing in parties, abandoned no political organization so long as he saw a chance of keeping it engaged in the reforms upon which he set his heart. Beginning his political life as a partisan of Clay, he did not give him up until he saw it was useless to expect the great Kentuckian to come out as the champion of freedom. He stood by other political friends with the same steadfastness, even when he had much to criticise in their conduct, and he never shirked the duty of criticising.[1] Nothing but the delicacy of his health, at critical times, prevented his being the candidate of his party for important places when a nomination was equivalent to an election, in the early part of his career. In a letter never before published, dated Haverhill, 8th mo., 1832, to an early and valued friend in Cincinnati, he wrote: —

"Six months ago I really considered myself a citizen of Cincinnati. I had determined upon going to the West. I left Hartford with regret,

[1] "His natural interest in affairs, and strong love of humanity, made him a willing and active worker in the field of politics and reform. For he was by instinct a political as well as a moral reformer, and dearly loved the conflict of ballots. He often gave expression to his views of public policy in the newspapers, in later life, and his opinions on political measures carried weight with leaders of national repute. His interest in party success sometimes brought him to the border line of expediency, jarring upon the uncompromising notions of his non-voting abolition friends. It was hard for him to abandon the Whig party, and impossible to cut loose from the Republican, but his political sagacity and judgment were maintained. While advocating the reëlection of Harrison in 1892, he foresaw and prophesied the success of Cleveland." — *W. L. Garrison in Brooklyn Address,* *December* 17, 1892.

for I had formed acquaintances there and established friendships which had become, as it were, a part of my being. I returned to Haverhill, and started for the South the first of December [1831]. Being a member of the National Republican convention [a delegate from Hartford] I intended to spend a part of the winter in Baltimore and Washington. On reaching Boston, I was taken with the influenza, which, added to previous ill health, kept me at home during the whole winter. In the spring [of 1832] the precarious state of my health, and some prospects which were held out to me by my political friends, induced me to remain in this section of the country. These prospects might have been realized before this but for a circumstance over which I had no control. You know what a tedious time we have had here relative to the choice of Representative to Congress. My political friends insisted upon my allowing myself to be a candidate. Astonished as I was at such an unexpected prospect, I could only assure them that my age presented, to say nothing of anything else, an insuperable barrier, the Constitution requiring twenty-five years, and my age being only twenty-four. . . . I should not have mentioned it but to account for my remaining in this section of the country. . . . I have written little for a long time save upon dry politics. I hate Jackson, or rather Jackson's measures, most cordially. I admire Clay, and shall do all I can to promote his success."

The "tedious time" referred to in the above letter was in connection with the candidacy of

Caleb Cushing, who began his efforts to get into Congress in 1826, and did not succeed until 1834. He had many enemies in his own party, which prevented his election in a district where his side was usually in the ascendant. He was occasionally disposed to transfer to some friend who could unite the factions of his party the burden of the candidacy. There were seventeen Congressional elections in the North Essex district between 1831 and 1833, and the seat in the national legislature to which this district was entitled was vacant during nearly the whole term. In the summer of 1832 there was a suggestion to unite the party by nominating Mr. Whittier. Mr. Thayer, editor of the Haverhill "Gazette," had been an opponent of Cushing, but could be depended upon to favor Whittier, and the young poet was quite willing to accept the position. His few years' experience in " practical politics " had fostered an ambition for power and patronage, of which those can have no idea who knew him only after he had devoted himself to philanthropic labors. After leaving his political editorship in Boston and Hartford, and coming back to his farm, he found his friend Edwin Harriman editing the Haverhill " Iris," a Cushing paper. He contributed many political articles to the " Iris," and one or two partisan poems, like the satirical verses addressed to the " Poetical Trio," given in a preceding chapter. Here is a private letter to Harriman which illustrates the motives and methods of Whittier's ambition, before the great change which came over his spirit a year or two later. He suggests that an election can be prevented in November by keeping Cushing in the field, if the Kittredge faction also nominate a candidate, while the Newburyport friends of Cushing may be encouraged to hope there will be no Kittredge candidate. After the November trial he will himself be old enough to go to Congress. The letter is dated " East Parish, Wednesday morning," probably in August, 1832.

" Since conversing with you yesterday, a new objection to our project has occurred to me, — the Constitution requires that the Representative shall be twenty-five years of age. I shall not be twenty-five till the 17th of December. So that I would not be eligible at the *next* trial in November. This, you will see, gives a different aspect to the whole affair. *Perhaps*, however, if the contest is *prolonged* till after the next time, the project might be put in execution.

" Suppose you advocate a holding on to Mr. C. in your Newburyport letter ? Suppose, too, that you nominate in your paper Mr. Cushing without any one-sided convention ? After the trial in November, you can *then* use the arguments in favor of our plan which you propose to do now ; and if it suits Mr. C. he can then *request* his friends to give their votes for some other individual for the sake of promoting peace in the district. The Kittredge committee would in that case probably nominate a candidate, — if one could be found, — but, I understand Mr. Thayer, not with the expectation of his being elected.

" If I were nominated after the November trial, Mr. Thayer, situated as he and I relatively are, would support the nomination, and let the other candidate go, as he did John Merrill. Purdy, the ' Telegraph,' and the ' Essex Register ' would do the same.

"The truth of the matter is, the thing would be peculiarly beneficial to me, — if not at home it would be so abroad. It would give me an opportunity of seeing and knowing our public characters, and in case of Mr. Clay's election might enable me to do something for myself or my friends. It would be worth more to me *now*, young as I am, than almost any office after I had reached the meridian of life.

"In this matter, if I know my own heart, I am not entirely selfish. I never yet *deserted a friend*, and I never will. If my friends enable me to acquire influence, it shall be exerted for *their benefit*. And give me once an opportunity of exercising it, my first object shall be to evince my gratitude by exertions in behalf of those who had conferred such a favor upon me.

"If you write to Newburyport to-day, you can say that we are willing and ready to do all we can at the next trial; say, too, that the Kittredge folks will scarcely find a candidate, and that there may be a chance for Cushing better than he has yet had ; that at all events it can do no harm ; and that if after that trial Mr. C. sees fit to request his friends not to vote for him for the 22d Congress, there will be as good a chance then of electing a Cushing man as there is now. Say, too, if you please, that I am ready to go on with the contest, and you had better recommend mildness in the process of electioneering."

In October, 1833, he wrote to his old Hartford friend, Jonathan Law : —

"I am happy to hear that the overthrow of our political party has not depressed thee. Alas for National Republicanism! It yet lingers here in this State, but desertions are rapidly thinning its once firm ranks, and in a year those who know it now will know it no more forever. I speak of the great majority. For myself, I see no reason for a change of opinion, and I should as soon think of worshiping the devil with the Manicheans, as to fall down and do homage to Andrew Jackson with the idolatrous 'spoils party' of the day. No, the old man is no better than he was when we battled him in Hartford; nay, I am inclined to think age has improved him, as death did Sheridan's fat friar, 'in the wrong way.' His late manifesto on the United States Bank is as full of egotistical authority as an imperial ukase, or a Turkish firman. And then, there is that 'foregone conclusion,' Martin Van Buren, clinging to the skirts of the old General, and whoever does homage to the latter is aiding the 'political grimalkin' (as Clinton called him) to slip into the Presidency, *nolens volens*. J. Q. Adams is nominated for governor by the anti-Masons in this State; he is a strong candidate, but he will not go down. John Davis, our candidate, is a very able man, and popular withal. There will probably be no choice by the people. Edward Everett has joined the anti-Masons, and there's a terrible hubbub about it. Daniel Webster, they say, is anti-Masonic, but Dan is crafty, and will

not hang out his flag at present. As for you in
Connecticut, you are disgracing yourselves as much
as possible by black laws and grog-shop laws.
God grant you a speedy deliverance from Jacksonism. . . . I am busy on my farm as a beaver
building his dam. My health is vastly improved;
the blues have left me; I go to husking frolics,
and all that sort of thing. I have put the veto
upon poetry; read all I can find, politics, history,
rhyme, reason, etc., and am happy, — at least I
believe I am. I have written some considerable
upon slavery, and have been pretty roughly handled by the Southerners. But so long as I can
intrench myself behind my Quakerism, as a tor-
toise does under his shell, I am perfectly safe.
The slavery question is getting to be an absorbing
one, and the recent noble act of Great Britain will
contribute to effect a change in this country. . . .
As to your suggestion about poetry, I must decline
attending to it. I have knocked Pegasus on the
head, as a tanner does his bark-mill donkey, when
he is past service. I am fixed at Haverhill, as
Pope says, —

> ' Fixed as a plant to one peculiar spot,
> To draw nutrition, propagate and rot.' "

The feeling against slavery had been growing
strong enough to have a marked effect upon the
National Republican party in Massachusetts, although for several years no third party took the
field. The abolitionists, led in Essex County by
Whittier, questioned the candidates as to their
opinion in regard to the right of petition and
slavery in the District of Columbia. They would

vote only for those who promised to present and
defend petitions for the abolition of slavery in the
District and in the Territories. Cushing was dis-
trusted by the anti-slavery men generally.   But
Whittier recognized his great ability, and wished
to turn it to account in aiding the cause of
liberty. Before each election, in 1834, 1836, and
1838, he secured Cushing's unqualified pledges in
favor of some of the measures demanded by the
abolitionists. He then used his whole influence,
and secured his election each time.   Cushing
acknowledged that he owed his success to his
young Quaker friend, and redeemed his pledge by
presenting the anti-slavery petitions which Whittier caused to be poured in upon him from every
part of the Essex district. That Cushing's heart
was not in it is shown by the disclaimers he made
as he presented the petitions. But he supported
John Quincy Adams in his demand that every
petition should be received, no matter what was
called for, and respectfully referred to the appro-
priate committee. His spirited speeches equaled
those of Adams himself, in eloquence and in courage. The "gag rule" introduced by Jarvis, of
Maine, was opposed by him with great ability,
but he took pains to say that he did not fully
approve of the petitions he insisted should be
received. Whittier kept him up to his work by
canvassing the Essex North district and forward-
ing petitions from every town where he could obtain signers to them.

As an illustration of the manner in which
Whittier plied Cushing with material for speeches

and sought to keep him in line, the following letters have an interest.

NEWBURYPORT, 25th of 10th mo., 1834.

I am disappointed in not seeing thee at this place and this time, as I called to apprise thee of the fact that at our meeting of the Essex County Anti-Slavery Society yesterday at Danvers, it was unanimously agreed upon to write letters to the candidates for Congress and state legislature on the subject of slavery and of their views of action in Congress and in the legislature upon it. Until after the passage of this resolution I did not reflect that it would embrace thyself and Osgood [his Democratic opponent], as we were thinking of Saltonstall and Rantoul [in the other Essex district]. As it is, however, I hope thee will favor the Society with an explicit answer, as the one hundred and twenty delegates present pledged themselves to vote for no man of any party who was not in favor of abolition in the District of Columbia. I heard, too, from a gentleman in the meeting, that two or three hundred of the legal voters of Lowell have pledged themselves to this effect.

HAVERHILL, 3d of 11th mo., 1834.

Several individuals, personally and politically thy friends, have suggested to me the idea of addressing thee in regard to thy sentiments in relation to slavery in the District of Columbia. From this I have uniformly dissuaded them by assuring them that, although friendly to Colonization and consequently opposed to Immediate Emancipation

and many of their views, I could have no manner
of doubt of thy willingness to do all in thy power
to remove slavery from the District, where it exists without warrant from the Constitution, and in
its most aggravated form.   By this assurance I
have, I believe, fully satisfied the individuals to
whom I allude.   Perhaps in making it I have
unintentionally misrepresented thy views and feelings.   If so, I can only say that my motives were
of the most friendly nature.   In the present pos-
ture of affairs in this district any formal inter-
rogation of candidates in reference to matters of
this kind is certainly to be deprecated.   But nothing is more certain than that the time is close
at hand when it cannot be avoided.   The spirit
working deep in the heart of New England will not
slumber.   Party machinery will not much longer
repress it.   If I have rightly represented thy views
it would be a great satisfaction to myself to be able
to put a line from thee to that effect in the hands
of two or three gentlemen previous to the coming
election.   If on the other hand I have mistaken
them, thee will oblige me by making no reply whatever in reference to the particular subject of this
letter.   Thayer has been acting with a great deal
of prudence as well as firmness in the support of
the Whig nominations.

20th of 2d mo., 1836.

I send thee three small petitions, and will
trouble thee no more for the present session.
Many thanks for thy defense of Adams, and of
the petitioners of Massachusetts.   We have just

got the question before the legislature in relation
to the right of petition, as violated by the resolution in Congress of the 18th of January. It will
probably be protested against on the part of our
legislature, and thus you will be fully supported
at home.

HAVERHILL, 1st of 3d mo., 1836.

I am greatly obliged to thee for thy account of
the state of politics at Washington. It is, however, pretty much as I had previously supposed.
My object in making the remark thee allude to
was to put thee on thy guard in reference to the
state of parties *here*. Our last election was omi-
nous. The Whig *party* cannot stand much
longer in Massachusetts. The Whig *men*, with
the exercise of a prudence and forecast perfectly
consistent with sound principles, may. I notice
that the Southern and Western Whigs take every
possible occasion in Congress to attack Van Buren
and his friends at the North. This course would
be fatal to the Massachusetts delegation. A firm
and steady support of Daniel Webster, without
playing into the hands of the White and Harrison parties, or volunteering attacks upon the Van
Buren party, is, it appears to me, the safest course
for yourselves, and the best for the true interests
of the State. Thy skirmish with Hardin, of Kentucky, and its triumphant result on thy part, has
gained thee no small degree of credit among *all*
parties here. It discovered an untrammeled and
independent spirit, and a determination to defend
the honor and the interests of thy constituents,

irrespective of partisan feelings. I like the old-
fashioned democratic tone of thy speech on the
right of petition. The Van Buren organ in this
district copied two paragraphs of it with approbation. On the right of free speech and communications there will be a splendid opportunity to
maintain the vital principles of democracy; to
hold up before the nation the now universally
detested Sedition Law; to speak of those who
suffered by it, and to set the Democrats of Virginia and South Carolina of 1800 in battle array
against the position of these " chivalrous " sov-
ereignties at the present time. It will be sport to
see the " engineer hoist with his own petard."
I wish that some one of the Massachusetts delegation would just tell the Southerners that the old
Bay State was *never* a slave State; that, although slavery existed here, it was recognized by
our laws only as an existing evil, and stood only
upon its own execrable foundation of robbery and
wrong; that our courts of justice were temples
of refuge for the slaves long before the Constitution of 1780. Thus, in 1770, a suit was instituted
by a slave in our judicial courts for freedom and
recompense for his services after attaining the age
of twenty-one years, and the court decided in his
favor. Other suits were in consequence instituted, and all terminated in favor of liberty.
(Vide Dr. Belknap's answer to Judge Tucker.)
On the part of the slave it was pleaded that servi-
tude was a violation of the colony's charter, and
of the fundamental law of England, that no person
could be deprived of liberty but by the judgment

of his peers. These facts are doubtless familiar to thee, and I only wish to call thy attention to them.

HAVERHILL, 12th of 12th mo., 1836.

I send thee three or four petitions, and there's "mair a-comin'." We need not tell thee that we want a hearing before Congress, and that we must have it somehow or other. The next year we shall send double the number, and so on, until the united voice of New England thunders upon the ear of Congress.

PHILADELPHIA, 16th of 1st mo., 1837.

I expected to have been in Washington ere this; but shall remain here until after the Harrisburg fanatical convention. . . . How are the abolition petitions received? I am looking with a good deal of anxiety for the presentment of the petitions from Essex County.

BOSTON, 13th of 3d mo., 1837.

I send with this a copy of the report and resolutions of the committee on the subject of slavery and the right of petition. These resolutions, or others stronger, will pass in both Houses. The message of Van Buren, and the course of the Van Buren party in Congress, have induced the leading Whigs to take this course. Many of the Van Buren men will go for the report. I am thankful that Massachusetts will thus nobly sustain her Representatives, and assert the right of her citizens "peaceably to assemble and petition for the

redress of grievances." I regret we have not yet
been favored with thy speech in Congress in the
great debate on the John Quincy Adams petition.
It would have done good [in promoting the passage of the resolutions before the legislature].
What is the meaning of Van Buren's message?
Is it the settled policy of " the government" to
" go to the death" for slavery? Will the old
Calhoun party accept the veto pledge of Van
Buren as a sufficient peace offering, ground their
arms, and wear the brands and ear-marks of " the
party"? I have been amused in looking at
Ritchie's comments on the message. They are full
of the childishness and garrulousness of dotage
gratified in its childish whims. But one thing is
certain: Van Buren will lose Rhode Island, Connecticut, and Pennsylvania by his extraordinary
veto threat. How much he will gain by it at the
South remains to be seen.

AMESBURY, 14th of 4th mo., 1837.

Our county anti-slavery society holds its quarterly
meeting in this place on the 21st. As the secretary of
the society and the person who forwarded the petitions to Congress, I wish to state to the meeting what
was the fate of their petitions. The reports of
Congressional proceedings are not accurate or full.
Next session our American society will have two
reporters in Washington. Could thee write me a letter in reference to the reception of the petitions, and
permit me to read it as a private but not strictly
confidential letter to myself? A similar request
will be made to Mr. Phillips. Of course I do not

expect you to avow yourselves to be other than what you are now understood to be, — anti-abolition. But as an abolitionist I am grateful to both of you for your defense of the character of the petitioners, and for your manly stand for the periled right of petition.

The first draft of Cushing's reply to the above note is folded with it among his papers. He gives the list of petitions, and tells which have been presented and which are to be hereafter offered.

The records of Congress show that Haverhill and Amesbury did more than their share in petitioning, and Mr. Whittier's hand is to be seen in the whole movement in that part of Massachusetts. The famous Haverhill petition of 1842 created a remarkable scene in the national House of Representatives. The Southern members were exasperated by the persistency with which these petitions were offered by John Quincy Adams and Caleb Cushing. They threatened a dissolution of the Union, unless even the right of petition was denied upon topics that directly or indirectly affected their "peculiar institution." It was in part to rebuke these hollow threats of dissolution that the Haverhill petition, with forty-three signers, was presented by John Quincy Adams. It read as follows : —

" The undersigned, citizens of Haverhill, in the Commonwealth of Massachusetts, pray that you will immediately adopt measures, peaceably to dissolve the union of these States : First, because no union can be agreeable or permanent which does not present prospects of reciprocal benefit; second, because a vast proportion of the resources of one section of the Union is annually drained to sustain the views and course of another section without any adequate return; third, because (judging from the history of past nations) this union, if persisted in, in the present course of things, will certainly overwhelm the whole nation in utter destruction."

The wildest storm ever witnessed in the House was raised by this petition. A resolution to expel Mr. Adams for presenting it was debated for four days, on the ground that he had offered the deepest indignity to the House, the greatest insult to the American people, and that he was even guilty of high treason. Mr. Adams's intrepid bearing throughout the tumult his action had caused saved that venerable statesman from an expulsion that was meant to be ignominious. He had explained at the outset that he did not favor the petition, but demanded that all respectful petitions should be considered. Whether this particular petition was written by Mr. Whittier is not certain, but as it came from his native town at a time when he was actively circulating petitions, it is probable he had something to do with it. One of the petitions sent to Adams, which, however, he did not present, though he tantalized his opponents by exhibiting it, was a satire upon the objection that most of the petitioners were women, who had no business to mingle in public affairs. This petition prayed that Congress would memorialize the British government to dethrone Victoria, on the ground that women had departed from their proper sphere of duty when they assumed the management of public affairs!

When nominated by the Whigs in 1838, Cushing was not inclined to pledge himself again to his anti-slavery constituents. He thought he was strong enough in his district to get along without making again the disagreeable pledges by which he had been bound in former years. Besides, Whittier had gone to Philadelphia, where he was editing the " Freeman," and Cushing thought he had a fair field for an unpledged election. But his hopes were dashed by the appearance of his Quaker friend on the scene at the last moment. Whether Whittier came home on purpose to manage this election does not appear ; but he was present at the Liberty party convention in Salem to which Cushing sent an ingeniously worded but non-committal letter, referring to his past record in the matter of the right of petition and the domestic slave trade in the District of Columbia. A question had been asked him in regard to the Territories ; and he replied that he objected to interfering with the institution in Florida, while a Territory. He called attention to the fact that in a previous session he voted against a resolution declaring that Congress ought not to interfere with slavery in the District. He had also voted against the admission of Arkansas as a slave State. He would do the same in the case of Florida, when it should call for statehood. He was in favor of restricting the domestic slave trade, which he said had not even the poor excuse of the foreign slave trade, that it

transfers men from a barbarous to a civilized community. But he declined to pledge himself to
specific measures, saying, "I cling to my personal
independence as the choicest and richest of all
possessions. I will take my place in Congress
as a freeman or not at all, pledged only to Truth,
Liberty, and the Constitution, with no terror before my eyes but the terror to do wrong. Thus,
or not at all, will I reascend the giant stairs of
the Capitol." Whittier was determined to get
a more explicit pledge or prevent his election.
At his suggestion, his friend Henry B. Stanton
read Cushing's letter and commented upon it in a
humorous and caustic way, and the convention
adjourned without any action in his favor. Cushing, who was anxious to secure the Liberty vote,
was in a corner of the gallery while his communication was being criticised. In the evening, he
met Whittier at the hotel, and expressed his
chagrin at the reception given his careful letter.
He said, "What shall I do?" Whittier replied,
"Thee cannot expect the votes of our people, unless
thee speaks more plainly." "But how can I do
that now?" said Cushing. Whittier suggested,
"Write a short letter to me, and do not hide thy
meaning under many words." Cushing did not
feel like doing it, but said at length, "Let me see
you in the morning." Whittier was to leave for
home by stage quite early, and promised to call for
Cushing. He found the anxious statesman half-
dressed, and waiting for him. He had decided to
sign any letter that Whittier would write. Whittier thereupon wrote the short letter that follows,

which Cushing copied and signed, and it was sent to all parts of the Essex district by special messengers : —

SALEM, November 8, 1838.

MY DEAR SIR, — I should regret to have any doubt remain on your mind as to the import of those points of my letter which are referred to by you. In respect to the District of Columbia, I am in favor of the abolition of slavery and the slave trade therein, by the earliest practicable legislation of Congress, regard being had for the just rights of all classes of the citizens, and I intended to be so understood.

In the concluding part of the letter, I stated that I felt bound to withhold stipulation in detail, as to my future course in Congress. But I did not design it to be understood that I entertained any desire or disposition to change my course in regard to the subjects embraced in the letter ; but, on the contrary, being resolved to continue to maintain on all suitable occasions, as I have heretofore done, the principles and spirit of the resolves of the legislature of Massachusetts, appertaining to the right of petition, and to slavery and the slave trade, in their various relations.

I am, very faithfully, yours,

CALEB CUSHING.[1]

To JOHN G. WHITTIER, Esq.

[1] This letter got into the papers at the South, and they taunted Cushing with having given a double pledge to the abolitionists. Whittier came to his defense in the *Pennsylvania Freeman*, explaining the matter as follows: " A private note from him in reply to one from ourself as his former neighbor and personal friend,

This letter was satisfactory, gave Cushing the Liberty votes, elected him by 1800 majority, and made him a third time indebted to Whittier for his election. He was kept up to his promises by constant reminders, and his course during this term also was in general satisfactory to his anti-slavery constituents. The tactics of Whittier in his dealings with Cushing, throughout the Congressional career of that statesman, are amusingly shown in a letter written from Haverhill, January 10, 1836, to his friend Thayer in Philadelphia : —

"The anti-slavery folks have circulated a petition to Congress in the village, and it has been signed by about one hundred and twenty legal voters. We shall plague Cushing with it, but he had as lief see the Old Enemy himself as see it. 'T is nothing to the dose we shall fix for Congress next year. We 'll haunt 'em, and torment 'em, till they behave better. We 'll prosecute our suit with a pertinacity which shall rival that of William Vans, or Walter Scott's Peter Peebles. . . . What has got into the Pennsylvania Quakers? Who would have expected to see them tossing their broadbrims into the air for the 'Hero of Tippecanoe'?"

asking an explanation of some points in his letter to the anti-slavery committee, was published and circulated in the district on our own responsibility. He was not elected as an abolitionist, but his whole course in Congress on this question has been honorable to himself — manly, open, and consistent. Whatever else the papers may say of him, they cannot accuse him of being a 'dough-face.' He has never betrayed his constituents, nor compromised the honor and dignity of the Pilgrim State, on the question of human liberty."

In 1840, all kinds of hat-brims were being tossed up for the " Hero of Tippecanoe," and in the midst of the general enthusiasm, Cushing thought he could safely cut loose from the bondage to the " anti-slavery folks " that had galled him for his first three terms in Congress. He made no pledges that year, and was nevertheless elected, but he found to his sorrow that he was not yet done with Whittier. In 1841, the Whigs came into power, and Cushing looked for some office of national importance. He would have obtained it but for the anti-slavery record Whittier had forced upon him, and perhaps in spite of that record, if Whittier had held his peace. President Tyler three times nominated him as Secretary of the Treasury; but the Senate rejected him each time with increasing majorities.[1] Whittier had taken pains to republish that letter of 1838, which Cushing had signed at his direction, and had prefaced it with these comments : —

" CALEB CUSHING. — As our distinguished and talented fellow-citizen of Essex North may erelong be before the Senate of the United States for a high post, we think it well to let them understand in good season that Mr. Cushing is no less an abolitionist than Edward Everett [whom the Senate had previously rejected]. When questioned by the abolitionists previous to his election in 1838, his reply was rather vague and unsatisfactory. It was so judged by the abolitionists in convention

---

[1] Ten years later, Cushing, then a member of the Massachusetts legislature, when trying to prevent the election of Sumner to the Senate, again came into unsuccessful collision with Whittier.

assembled, and the prospect was that he would lose
his election. At the eleventh hour, his personal
friend, John G. Whittier, went to him and told
him of his danger, and he penned the following
explanation, which saved his election by 1800
votes. We shall see whether he will eat back this
explanation for the sake of being premier or anything else under John Tyler of Virginia."

Whittier's skill in handling all the weapons of
politics in behalf of a cause which both the great
parties at the North were then doing their best to
keep out of the field of their controversies, was
shown in many ways even before he assisted in
forming the great party of freedom which in
twenty years placed Abraham Lincoln at the head
of our government. From first to last, he refused
to come out from his party until he had done all
that could be done to induce it to assist in the
work of reform. He would not cast aside a strong
man, if he could get ever so little of his strength
committed to the cause he had at heart. This was
strikingly illustrated in the Cushing incident, related above, and it is to be noticed in his whole
career as a philanthropist. When he entered the
field as an opponent of slavery, he took with him
every weapon he could handle, and refused to
throw away the ballot, as did many of his associates. In an editorial article written in those days
he says: "What an absurdity is moral action
apart from political!" His pen was consecrated
to the cause, and he refused editorial positions
that would keep him off the field toward which
a sense of duty urged him. In 1835-36, his

friend Thayer was, as we have seen, calling him to Philadelphia to engage in a promising newspaper enterprise. Here is an extract from one of his letters in reply : —

" I should like to be in Philadelphia, — more especially since thee and thy folks are there, but . . . I feel too deep an interest in the struggle now going on between Slavery and Freedom, especially as I have been somewhat active in the cause of Emancipation, and as my *apparent* withdrawal from it might be construed very unfavorably to the cause as well as to myself. I have, I hope, no fanaticism about me ; cant of all kinds, religious, political, or moral, I abhor. But I regard the contest now going on as of vital interest to the welfare of mankind, not in our country alone, but in all the world. It is a struggle for the rights of man everywhere. In such a cause, I must not *seem* to yield, especially at a time like this, when its advocacy is so unpopular that its abandonment would subject me to the charge of cowardice and insincerity. I must, therefore, with many thanks for thy offer, which under other circumstances might have been most acceptable, decline accepting it. Believe me, I should like to be with you, but I cannot there be entirely free." [1]

---

[1] Another extract from the letter above quoted, written in midwinter from the old homestead at East Haverhill, shows how his hands were employed in these days when his heart was so fully occupied with philanthropic work. He says, " I live out of the way of the post office, and only see it about once a fortnight. . . . I have been teaming and sledding and feeding my cattle, for

> " From the hens on the roost to the pigs in the sty
> I am lord of the fowl and the brute."

In explanation of Mr. Whittier's frequent assistance to politicians who were not at heart in favor of the cause to which he had consecrated all his powers, it may be said that it was the policy of his life to accept whatever aid he could obtain by indirect as well as by direct methods. He did not expect even from the politicians of his own party the same unselfish devotion to duty which he exacted of himself, and much less did he expect it of others. He took men as he found them, encouraged them to go part way with him, and was not inclined to lose any little advantage to his cause which they might render. This habit of charitable allowances for men who had a capacity for serving a cause he had at heart, even if they sometimes made grave mistakes, is shown in his reply to a friend who was complaining of a party leader who had been accused of wrong-doing. "Has thee found many saints or angels in thy dealings with either political party? Do not expect too much of human nature." He had a genius for coalitions, and could accept assistance from unfriendly sources in furtherance of a philanthropic object. While he did not purchase such aid by an abandonment of principle, he secured it sometimes by appeals to the selfish ambitions of statesmen. His letters to Rantoul and Cushing show his skill in dealing with strong men who were not of his party. Through Rantoul he secured, in 1837, the almost unanimous condemnation of President Van Buren's pro-slavery course from the Massachusetts legislature. Through Cushing he held up the hands of John Quincy Adams in his memorable contest in

Congress for the right of petition. Neither of these objects could have been secured but by the means he adopted. Although one of a small minority, he was often able by his tactics to turn the scale of the great parties in his district and in the State, and secure ·for the cause of freedom important advantages. It will be seen later how largely he contributed to the election of Charles Sumner to the United States Senate, by holding the anti-slavery vote to a coalition distasteful to many of his followers, which gave to pro-slavery Democrats the governorship of Massachusetts, and the principal state offices. He thought it of the first importance, at that time, to secure a voice for freedom in the Senate, and was willing to give up a great deal to secure it.

Whittier has been called the Laureate of the Liberty party, but it will be found that he did a great deal more than write verse for it. He was active in conventions that inaugurated and shaped the policy of the party, beginning his work for a third party only when all hope of reforming the others had to be given up. If not in personal attendance as a delegate, he wrote letters expressing his views, so as to have a voice in the councils of the party. This brought him into collision with a large number of his friends among the abolitionists, who believed in the policy of abstaining from all political action under a Constitution which they called "a covenant with death and a league with hell," and who spent much time in denouncing churches that failed to do their whole duty to the slave. Whittier's position in regard to this mat-

ter is explained in a letter written to the anti-
Texas convention of 1845, in which he said " that
though as an abolitionist he was no blind worshiper
of the Union, he saw nothing to be gained by an
effort, necessarily limited and futile, to dissolve it.
The moral and political power requisite for dissolving the Union could far more easily abolish
every vestige of slavery."

Though running counter to the teachings of Garrison in this matter, and coming under the censure
of his friend, he maintained his position with
steadiness. He was ready to go with any party
that was marching in his general direction, even if
he could not keep step to all its music. He refused to enter into controversy about non-essentials,
and thought that the contest into which Garrison
led the American Anti-Slavery Society against the
Constitution and the church was a waste of strength
that had better be applied more directly to the
overthrow of the system of slavery. As a Quaker,
he had been a " come-outer " all his life, and had
learned the art of coming out quietly and in order.
Many of the leading abolitionists had recently left
Orthodox churches, and were ablaze with the excitement of the act. The Quaker of course did
not disapprove of their cutting loose from a church
that hampered them, but thought they made an
unnecessary fuss about it. They considered it
their duty to hammer away not only at the church,
but at all abolitionists whose consciences allowed
them to remain in the church. Against this spirit
Whittier constantly protested, and continued to
make his influence felt in politics by questioning

candidates, and supporting only those who pledged themselves to the cause of freedom.

When a state legislature was to be influenced to pass an act or a resolve bearing upon any scheme of philanthropy in which he was interested, Whittier was a most skillful and efficient "lobbyist," in the best sense of that word. Though he served but a single term in the legislature, and after 1837 could not have been elected, yet his was a familiar form in the lobby of the State House for many years. He was a shrewd judge of men, knew how to touch their weak points, and scrupled not to reach their consciences along the line of least resistance. He was by nature and by study a practical politician, never taking the motto, "My party, right or wrong," but rather, "My party in preference to a worse one," or, "My party as I am trying to make it." Wendell Phillips once said of him that he was a superb hand at lobbying. He never worked for any personal advantage, but only for a cause he considered worthy of conscientious effort. His keen sense of the ridiculous kept him from being in the least degree "cranky" in his philanthropy.[1]

---

[1] Mr. Whittier once related this incident of his early political life in Haverhill: A drunken neighbor of his asked to be taken to the town-house on election day in Mr. Whittier's wagon, promising to vote for Whittier, then a candidate for the legislature, if he could be thus accommodated. As his affiliation had heretofore been with the opposite party, Whittier thought it best to watch him carefully. He could not be prevented from stopping at a liquor saloon on the way, and being already drunk when he started, became difficult to manage upon arrival at the polls. But he was not too drunk to determine to vote against Whittier, whom he tried to shake off. He was, however, started for the ballot-box,

In May, 1836, Mr. Whittier assumed editorial charge of the Haverhill "Gazette," and retired from the position on the 17th of December of the same year. His opposition to Governor Everett led to dissatisfaction among some of the Whig readers of that paper, who did not like the anti-slavery tone he gave to their party organ. The "Gazette" was owned by Jacob Caldwell, husband of Whittier's older sister. To placate the friends of Everett, Mr. Caldwell sold half his interest in the paper to Dr. Jeremiah Spofford, of East Bradford, now Groveland, and it was announced that while Whittier was to edit the literary and poetical departments, Spofford was to be the political editor. Whittier's hand is nevertheless to be seen in many anti-slavery touches in the editorial columns, though Everett was not directly attacked. The following extracts from letters to Spofford show the spirit with which Whittier accepted the situation, and the interest which he still had in the success of the Whig party. He was at this time living in Amesbury, but was considering a plan of buying Caldwell's interest in the "Gazette," and returning to his native town, but his abolitionism proved an insurmountable obstacle.

with the right vote in his hand, and carefully supported by his Quaker neighbor. But at the last moment, an opposition vote was handed him, and Whittier had the mortification to see this deposited in the box. "Did not take the man home, did you?" Mr. Whittier was asked, when he told this story. "Oh yes, I did," he said; "I promised his wife I would see him home safely, and I had to do it. I took him home dead drunk in the bottom of my wagon!"

HAVERHILL, 27th 8th mo., 1836.

Having a proof-sheet of a work I am publishing in Boston [1] to examine and alter, I suppose that nothing will be gained by visiting Bradford, beyond what may be by my writing. I have received a long letter in relation to Governor Everett from one of his personal friends, who says that if the " Gazette " supports him after what I have said, it will surprise and mortify my friends everywhere. On this point I do feel as if it would not do for me to act inconsistently. I should lower myself in my own estimation, and in that of the public. It seems to me that there are many advantages which will result from thy coming in as editor *after* the election. If we bend our whole energies to the Whig cause, if we fill our paper with Whiggism, and resolve to sink or swim with it, why, *if* that cause is unsuccessful, we shall go down with it. If, on the other hand, the paper pursues the even tenor of its way until after the election, on thy coming in it can then, so far as is consistent with principle and truth, govern its course by the circumstances and result of the great struggle. We shall have a meeting here this week to choose delegates to Worcester. I expect Webster will be present and speak on the occasion. I have thought some of thy name as a candidate for elector; probably, however, some Salem man will be designated.

[1] *Mogg Megone.*

HAVERHILL, 23d of 11th mo., 1836.

DEAR DOCTOR, — I have just learned that a good deal of dissatisfaction exists in this village in regard to my connection with the "Gazette." Many say they will not take the paper so long as I am the editor. They want a thorough-going exclusive Whig press. My aim has been to make the paper as interesting as possible, and at the same time temperately advocate my sentiments on the subject of slavery. In so doing I have had no compensation except $90, and the pay for my expenses in circulating petitions in Essex County. I did not expect to make money; on the contrary, I did not by any means consult my pecuniary interest in the matter. I am attached to Haverhill, and would like to stay here. Of late, however, some of the Whigs have told Caldwell that he must get rid of me, that my abolition made me indifferent as to politics. Caldwell is uneasy about it, but I cannot promise that next year I will go for Everett; on the contrary I must oppose him. Of the two I prefer Marcus Morton. Situated as we are I have been willing to sacrifice many of my feelings, but on this subject I cannot. I have had some idea of buying Caldwell's half myself, but if the Whig leaders are against me I shall hardly have courage to do it, much as I wish to permanently locate myself in this village. I did not before to-day understand that there was any particular opposition to me.

HAVERHILL, 1st of 12th mo., 1836.

DEAR DOCTOR, — I have felt rather unpleasantly about leaving the paper, and could I consistently with what I conceive to be my duty take such a course as would be satisfactory to its patrons, I would do so. . . . In case thee assume the entire control of the editorial department, it is important that it should not be supposed that there is any personal difficulty between ourselves. The truth is, we have always been friends, and I trust we always shall be so. So far as my influence can go, I shall do all I can to procure thy election as a member of the Executive Council this winter. As far as I can judge, few if any of the anti-slavery folks out of town will drop the paper in consequence of my leaving it. Two or three individuals in the village will probably discontinue it. But on the other hand from twenty to thirty will take hold of it. Our anti-slavery folks generally understand thee to be a friend of free discussion, although not an abolitionist, and that is sufficient, provided the paper does not say anything against them. Nothing ought to be said publicly about my being compelled to leave the paper, as it would only irritate some of my friends. For my own part, I shall have it understood, so far as I am able, that it is only a business transaction between my brother-in-law and thyself or others.

In January, 1837, he started for Washington, where John Quincy Adams, assisted by Caleb Cushing, and the entire Massachusetts delegation in Congress, were battling for the right of petition. His intention was to help them in their preparation for the debates, but when he arrived at Philadelphia he learned that a despotic rule had been passed cutting off debate and annihilating the right of petition. He therefore gave up his intended visit to Washington, and went to Harrisburg, to attend an anti-slavery state convention. Here he met Governor Ritner, " who alone of all the governors of the Union in 1836 met the insulting demands and measures of the South in a manner becoming a freeman," as he says in his preface to his poetical tribute to this independent farmer and high-souled statesman. The poem entitled " Ritner " was written immediately after his return to Boston from Pennsylvania.

Massachusetts had a governor in 1836 who in his inaugural address invoked " the patriotism of all classes to abstain from discussion of the subject of slavery," and to Edward Everett at once Mr. Whittier made indignant reply : " We can neither permit the gag to be thrust in our mouths by others, nor deem it the part of 'patriotism' to place it there ourselves." This letter fills five columns as printed in the " Liberator " of February 20, 1836. Its tone may be judged from this paragraph : —

" Is this the age, are ours the laws, are the sons of the Pilgrims the men, for advice like this ? . . . Far fitter is it for the banks of the Bosphorus and the Neva than for those of the Connecticut and the Merrimac. It is not suited to our hard-handed artisans and free farmers. . . . They have seen demands gravely made by slaveholding legislatures and governors upon the authorities of free and sovereign States for the delivery of their fellow-citizens to torture and death, and for the passage of laws against the liberty of speech and of the press. By things like these has the Northern laborer been summoned to discussion."

In reply to Governor Everett's statement that the framers of the Constitution provided for the perpetuity of the institution of slavery, he quotes passages from Washington, Jefferson, Franklin, and others, to show that they looked for its speedy extinction. Then comes this memorable passage:

" George Washington was another signer of the Constitution. I know that he was a slaveholder; and I have not forgotten the emotions which swelled my bosom, when in the metropolis of New England, the Cradle of Liberty, a degenerate son [1] of the Pilgrims pointed to his portrait, which adorns the wall, with the thrice-repeated exclamation, 'That slaveholder!' I saw the only blot on the otherwise bright and spotless character of the Father of his Country held to open view, exposed by remorseless hands to sanction a system of oppression and blood. It seemed to me like sacrilege. I looked upon those venerable and awful features, while the echoes, once wakened in that old Hall by the voice of ancient Liberty, warm from the lips of Adams and Hancock and the fiery heart of James Otis, gave back from wall and gallery the exulting cry of 'Slaveholder,' half expecting to see the still canvas darken with a frown, and the pic-

[1] Peleg Sprague.

tured lips part asunder with words of rebuke and
sorrow.[1] I felt it, as did hundreds more on that
occasion, to be a reproach and a cruel insult to the
memory of the illustrious dead. Did not the
speaker know that the dying testimony of Washington was against slavery ? "

Mr. Whittier took occasion, while commenting
upon the message, to refer with cutting severity to
some pro-slavery utterances which Everett had
made while he was in Congress.   The boldness
and spirit of the letter attracted much attention,
and the governor was greatly annoyed by it. Until
they met in the electoral college, in 1864, Everett
did not again encounter his unwelcome correspondent. On that occasion he came up cordially
to Whittier, and expressed his pleasure that at last
they were agreed.

The whole month of March, 1837, Mr. Whittier
spent in Boston in work among the members of
the legislature, to secure the passage of acts and
resolves to show that Massachusetts did not respond favorably to the inaugural address of President Van Buren. This message, by its tone of
subserviency to the South, created great indignation

[1] The famous sentence of Wendell Phillips, " I thought those
pictured lips would have broken into voice, to rebuke the rec-
reant American," was clearly plagiarized, says Kennedy, by an
unconscious act of memory, from the above eloquent passage by
Whittier, written nearly two years previous to the Faneuil Hall
speech by Phillips. Young Phillips had been mightily aroused
by the Garrison mob, some months before the date of Whittier's
open letter to Everett, and had resolved to devote his life to the
cause of Freedom. He had undoubtedly, therefore, read Whittier's strong and manly letter to the governor, and remembered,
dimly, the passage in question.

throughout the North, wherever the abolitionists had been educating the consciences of the people. Whittier saw the opportunity to commit the State to anti-slavery action, and promptly made the effort. On the last day of March he wrote to his friend Thayer : —

" Just look at old Massachusetts ! The legislature is abolitionized, the whole State is coming. For the last four weeks I have been in Boston, aiding and abetting in the plan of tumbling our six hundred representatives off the fence upon the abolition side. We have caucused in season and out of season, threatened and coaxed, plead and scolded, until we 've got the day. The Van Buren men are persuaded to look to the people of Massachusetts, and not to orders from Washington. And they have done as we advised : to save themselves they have joined hands with the abolitionists. . . . We shall get a bill through, moreover, granting a jury trial for fugitive slaves. Rantoul, the Van Buren leader, will make a great effort for it. Among those who have been 'taking care' of the legislature with myself, I would mention Gardner B. Perry, Dr. Farnsworth of Groton, George Bancroft of Springfield, and a number of other abolitionists."

The " orders from Washington," to which reference is made in this letter, were contained in the inaugural address, in which the President announces that he is " an uncompromising opponent of every attempt on the part of Congress to abolish slavery, in the District of Columbia, against the wishes of the slaveholding States," and calls for a

cessation of discussion about the matter. The
Boston papers of both parties opposed the introduction of the resolves favoring the rights of petition and the abolition of slavery in the District;
but, in spite of them, Whittier and his little band
of abolitionists secured a unanimous vote of the
Massachusetts Senate in favor of the resolutions,
and there were only sixteen who voted against
them in the House. The Boston " Atlas " of the
day complainingly says that John G. Whittier, the
Quaker poet, and others whom it names, " were
indiscriminately mingled with the members in the
Representatives' Hall during the whole debate."
The journals that had been angered by the introduction of the resolves were silenced by the una-
nimity of the vote. The bill securing jury trial
for runaway slaves was passed by both Houses with
scarcely a dissenting voice. It was while Mr.
Whittier was engaged in influencing the legislature
to pass the acts and resolves to which reference
has just been made, that he wrote the following
letter to his friend Robert Rantoul, Jr., the Democratic leader in the House of Representatives. It
was written from No. 1 Pitts Street, Boston, on
the 13th of March, 1837 : —

" I am fearful that I am troubling thee too often
with the question of slavery, but the deep interest
I feel must be my excuse. To thee, as to a friend,
I have spoken freely. I am certain that the resolutions [favoring the right of petition and the
abolition of slavery in the District of Columbia]
would pass even without thy aid. But, if they did
so, there would be a *party* aspect given to the mat-

ter, which I should regret exceedingly. It would insure, I fear, the reëlection of Edward Everett, as long as he pleased to occupy the Chair of State, and upon thyself, as far as Massachusetts or New England is concerned, the effect would be injurious. No party in the country is now so thoroughly organized and so united as the Abolitionist. Asking nothing for themselves, and contending only for great principles, under the impulse of duty, there is nothing but harmony and unison among them. They move in a mass, and that without concert, because they are governed, under all circumstances, by the same principles of action. So long as they remain thus they are invincible.

" It does seem to me that the present responsibility of thyself in this matter is very great. Thy talents, eloquence, and thus far steady devotion to equal rights, thy influence almost unbounded with the administrative party of the State, all combine to render thy decision, whatever it may be, of no trifling importance. Whatever may be thought of it now, the present is a crisis in the affairs of this State. Thy course on this question will be a matter of history. Never since Patrick Henry electrified the Assembly of Virginia has there been a nobler opportunity for advancing the cause of righteous liberty. What are the paltry offices which men contend for, which the vile, the imbecile, the sordid struggle for, as the *reward* of partisan fraud and management, to that which is received from a grateful, intelligent, and virtuous people, not for services rendered to themselves,

but for those rendered to the cause of pure democracy, humanity, and truth! In coming years the
greenest wreath in the memory of Jefferson will
be the record of his sentiments on the subject of
slavery. I know that thy own sentiments are
similar to those of Jefferson. I feel assured that
slavery, in any form, is odious to thy feelings.
Why not, then, say so; carry out thy democratic
principles, and insure the approbation of the wise
and good, throughout the world, and for all time;
nay more, secure that self-approval, that answer of
a good conscience, which, when the exciting ambitions and hopes of the partisan are lost, in the hour
of sickness, and in the decline of life, will be
dearer than any earthly honor. Never had any
one a more excellent opportunity of doing honor
to himself and to the cause of republican liberty
than thyself at this time. It would prove to the
people of Massachusetts that thy democracy is not
a partial and time-serving principle, but radical
and based upon the equality of the human family,
and zealous for the rights of all classes. In a word,
it would prove that to be a friend of the policy
and principles of Mr. Van Buren, as regards
other matters, does not necessarily imply a slavish
acquiescence in his extraordinary views on the
subject of liberty and slavery. It would win the
respect and command the admiration of all parties.
It would *disappoint* thy enemies; it would increase the esteem of all thy present friends, and
add to their number. It would do much for the
cause of humanity, and truth, and justice. May
we not hope that it will be done ? Excuse the lib-

erty I have taken, and believe me cordially thy
friend,   JOHN G. WHITTIER.

P. S.   Ill health prevents me from getting out
much in the evening; will it be in thy power to
call at this place to-morrow evening?

The poems written by Mr. Whittier during the
first years of his anti-slavery work, from 1833 to
1837, were with few exceptions devoted to the
cause he had so warmly espoused. They were
published in the " Liberator," the Boston " Courier," the " Anti-Slavery Reporter," the " New
England Magazine," and the Haverhill " Gazette."
They include "Toussaint L'Ouverture," "The
Yankee Girl," "Our Fellow Countrymen in
Chains," "The Hunters of Men," "Song of the
Free," "Is This the Land Our Fathers loved,"
"Ritner," "O Thou Whose Presence went before,"
and several poems not to be found in any collection
of his works.   In the "Liberator" of September
3, 1836, is a poem of his "To the Daughters of
James Forten," beginning : —

"Sisters! the vain and proud may pass you by."

The poem " Mogg Megone " belongs to this period.
It was published originally in the " New England
Magazine," in the numbers for March and April,
1835, and Mr. Whittier never tried so persistently
and unsuccessfully to suppress any other poem.
In the edition of 1888 he succeeded in relegating
it to the appendix. He began writing it while at
home, in the spring of 1830, and laid it aside when
he went to Hartford to edit the " Review."   The

finishing touches were given to it in 1834, while he was managing his farm at Haverhill, and busying himself with the politics of his county.   It probably would not have been finished but for material which came to his hand in two books of history [1] published after some lines of it had been written.   "Mogg Megone" was the first bound volume, exclusively of verse, ever issued by Whittier.   It was published in 1836, by Messrs. Light & Stevens, Cornhill, Boston, making a tiny book of sixty-nine pages, 24mo.   It was so very modest in its size that it seems to have escaped the attention of reviewers for several months after its publication.   But the "North American Review" for April, 1837, contains an appreciative notice from the pen of Professor C. C. Felton, which concludes with these words: "He has in various forms displayed his power, and if he will choose a less revolting theme, and construct his fable skillfully, and give to the execution all the finish of which he is capable, he will make a poem that shall live."

In a letter to Lucy Hooper, written in August, 1837, Mr. Whittier says: "I send thee a copy of 'Mogg Megone.' I was unable to finish it as I could have wished. It is, in my mind, liable to one grave objection. It is not, I fear, calculated to do good. But a small edition, however, was printed, and it is some satisfaction to believe that it cannot do much evil. The 'North Ameri-

---

[1] These were Folsom's *History of Saco and Biddeford*, and Williamson's *History of Maine*, published respectively in 1830 and 1832.

can Review,' I understand, gave a very favorable notice of it."

In 1837, he spent a few months in New York, acting as one of the secretaries of the American Anti-Slavery Society. He also occasionally wrote for Joshua Leavitt's " Emancipator." He occupied a room in which James G. Birney, Theodore D. Weld, Elizur Wright, Henry B. Stanton, and Joshua Leavitt had desks. The editing of the " Emancipator" and the " Anti-Slavery Reporter" was but a small part of their work. They wrote personal appeals to public men, distributed petitions to Congress against the interstate slave trade, in favor of freedom in the District of Columbia, and in opposition to the annexation of Texas. They wrote tracts, operated an " underground railroad" for fugitive slaves, and employed lecturers. There were several wealthy men like Gerrit Smith, Lewis and Arthur Tappan, and Joseph Sturge of England, who supplied a large part of the needed funds. Weld and Stanton were brilliant orators; Birney, the candidate of the Liberty party for the Presidency, wrote long and elaborate letters and essays; Elizur Wright and Leavitt were writers of sharp and pungent editorials; Whittier was sagacious in counsel, and was occasionally inspired to write a poem that electrified the North. The state of his health did not allow him to keep regular office hours, but he came and went as he pleased, boarding in Brooklyn, and crossing the ferry to reach the office on Nassau Street. Mr. Weld says that Whittier and he were much together in those days, and held long discussions upon themes in which they were both interested. One summer evening, at about nine o'clock, they went up to the balcony over the entrance to the New York City Hall, and the topic under discussion was so interesting to them both that they paid no heed to the great clock that tolled the hours over their head, and it was nearly daylight before it had occurred to them that it was time to seek their homes.

TO ELIZABETH H. WHITTIER.

NEWPORT, 6th mo. 14, 1837.

Thee hardly expected to hear from me at this place; certainly I did not expect to be here when I left Amesbury. On reaching Boston, I found none of the Portland people at the convention, and after waiting a week in Boston I received a letter from General [James] Appleton, stating that, owing to the present pecuniary embarrassments, it was impossible to obtain a sufficient number of subscribers to warrant the undertaking of a paper in Portland at present. Thus situated, I came on to the Yearly Meeting, and agreeably to the request of Professor [Elizur] Wright, I shall spend two or three months with him as one of the corresponding secretaries of the American Anti-Slavery Society, after which time there will probably be an opening for me in Portland or Philadelphia. I shall leave to-day or to-morrow for New York, and on arriving there will take an early opportunity to write more fully. The Yearly Meeting, at the suggestion of some Philadelphia Friends, has concluded to shut our meeting-houses against anti-slavery lecturers. I regret the step exceedingly. Sarah M. and Angelina E. Grimké are now in Boston. Next week they go to Lynn and Salem, and next to Ipswich, Newburyport and Amesbury. They are excellent speakers, and cannot fail to make a good impression wherever they go.

TO THE SAME.

NEW YORK, 4th of 7th mo., 1837.

I have now been in this city between two and three weeks, and shall perhaps stay here three weeks longer, or more. My paper will not start in Maine until the Ninth month, if it does then,[1] and I have some doubts about its agreeing with me to write very steadily, as since the warm weather I have been troubled with my old complaint of palpitation. I am lounging away my time here, not closely applying myself to anything, overseeing the sending out of petitions.

There had been a division in the ranks of the abolitionists, and the "new organization," which included Whittier, the Tappans, J. G. Birney, Samuel E. Sewall, H. B. Stanton, Joshua Leavitt, Amos A. Phelps, and Gerrit Smith, favored political action, while Garrison, and those who adhered to him, refused to recognize the possibility of attaining their end without the overthrow of the

[1] The plan of starting an anti-slavery paper in Portland, which he was to edit, was given up because of business troubles in Maine growing out of ruinous land speculations, which made it an unpropitious time for beginning the publication of such a paper.

Constitution. From first to last, as we have said, Whittier never wavered in his determination to fight slavery at the ballot-box, and he considered it useless waste of strength to tug at the pillars of the Union, and attempt to overthrow the church or to carry along reforms for which the time was not yet ripe. To the criticism he received from his friends of the "old organization" he made temperate and good-natured replies, reserving all his sharpest arrows for the common enemy.

It was in 1837 that he wrote "The Pastoral Letter," called out by the action of an association of clergymen which met at Brookfield, Mass., and issued a letter to the churches warning them against discussions of "agitating and perplexing subjects," and especially against the mission of the South Carolina sisters Grimké, which "threatens the female character with widespread and permanent injury."

In 1837, John Quincy Adams wrote a series of remarkable letters to his constituents, telling the whole story of his great fight in Congress for the right of petition. These letters were published in the Quincy "Patriot," which had a small circulation, limited to his Congressional district. As Adams at this time belonged to neither of the great parties that divided the country, none of the party organs copied these letters, the spirit and brilliancy of which would have insured their appearance in every leading journal of the country if the journalistic enterprise of the present time had prevailed in those days. The friends of liberty were not willing that this record of a splendid forensic contest should be thus smothered. It was decided to publish the letters in a pamphlet for general circulation, and Mr. Whittier was called upon to edit them. He went to Quincy and conferred with Mr. Adams, who was glad to have added publicity given to what he justly regarded as the crowning work of his long and useful life. The pamphlet was published by Isaac Knapp, of Boston, and its pages cannot be read even now without such a thrill as the highest eloquence and most pungent satire impart to sympathetic nerves.

TO HARRIET MINOT.

NEW YORK, 8th mo. 6, 1837.

I am now boarding in the family of Don F. Del Floys, a Spanish refugee, whose wife is a sister of Captain Charles Stuart.[1] I see all the French and Spanish ladies in the city. As a general thing they are not so beautiful as the American ladies. There is more dignity and haughtiness in the Spanish ladies; yet on acquaintance they are very agreeable. . . . Dr. Channing has written a long letter to Henry Clay on the Texas question. The good cause of emancipation goes on with unprecedented rapidity. . . . I am sorry to learn that —— is offended with me. She is certainly wrong. I never give my friends occasion for offense. Phrenologically, I have too much self-esteem to be troubled by the opinions of others, and I love my old friends too well to deny them the gratification, if it be one, of abusing me to their hearts' content.

---

[1] An officer in the English army who came to this country and threw himself heart and soul into anti-slavery work.

But I fear nothing from you Haverhill folks in the way of slander ; you never speak evil of any one ; no prying into the business of others ; no society small-talk ; no tea-table scandals ; no adepts in the science of dissecting characters ; all is peace and harmony and good will. . . . Thee would not judge perhaps from the tone of this letter that my mind has been a good deal exercised of late on the subject of religious obligation. Yet such is the fact. The prayer of Cowper is sometimes in my mind, " Oh, for a closer walk with God." I feel that there are too many things of the world between me and the realization of a quiet communion with the pure and Holy Spirit. Why is it that we go on from day to day, and week to week, in this manner ? Alas for human nature in its best estate. There is no upward tendency in it. It looks downward. It is indeed of the earth.

It was in the summer of 1837, while residing in New York, that Mr. Whittier made the acquaintance of Lucy Hooper, who was then only twenty years of age. She was a native of Essex County, and was at that time living with her parents in Brooklyn. Mr. Whittier had a boarding-place in the same city, and was a frequent visitor at the house of the Hoopers. He encouraged the literary ambition of the charming young poetess, who had already published many verses, and who was considering the advisability of collecting them in a book. The next year, when Mr. Whittier was editing the " Pennsylvania Freeman," he called for and received occasional poems from her. It was in 1839 that one August afternoon he walked with her by the river of their childhood, an event commemorated in the elegy he wrote on the occasion of her death in 1841.

TO LUCY HOOPER.

NEW YORK, 8th mo. 21, 1837.

In perusing some of thy brief and fugitive pieces of poetry, I have been impressed with the belief that it is in thy power to write a poem of some considerable length, which would be worth infinitely more to thee and to the literature of the country than all the hurried sketches and " bits of poetry " which thou and myself and a score of others who might be named have ever written. The truth is, the " small craft " of poetry in which we have indulged ourselves is not fitted for the voyage of Immortality. We shall perish, and verily *our works will follow us.* The hearts which now know us and love us will also soon cease to beat, and with them our very memories will die. The utilitarian of the twentieth century will not heed whether, in treading on our graves, he shakes the dust of prose or poetry from his feet. And after all what matters it? Who cares for the opinions of the twentieth century? Not I, for one. But we *do* all care for the opinions of the good and the wise and the pure-hearted around us! If we strive for fame, or riches, or honor, it is because we wish to share their smile with the friends whom we love, and in the matter of poetry, a poetical reputation.

If we write at all, why not use our talents to the best advantage? Why not write a poem upon which we can concentrate all our powers? I have long thought of doing this myself, but I have nearly abandoned the idea. An accumulating pressure of other matters compels me to forego the undertaking. But what should hinder thee from doing it? Nothing that I can conceive of.

I send thee with this a poem by Mrs. Maria G. Brooks, a Massachusetts lady. The poem ["Zophiel, or the Bride of Seven"] was written, I believe, in the West Indies. It has been republished in fine style in England, edited by, and under the sanction of Southey. There are some very exquisite passages, but as a whole the poem is defective in plot, and full of weaknesses and hard, ungraceful rhyme. Yet the true gems in it are none the less conspicuous for the foil of bad taste and the lack of general interest.

Now I do not wish to flatter thee; first, because I should despise myself for the meanness of the attempt, and second, because I know that by so doing I should deservedly forfeit thy esteem. But in perfect sincerity allow me to say that I believe thee able to produce within six months of this time a poem which would be received with general commendation on both sides of the Atlantic. Pray think of it! I wish very much to have the pleasure of the walk proposed so long since, but fear I shall not find leisure before I go to New England. I will try, however, and call again before I leave.

Boston, 8th mo. 27, 1837.

I did not receive thy note until after my return from Brooklyn the other day, or I should have alluded to it when I saw thee. I did not wish to throw any obstacle in the way of thy publishing thy fugitive poems, but simply to suggest the expediency of deferring their publication until thou couldst have time for the completion of a longer and more elaborate poem. I know it would require a good deal of patient perseverance and severe intellectual toil; and for myself I frankly confess that I have not resolution to attempt anything of the kind. Besides, unless consecrated to the sacred interests of religion and humanity, it would be a criminal waste of life, and abuse of the powers which God has given for his own glory and the welfare of the world. Mere intellectual renown is valueless. Do the best that we can, in the matter of intellect, the devil is wiser than any of us. The humblest and weakest follower of the meek and lowly Redeemer is more to be envied than a Voltaire, a Rousseau, or a Byron, and the lowliest teacher of that sublime philosophy which " the wisdom of the world accounteth foolishness " is wiser and better than the prodigies of intellect, whose learning and acquirements only enable them, in the words of another, " *sapienter descendere ad infernum.*"

Shouldst thou conclude to publish a small and select volume of thy poems, I have no doubt of their success. They are better than a great proportion of Mrs. —— 's, although the *sentiment* and the *moral* are not always so good as hers, in a religious point of view. There is an originality and a freshness of poetic feeling in them which cannot be found in Mrs. ——'s writings. She says, besides, a great deal too much of "babies," "dead infants," "sick infants," "sleeping infants," "smiling infants," infants *ad infinitum,* so that her book might not be inaptly termed "The Chronicles of the Nursery." This no doubt results from the fact that her affections have all been forced into one channel. If I can do anything to promote the publication of thy poems, I herewith cheerfully, and grateful for the opportunity of so doing, tender my services. Please write me thy intention.

For the coming fortnight I shall probably be at Amesbury, and should be happy to hear from thee at any time. My health has suffered from my residence in New York, — a place which, with all due deference to thyself, I must consider unfit for Christian, or heathen even, to dwell in. The present is a favorable time, in some respects, to publish. There are few new books in the market. Remember me kindly to thy sisters, mother, and brother, and believe me, very sincerely thy friend.

In 1837, while Mr. Whittier was in New York, Isaac Knapp, of Boston, publisher of the "Liberator," without consulting him, published a volume of over one hundred pages, entitled "Poems written during the Progress of the Abolition Question in the United States, between the years 1830 and 1838. By John G. Whittier." This was the first edition of Whittier's poems ever published.

CHAPTER VI.

1837–1840.

THE political and in a measure the literary interests of Mr. Whittier had made the editorial occupation a natural one, and but for family reasons he might have continued in it. His devotion to the anti-slavery cause led to his return to this work. Late in the autumn of 1837, he heeded a call to Philadelphia, and went to the assistance of the venerable anti-slavery pioneer, Benjamin Lundy, who was editing the "National Enquirer." In March, 1838, Lundy, worn out in the cause to which he had devoted his life, retired from the management of the paper, the name of which was changed to "Pennsylvania Freeman," and in the issue of March 15 Whittier pledged the entire devotion of his energies to the cause of Universal Freedom, as he became the responsible editor.

In Philadelphia, Mr. Whittier made his home again with his good Haverhill friends, the Thayers, and among the Quakers found congenial companionship in many families ; one of his steadfast friends was John Dickinson, father of Anna E. Dickinson, who in later years became celebrated as a public speaker, and of Susan E. Dickinson, well known as a writer. The last-named daughter contributes these reminiscences of Whittier's Philadelphia life : —

"I saw him once, when, a young child clinging to my mother's hand on the way home from Twelfth Street meeting, she said to me, 'Look at the young man walking with thy father; that is the poet, John G. Whittier.' Young as I was I knew his name; for I had heard from her lips already the story of how some years before she had rushed bareheaded from her home on Arch Street, near Third, up to Sixth Street, as the fire bells clanged out, and the word came that Pennsylvania Hall was mobbed and on fire; and but half an hour before her husband had left her to join Whittier and Thomas Shipley and a few other faithful ones, for the first meeting there after the dedication. She told how calm and quiet Whittier was *outwardly*, looking on at the destruction of the hall, his office, and his books and his papers, and how helpful to others in the rush of the mob and the whirl of the flames. The late Edward M. Davis, son-in-law of Lucretia Mott, once wrote to me that it was difficult to give many incidents of Whittier's life in Philadelphia; he went so little into social circles, was so quiet, doing steadfast and indefatigable work on the paper, and on committees; a great amount of writing, but very little public speaking; his work was far more prominent than he was. Mr. Whittier himself told me, in 1867, that my father and he went to Harrisburg as delegates to form the state anti-slavery society, and that he was one of the committee that drafted the constitution of the society. The time at which

I mentioned first seeing him must have been when he stopped for two or three days on his return from Washington, whither he was sent in 1845 as one of the commissioners to present the remonstrance of Massachusetts against the annexation of Texas. Perhaps the dark, spirituelle beauty of his face which stamped itself on my childish memory was made clearer by the likeness (a daguerreotype) of him sent to one of my Western schoolmates a few years later, and which kindled the enthusiasm of all the pupils over him into flame. Two of my classmates there were the daughters of Joseph Healy, who did most of the anti-slavery printing and publishing in Philadelphia for years ; and one of my most treasured possessions is the little paper-covered revised edition of 'Moll Pitcher and the Minstrel Girl,' presented by one of them. Among the young women to whom we girls looked up with interest and admiration in those days was Elizabeth Lloyd, Jr., author of many beautiful poems,[1] and there was a special glamour attached to her because she was understood to be one of the very few with whom Whittier was really on terms of warm personal friendship, outside of his firm and faithful comradeship with his anti-slavery friends. My father died suddenly but a few weeks after the time when he and Whittier walked from meeting together, which explains why I can tell nothing from the lips of the friend who was so dear to him."

Some of the Philadelphia Friends, who were

[1] The best known of these is *Milton on his Blindness*.

accustomed to hear the voices of women raised in their meetings, objected to the appearance on the anti-slavery platform of several young women who had trained themselves for public speaking in a lyceum of their own; and one of the young women wittily said that the conservative Friends believed that Paul meant to say that women were bound to keep silence *except* in the churches! In those days Mr. Whittier was accustomed in a humorous vein to discourage the would-be feminine orators; his real attitude is set forth in this letter to Elizabeth Neall: —

TO ELIZABETH NEALL.

1839.

For myself, abolition has been to me its own "exceeding great reward." It has repaid every sacrifice of time, of money, of reputation, of health, of ease, with the answer of a good conscience, and the happiness which grows out of benevolent exertions for the welfare of others. It has led me to examine myself. It has given me the acquaintance of some of the noblest and best of men and women. *It owes me nothing.* So, then, two of the youngest members of the Women's Society are to hold forth. . . . Shade of the Apostle Paul! What is this world coming to? Never mind, "I like it hugely," as Tristram Shandy said of Yorick's sermon, and would like it better to see them wield in their delicate fingers the thunderbolts of abolition oratory. As the author of John Gilpin said of the hero and his horse,

"And when he next doth ride abroad,
May I be there to see!"

Seriously, I see no good reason why they should not speak as well as their elders. "Let the daughters prophesy," agreeably to the promise of the prophet Joel, and let the doors be thrown open to all without distinction of sex, and then another part of the promise will be verified, — "the young men shall see visions"! I go the whole length as regards the rights of women, however, although I sometimes joke a little about it. I am afraid it is a besetting sin of mine to do so in reference to many things in which I feel a sober and real interest. I have repented of it a thousand times, especially as it gave those who were not intimately acquainted with me a false idea of my character. . . .

Of his life in Philadelphia, his cousin, Ann E. Wendell, contributes these reminiscences : —

"I can recall but little of Greenleaf's first visit to us in the winter of 1836–1837, but the picture of the first evening is very vivid. I remember his dignified entrance, his dress a light overcoat and a sealskin cap, — there my memory of that evening closes ; but that he was in a genial mood, ready to enjoy what came, I judge from his accepting an invitation from my brother Isaac to visit him at his home ten miles out of town, and to take with him my sister Margaret and my little brother Evert. The winter was very cold, and the sleighing good, so they were to go in a sleigh. Greenleaf became much interested in telling Margaret some interesting story, and the result was an upset in a snow-drift, which was a source

of much merriment then and afterward.   He came
several times, talked a good deal, and was very
entertaining.   I cannot now recollect much of
his conversation, except what he said of his fear
of ghosts, and his dread of passing the grave-yard.
We did not see him again until 1838, when he
came to edit the 'Pennsylvania Freeman.'   He
was with us a good deal during the next winter.
I think the portrait of him by Bass Otis was
painted at about this time, and not in 1836.   I recollect sitting on a sofa and holding this portrait
before Joseph Sturge for his inspection, and his
remark, ' John, I do not quite like it.'   I do not
recollect the objection.   I always fancied there
was a similarity in a smile in all the portraits by
Otis, and perhaps he saw it did not look quite
natural.   But the position was lifelike.   Otis
placed him at the table, turned his attention to
something else, and then addressed him a little
suddenly with, ' Mr. Whittier ! '   When Greenleaf
started up to respond, he said, ' Keep that position,' and he was so taken.[1] . . . Joseph Healy at
that time lived on Seventh Street, and his house
was a gathering-place for the abolitionists.   Green-

[1] It was after this painting that the engraving in the first volume of the edition of 1888 was executed.   A few years after this
portrait was painted, the ladies of Philadelphia had an anti-
slavery bazaar, and wished to have an engraving of it made by
Sartain to be sold at the fair.   One of them wrote to Mr. Whittier, asking his permission, and this was his reply : " I have no
great fancy for having my face made use of in the manner thee
suggests ; but if it will be of any service to the bazaar it would
perhaps be foolish to object to it.   My *heart* has been too long
devoted to the good cause in which you are laboring to allow me
to withhold my *head* when it is needed."

leaf was there a good deal, but I think he boarded
with his old friend and townsman, A. W. Thayer.
Abolitionism at that time was so blended with
transcendentalism and ultra-liberalism, in both the
social and religious point of view, that the Orthodox Friends of Philadelphia, although fully believing in the right of abolition, were very shy of
joining in the public movements of the abolitionists. This threw Greenleaf almost entirely with
the Hicksite division of the society, and he being
always retiring did not soon make many personal
acquaintances on our side, although he belonged to
the Orthodox division.

"When Pennsylvania Hall was burned we lived
on the same street, six or seven squares from it.
Greenleaf did not come to see us that night, as he
was in the midst of the crowd at the fire. There
were other riots about that time. One evening the
mob attacked a colored institution not far from us,
and the police were ordered there. They came, a
line of men reaching from one side to the other of
the street, and stopped in front of our house. Another line came, another and another, until they
formed a solid square of men. At a given signal
all sprang their rattles together, and marched down
to the scene of trouble.

"One incident I recall, of 1838. My sister Margaret entertained a small company at our house,
and the amusement of the evening was taking pro-
files on the wall, from the shadow cast upon a
paper pinned upon it. I have kept Greenleaf's
until this time, and not long ago pasted it on
black cloth and had it photographed. It is like

the old-fashioned silhouettes, and I think it a perfect likeness. I prize it for the curiosity of its origin. When the last collection of his works was made, I asked him if he wanted this likeness engraved; but he wrote to me he had a side face taken[1] by William Gray's grand-daughter. I suspect he thought it would be a rather ridiculous affair, but I don't think it is.

" Greenleaf was with us a great deal during the next two or three years. I very rarely went from home, and was much confined to the sofa. In the evening, the centre table was rolled to the sofa so that I could enjoy the light. Greenleaf often came home very weary, and seated himself at the table, looking as though he felt there was nothing more to do, and both body and soul could rest. That memory makes the picture taken from Miss Gray's photograph valuable to me, as it looks as he did at such times, although William J. Allinson said it looked as though he had never received the breath of life.

" He was very uncertain; we could never make an engagement and be sure he would be with us. Elizabeth Stuart Phelps Ward, in the ' Century,' describes our experience exactly. He did not like little companies, where he would be an object of particular interest. On one occasion he did, I think, intend to be present, and then gave up the intention; but knowing how much sister Margaret would be disappointed, he sent the following lines : —

[1] The picture in the fourth volume.

'To cousin Margaret Wendell, greeting :
This may inform thee that to-night
There 'll be an anti-slavery meeting,
To set the world and so forth right !
And I, bear witness all slaveholders,
Must hold therein a lofty station —
A moral Atlas on whose shoulders
Shall rest the ark of reformation.
And therefore, cousin Margaret, seeing
My present duty — pardon me !
Since nothing but the *world's* well-being
Shall keep me, dearest coz, from *thee*.

'12th mo., 12th, 1839.'

"The poem 'To a Friend on her Return from Europe' was addressed to Elizabeth Neall [Mrs. Sidney Howard Gay]. The lines, in the edition of 1838, 'In the Commonplace Book of a Young Lady' were written for my sister Margaret, at least the prelude was. 'The Quaker of Olden Time' and the poem 'The Relic' were written at our house in Philadelphia in 1839. In the winter of 1840, Mr. Whittier edited a small collection of poems for an anti-slavery fair, entitled 'The North Star.' The poems were contributed by friends interested in the cause ; among them were John Quincy Adams, James T. Fields, Lucy Hooper, John Pierpont, Greenleaf, and his sister Elizabeth.[1] . . . It was his intention at that time to go to the World's Convention held in London the next summer, and we did not know his reason for remaining at home, although aware that he was ill during the winter."

The following incident of Mr. Whittier's resi-

---

[1] Whittier's own contributions to the collection were *The Exiles* and *The World's Convention*.

dence in Philadelphia is told by Mr. Edwin H. Coates, who was one of a committee of twelve persons organized in 1834, and acting with a still larger association, for the purpose of aiding fugitives from slavery. One member of this committee was John P. Burr, a natural son of Aaron Burr. Mr. Coates says that when Mr. Whittier took up his residence in Philadelphia he came to him to learn the workings of the "underground railroad" : —

"Like all of us he learned that the great secret of our success was to be cautious, discerning, and *never to make a mistake.* A mistake, a blunder, meant the penitentiary, and years of painful imprisonment. A Virginia slave named Douglass applied to the committee for help to get his wife and children into a free State. We dispatched an agent to Baltimore to consult with the vigilance committee there, and finally a letter was sent to the family by an efficient female agent by the name of Butler, who worked her plans and ours so well that in a short time the little party landed in Philadelphia. At eleven o'clock that night there came to my house a consequential-looking individual who handed me a copy of the Washington 'Globe,' at the same time pointing to an advertisement containing a reward for the recovery of the runaways, and a full description of each one. As may well be imagined, I began to grow alarmed. So as soon as this person had withdrawn, I started for the residence of Whittier, and was closeted with him for an hour. A conviction for complicity in this scheme meant personal

injury, or at least imprisonment for a long and
indefinite term. Without coming to any conclusion as to the best course to pursue I went home
and to bed. I know I kept looking at the penitentiary with one eye and on the God of the
oppressed with the other. But it providentially
turned out all right, and I had the unspeakable
pleasure of soon meeting the family in a secure
place and shaking hands with them all. I then
with joy rushed to Whittier's house, at the still
hour of midnight, and called my anxious friend
out of bed. From the room below I cried, ' Whittier ! Whittier ! the Douglass family is safe ! '
From his chamber came the exclamation : ' Glory !
Hallelujah ! ' — and this is the first time I remember hearing a Quaker shout. But he did, and it
came from his very soul. We soon had barbers
and dressmakers and others to assist in changing
the personal appearance and effecting a complete
disguise of the determined slaves, and when they
left that house, with their wigs, strange clothes,
and other changes, they could not have been
recognized as the same party who entered it."

In May, 1838, Mr. Whittier, accompanied by
his cousin, Joseph Cartland, visited Joseph
Healy's place in Bucks County, and in a letter
from there to a friend he says in regard to the
divisions in the Society of Friends : —

"Here as everywhere else in Bucks County,
the 'heretics' [Hicksites] have the ascendency in
point of numbers, and I fear that even those who
have in some degree maintained their integrity
have not always given evidence of soundness in *all*

respects. . . . What will it avail us if, while boasting of our soundness and of our enmity to the delusion of Hicksism, we neglect to make a practical application of our belief to ourselves ? if we neglect to seek for ourselves that precious atonement which we are so ready to argue in favor of ? I do not undervalue a sound belief. The truth should be held, but at the same time I believe it may be 'held' in unrighteousness. I do not dare to claim to be any the better for my orthodox principles. The mercy of God is my only hope. . . . I cannot forbear to mention one fact which has come under my notice, as showing that prejudice against color is not confined to human bipeds. A hen at this place has disowned two of a fine brood of chickens who happen to be black! Let this be communicated to Elliott Cresson [an agent of the Colonization Society]."

Notwithstanding his well-known abolition sentiments, Mr. Whittier was invited to contribute to the first number of the " Democratic Review," published at Washington, October, 1837. His poem " Palestine " appeared in that number, which also contained William Cullen Bryant's "The Battle-Field." To the second number he contributed " The Familist's Hymn," and thereafter for nearly ten years he sent to the " Review " most of his best work.

Busy as Mr. Whittier was with his work in the fields of philanthropy and reform, while in Philadelphia, he then laid a plan that the state of his health did not permit him to execute, for a literary undertaking of considerable magnitude, the exact

nature of which cannot now be known. But
among his papers is found a letter from an intimate literary friend of his which gives some hint
of it. This friend writes : —

" I am delighted with thy idea ; thou givest form
and substance to a vague desire of seeing something like a corner-stone laid for a Quaker temple
of literature. Thou art the man to undertake it.
. . . I have never seen the Wordsworth sonnets
alluded to, but will look at them to understand
thy plan. Thy idea only needs the setting of J.
G. Whittier's poetry to make it the richest jewel
in his crown of fame. But I would have thee lay
it by, uncut and unpolished, till restored health
and the quiet occupation of a home life will allow
thee to work upon it, without paying the price
which has been the penalty of too many of thy
literary labors."

Slave-hunters were often following their prey
into Pennsylvania in those days, and many in-
stances are given in the newspapers of the time of
free colored people being kidnapped and taken to
the Southern States, either without giving them a
chance to prove their right to freedom in the
courts, or by false swearing as to their identity.
Mr. Whittier called attention, in the following
paragraph in the " Freeman," to what he properly
called " a desecration of the Hall of Independence " : —

" It may not be generally known to our readers
that the building in which our National Independence was first proclaimed is not unfrequently
devoted to the vile purpose of trying colored

Americans charged, in the quaint language of a New York mechanic, with having been ' born contrary to the Declaration of '76,' and that from its doors many a poor wretch has been borne away into helpless bondage. Our indefatigable friend, Samuel Webb, of Philadelphia, lately presented a petition to the city council, praying that the building wherein, in the year 1776, was proclaimed to an admiring world the sublime truth that all men are created equal, may no longer be prostituted to the purpose of sending men, women, and children, unconvicted of crime, into hopeless, helpless, endless bondage, a purpose inconsistent with the uses to which that building should be applied, which was selected by the founders of the Republic in which to ' proclaim Liberty throughout the land, and to *all* the inhabitants thereof.' The memorial was presented to the council, and it was respectfully received and referred to the committee on city property. What action has been taken on it we have not learned. The first trial of a man charged with being a chattel, at which we were ever present, was held not long ago in that very hall ! "

He goes on to tell of a respectable-looking man, who asserted his right to freedom, being delivered to slave-hunters from Maryland, their word being taken as sufficient evidence that he was a slave who had escaped from his master. The justice decided against him, and at once, in that sacred hall, one of the slave-hunters drew from his pocket a pair of handcuffs and took him away in triumph. It was to arouse a people who had become accus-

tomed to such scenes, to the wickedness and inconsistency of permitting them to happen in a free
country, that Mr. Whittier was now devoting all
his energies. His connection with the "Freeman"
during the years 1838–39 was interrupted by excursions to western Pennsylvania, to New York,
and to his home in Massachusetts; at times he was
incapacitated for work by serious illness. Very
few of his poems appear in the "Freeman" during
these two years of hard work, harassed by contin-
uous invalidism. In the second number after he
took charge appeared the pathetic "Farewell of
a Virginia Slave Mother : " —

> " Gone, gone, sold and gone
> To the rice-swamp dank and lone."

The other poems of this period are " The Familist's Hymn," which he copied into his own paper
from the "Democratic Review;" a New Year's
Address in which he severely lashed C. G. Ather-
ton, of New Hampshire, author of the "gag rule"
in Congress ; the ode read at the opening of Pennsylvania Hall; a philippic against Governor
Porter of Pennsylvania, whose inaugural address
took strong grounds against the anti-slavery agitation, and recommended a law to punish sedition;[1]

---

[1] This poem, published February 28, 1839, does not appear
in his collected works. The physician named in the following
stanza of it was Dr. Bartholomew Fussell, of Chester County, an
active abolitionist : —

> "Go hunt sedition ! Search for that
> In every pedlar's cart of rags ;
> Pry into every Quaker's hat
> And Dr. Fussell's saddle-bags,
> Lest treason wrap, with all its ills,
> Around his powders and his pills."

"Lines on Receiving a Cane," made from wood-work of Pennsylvania Hall, which the fire had spared; and a poem suggested by being present at the trial of a fugitive slave in the immediate vicinity of Independence Hall, entitled "Republican Man-Robbery." The slave referred to in the last-named poem was handcuffed in the presence of the court and spectators and sent South. These, with the hymn "Worship," are the only verses of Whittier's that appeared in the "Freeman" during the two years he conducted it.

He refused to discuss, or to allow his correspondents to dwell upon, political, religious, or reform topics not bearing directly upon the main object of his paper. To a correspondent who asked him to take up the cause of Peace he replied: —

"We will not use the funds collected from persons of all sects and parties and opinions for the sole and express object of promoting the abolition of slavery for other purposes. Common honesty forbids."

On another occasion, he illustrated the same policy with the following parable: —

"When Anthony of Bourbon, during the French King's minority, held the regency of France, he informed the Danish ambassador that he hoped in a short time to procure a free passage for the gospel throughout France. The ambassador, a zealous Lutheran, expressed his pleasure, but hoped that Luther's, not Calvin's, doctrines might pass current. 'Luther and Calvin,' answered the Regent, 'agree in forty points, and differ but in one. Let those therefore that follow the tenets of

those two unite their strength against the common
enemy, and at better leisure, in a more convenient
season, compound their own differences.'"

Early in May, 1838, Mr. Whittier attended the
annual meeting of the American Anti-Slavery
Society in New York, where he offered a resolution that led to an animated debate. This resolution advised members and agents of the society
not to rely upon physical force for protection
against the violence of their enemies. There was
a small majority against this proposition. He returned to Philadelphia in season to see his office
destroyed by the mob of May 17, 1838, spent a
week in straightening out matters, and then
started for Boston, where he attended the annual
meeting of the New England Anti-Slavery Society, and was a member of the business committee.
During his absence he sent letters to the "Freeman." The New England convention was held in
Marlboro chapel, and a mob gathered as in Philadelphia, threatening to destroy the hall, but the
mayor promptly took measures to protect the convention. Mr. Whittier says of the Marlboro
chapel that it was nearly equal in size and beauty
to Pennsylvania Hall. He describes a visit on
a June day to the ruins of the Ursuline convent
in Charlestown, which was destroyed by a mob
in 1834. He says: "The stone literally ' cries
out from the wall,' and the scorched timber
answers it. Would it not be well to let the walls
of our beautiful Hall remain like those of the
Charlestown convent, a monument and a warning?" He returned to his work in Philadelphia

the last week in June. Fortunately the printing-
office of the "Freeman" was not in the building
that had been destroyed by the populace, and the
publication of the paper was not interrupted.

Pennsylvania Hall was the largest and finest
edifice of its kind in Philadelphia. It had been
built by an association of citizens, at a cost of
$43,000, that they might have a room in which
the principles of liberty and equality of civil rights
could be fully discussed, and the evils of slavery
portrayed. The dedicatory exercises had been in
progress three days, with crowded audiences in
attendance; addresses had been delivered by
David Paul Brown, William Lloyd Garrison,
Arnold Buffum, Angelina Grimké Weld, and
others; letters read from John Quincy Adams,
Thaddeus Stevens, William Jay, and Gerrit Smith;
and also an ode written for the occasion by John
G. Whittier. There were threats of violence from
a rabble in the streets, incited, it is said, by Southern men sojourning in the city. On the evening
of the third day, May 16th, while Garrison was
addressing a woman's meeting, the windows were
broken by stones, but the inner blinds prevented
injury to the audience. Mrs. Weld, a native of
South Carolina, delivered an eloquent address in
the midst of pauses in the tumult, and Lucretia
Mott and Maria W. Chapman, by the grace and
dignity of their presence, and the discretion of
their speech, prevented an outbreak of violence,
which was threatened in the crowded hall. Abby
Kelley, of Lynn, on this occasion made her first
public address. She said : —

"It is not the crashing of those windows, nor the maddening rush of those voices, that calls me before you. Those pass unheeded by me. But it is the small voice within, which may not be withstood, that bids me open my mouth for the dumb, that bids me plead the cause of God's perishing poor."

When the meeting adjourned, the women passed unharmed through the angry mob that blocked the streets outside. The next morning, a crowd again assembled in the streets, and Daniel Neall, president of the managers of the hall, called upon the mayor for protection. The mayor replied: "It is public opinion that makes mobs, and ninety-nine out of a hundred of those with whom I converse are against you." The city solicitor gave orders to the police not to arrest a single man. Placards had been posted calling for mob violence. The day passed, and nothing was done by the authorities to insure order. In the evening there were fifteen thousand persons assembled in the streets. The mayor gave notice that he would disperse the mob, if he could have possession of the building. The keys were at once given him, and he made this singular speech : —

"There will be no meeting here this evening. This house has been given up to me. The managers had the right to hold their meeting, but as good citizens they have at my request suspended their meeting for this evening. *We never call out the military here.* I would, fellow-citizens, look upon you as my police, and I trust you will keep order. I now bid you farewell, *for the night!* "

The mob gave three cheers for their friend the mayor, and commenced the attack as soon as he was gone. The doors were forced open, the papers from Mr. Whittier's editorial room, the window-blinds, and other inflammable materials were piled upon the speaker's platform in the large hall above. They were set on fire, the gas was turned on, and in a few hours only the blackened walls of the beautiful building were standing. The fire department was called out, but the mob prevented a drop of water from being thrown upon the flames. They were allowed to save only adjoining property. With a change of dress to avoid recognition and assault,[1] Mr. Whittier was active during the fire in saving what he could from his office, which was in the lower story. His paper went to press early the next morning, with this brief account of the outrage from his pen : —

"18th of Fifth month, half past seven o'clock. — Pennsylvania Hall is in ashes! The beautiful temple consecrated to Liberty has been offered a smoking sacrifice to the Demon of Slavery. In the heart of this city a flame has gone up to Heaven. It will be seen from Maine to Georgia. In its red and lurid light, men will see more

---

[1] Mr. Whittier went out to visit his office, found an excited multitude in the street, and knowing that his life was imperiled if he was recognized, went to the house of his friend, Dr. Parrish, put on a wig and a long white overcoat, and again ventured into the midst of the mob. It added to his security, that having resided in Philadelphia only a few months, he was not much known outside the circle of his friends. When his office was being sacked, he went in with the crowd and secured some things he wished to save from destruction.

clearly than ever the black abominations of the
fiend at whose instigation it was kindled. . . . We
have no time for comment. Let the abhorred
deed speak for itself. Let all men see by what a
frail tenure they hold property and life in a land
overshadowed by the curse of slavery."

The convention that had been holding its annual
meeting in the hall adjourned to meet on the morning of the 18th, to elect officers and transact other
business. The meeting was held according to
adjournment, and its business transacted in the
open street, in front of the smoking ruins, and
surrounded by a mob not yet satisfied with violence, though cowed into silence for the time by
the dignity and solemnity of the proceedings.
Mr. Whittier took part in this meeting, to sustain
a resolution he had offered to the effect that the
right of suffrage should be held sacred to the cause
of freedom, and votes withheld from candidates
opposed to the abolition of slavery within the ju-
risdiction of Congress, who encouraged or in any
way sustained mob-law in its attempts to put down
freedom of speech and of the press, or favored the
disfranchising of colored citizens.

The excitement in the city did not subside for
several days. Outrages were frequent against
innocent negroes, and against newspapers and
individuals that ventured to oppose the mob-spirit.
On the evening of the 18th the rioters attacked
and set fire to a new building intended as a
" Shelter for Colored Orphans," and the next
day spent their fury on a Bethel church belonging
to colored people. The office of the " Public

Ledger " was threatened, because it had advocated
free discussion, but preparations for defense had
been made, and the mob did not venture upon an
attack.   The governor of the commonwealth, to
whom Whittier had the year before addressed the
poem " Ritner," promptly issued a proclamation
expressing the deepest regret that the soil of Pennsylvania had been disgraced by acts of lawless
riot, and offering a reward of $500 for the appre-
hension and conviction of each and every person
engaged in the outrage.   This action shamed the
mayor into issuing a similar proclamation, but he
took pains to word it so that only the person who
set the fire was to be apprehended.

The jury of inquiry to which was referred the
matter of damages the county would be required
to pay on account of the destruction of Pennsylvania Hall were three years in making up their
decision.   They reported in 1841 that the loss
amounted to $33,000.   The value of the lot was
from $10,000 to $15,000.   The lot was eventually
sold to the order of Odd Fellows, by which a hall
for their own purposes was erected and dedicated
in 1846.

Reference has been made above to an address
made by Mrs. Weld, a native of South Carolina.
It was a singular episode of those exciting days
that the marriage of Angelina Grimké to Mr.
Weld took place the night before the burning of
the hall.   Miss Grimké was a Quakeress who had
freed her slaves, and was delivering eloquent abolition addresses at the North.   Mr. Whittier, then
editor of the " Freeman," was invited to the wed-

ding, which was attended by a large number of the foremost anti-slavery agitators in the country, Mr. Garrison included. But, as Miss Grimké was marrying " out of society," an orthodox Friend like Mr. Whittier could not lend his countenance to the wedding by assisting at the ceremony. He therefore was absent, but compromised his orthodoxy by escorting a young lady to the house, and the next morning he called again at the door with a congratulatory poem he had written during the night! Both bride and groom were numbered among his dearest friends.

The burning of Pennsylvania Hall was but one sign of the terrible struggle which was at hand. How deeply Whittier was moved, and how instinctively he sought the use of political instruments, will be seen from the two letters which follow : —

TO CALEB CUSHING.

PHILADELPHIA, 3d 6th mo., 1838.

In regard to some political queries in thy letter of last spring, touching the course of the abolitionists in the presidential contest, I will answer briefly. The abolitionists will not lend any support to Van Buren. The Clay resolutions have cost him the votes of thousands. Yet even they will not satisfy the South. He will be pressed to commit himself entirely to the interest of slavery. He will be required to write another North Carolina letter, *à la* Van Buren. A veto pledge will be required. Now will Henry Clay do this ? — our Henry Clay, the man we have all loved and

honored and *forgiven* — will he stoop to meanness
so ineffable ?   I should greatly prefer him to Van
Buren or General Harrison.   But his course in
the Senate has surprised and grieved me.   Our
friends in Vermont, Rhode Island, Massachusetts,
New York, Michigan, and Ohio are not yet wholly
prepared to give him up.   But a single further
" bowing of the knee " to slavery will drive them
from him.   The extra ounce will break the camel's
back.   As it is now, Henry Clay stands tolerably
well in the South.   The extracts from the
" Emancipator " and from my paper, commenting
severely on his course, have been industriously
circulated at the South by his friends, in order
to prove that he is regarded by the abolitionists
as their sworn enemy.   They have been (as I
anticipated they would) of essential service to his
cause.

Let him, if he has any regard for his former
professions, to opinions of the wise and good all
over the world, and to the suffrages of the people
of the free States, make no further effort to con-
ciliate the slaveholder.   I say advisedly, and from
personal interviews and correspondence with abolitionists all over the country, that they *will have
no more*.   Has it come to this, that even to be a
slaveholder and a colonizationist is not enough to
satisfy the slavery interest !   What then ought
the free North to demand of a candidate for her
suffrage ?   What ought abolitionists, whose lives
and liberty may be at stake on the issue of the
question, to ask?

TO J. E. FULLER, BOSTON.

PHILADELPHIA, 8th mo., 16, 1838.

Our cause here is slowly, and against unnumbered obstacles, going ahead. *You* in New England have got *pro*-slavery to contend with; *we* have got into a death-grapple with slavery itself. They leave no stone unturned to put us down. The clergy of all denominations are preaching against us. The politicians are abusing us in their filthy papers; and dirty penny sheets, with most outrageous caricatures of Garrison, Thompson, Angelina Grimké Weld, are hawked daily about the streets. But we shall go ahead nevertheless. We are slow-moulded, heavy-sterned, Dutch-built, out hereaway; but when once started on the right track, there is no backing out with us. The abolitionists of old Pennsylvania are of the right material; many of them don't believe in the devil, and those who do are n't afraid of him. I admire and honor their stern moral courage, in manfully maintaining their ground against a fiendish and bitter opposition.

Mr. Whittier, much broken in health, returned to his home in Massachusetts, in October, 1838, took a hand in the Congressional election, and continued editorial work upon the "Freeman," sending his articles by mail, until April, 1839, when we find him again in Philadelphia. During his absence, early in November, a small volume of his poems was issued by Joseph Healy, the financial agent of the Anti-Slavery Society of Pennsylvania. It was a book of 180 pages, half of it devoted to

poems bearing upon the subject of slavery, and the
remaining pages filled with selections from his
miscellaneous works.   There are fifty poems in this
collection, none of them copied from "The Legends of New England," and only eleven of them
to be found in the edition of his complete works
published just fifty years afterward.   The volume
is dedicated to Henry B. Stanton, "as a token of
the author's personal friendship, and his respect
for the unreserved devotion of exalted talents to
the cause of humanity and freedom."   The poems
in this volume were collected and arranged by Mr.
Whittier during the summer of 1838.   Reference
to it is made in this letter to his sister, at Amesbury, written August 3, 1838 : —

"What I want of thee is (if thee can do it) to
send by mail copies of 'The Fratricide' and
'The Pharisee.'   An edition of my poetry is publishing in this city, and I want them very much.
. . . My paper is beginning to attract attention,
and I should not think it strange if it got pretty es-
sentially mobbed before the summer is out.   The
colonizationists can set on the dog of the mob just
when they choose.   I wish I could escape from
the duties of an editor for a month or so.   My
health needs it.   I may go out into the country a
while, if I can get anybody to supply my place.
Last evening I had a delightful walk about one
mile and a half out of the city to the Fairmount
water works, with a company of 'young friends.'
It is a beautiful place; nature has done much, but
art infinitely more : fountains are made to gush
up from the rocks of the cliffs which overhang

the Schuylkill, through the mouths of images carved out of marble. The view of the river winding down to the city is very fine. My health is better than I could expect, but I have suffered a great deal. I have been out in the country frequently. Send me the two 'poetries' as soon as possible."

The poem "The Fratricide," written in 1831, may be found in the appendix to the Riverside edition of Mr. Whittier's works, but "The Pharisee" is omitted. It is the story of Paul's conversion, told in blank verse.

Whittier struck the keynote of his whole career as a reformer when he quoted, upon the title-page of this first authorized collection of his anti-slavery poems, these noble words of S. T. Coleridge : —

" 'There is a time to keep silence,' saith Solomon. But when I proceeded to the first verse of the fourth chapter of the Ecclesiastes, 'and considered all the oppressions that are done under the sun, and beheld the tears of such as are oppressed, and they have had no comforter ; and on the side of the oppressors there was power,' I concluded this was *not* the time to keep silence ; for Truth should be spoken at all times, but more especially at those times when to speak Truth is dangerous."

It was during this visit to his home in the fall of 1838, and just before returning to his editorial duties in Philadelphia, that he wrote in the album of Mary Pillsbury, of West Newbury, the following lines, expressing his love of his New England home :—

Pardon a stranger hand that gives
Its impress to these gilded leaves.
As one who graves in idle mood
An idler's name on rock or wood,
So in a careless hour I claim
A page to leave my humble name.
Accept it; and when o'er my head
A Pennsylvanian sky is spread,
And but in dreams my eye looks back
On broad and lovely Merrimac,
And on my ear no longer breaks
The murmuring music which it makes,
When but in dreams I look again
On Salisbury beach — Grasshopper plain, —
Or Powow stream — or Amesbury mills,
Or old Crane neck, or Pipestave hills,
Think of me then as one who keeps,
Where Delaware's broad current sweeps,
And down its rugged limestone-bed
The Schuylkill's arrowy flight is sped,
Deep in his heart the scenes which grace
And glorify his " native place ; "
Loves every spot to childhood dear,
And leaves his heart " untraveled " here;
Longs, 'midst the Dutchman's kraut and greens,
For pumpkin-pie and pork and beans,
And sighs to think when, sweetly near,
The soft piano greets his ear
That the fair hands which, small and white,
Glance on its ivory polished light,
Have ne'er an Indian pudding made,
Nor fashioned rye and Indian bread.
And oh! whene'er his footsteps turn,
Whatever stars above him burn,
Though dwelling where a Yankee's name
Is coupled with reproach or shame,
Still true to his New England birth,
Still faithful to his home and hearth,
Even 'midst the scornful stranger band
His boast shall be of YANKEE LAND.

Something of the same spirit appears in this
letter : —

My fugitive poems have never been published, except a few in a late volume bound up with my abolition and incendiary verses. I am glad thou hast undertaken to say something of our own Merrimac, endeared to me by all the recollections of childhood, and the ripple of whose waters I still hear in my dreams, even on the banks of the Schuylkill and the Delaware. Some time ago I wrote a prose tale called " Passaconway," the scene of which is on the banks of the Merrimac. I long to return once more to New England, but when I shall it is out of my power to decide. I like the Quaker purity of this city, and its Quaker hospitality, but I would rather live as an obscure New England farmer. I would rather see the sunset light streaming through the valley of the Merrimac than to look out for many months upon brick walls and Sam Weller's "werry beautiful landscape of chimney pots.". . . I am sorry, but I fear Van Buren will be reëlected ; it will be hard to give the New England States to Clay.

In July, 1839, he found it necessary, as already mentioned, to give up the drudgery of editorial work, and he called his cousin, Moses A. Cartland, afterwards widely known as a successful teacher, to take his place for a few weeks. He made a tour to western Pennsylvania, working for the cause of anti-slavery reform wherever he went, and sending occasional letters to his paper. Mr. Cartland says of him, " He goes with the hope of restoring the tone of his worn and wasted energies, exhausted as they have been by unremitting toil in that cause which lies deepest in his affections, the cause of freedom and humanity."

The election of Caleb Cushing having been secured in the North Essex district, Mr. Whittier did not return to his editorial duties in Philadelphia until he had arranged for the sending of petitions from every part of his home district to the next session of Congress, calling for the abolition of slavery in the District of Columbia, and for the restriction of the interstate slave trade. His first effort when he resumed his duties as editor of the "Freeman" was to wake up the anti-slavery people of Pennsylvania to the importance of giving their Congressmen no rest until their object was attained. The petitions sent in response to this call were refused reception by a rule adopted by Congress, and the Northern author of this rule received a terrible poetical castigation at the hands of Whittier, in his New Year's address to the patrons of the "Freeman."

On the 14th of March, 1839, Miss Minot wrote to her friend, Elizabeth Whittier, of an interesting rumor, which had, however, no foundation in fact : —

"We have just heard of your brother's engagement. Mr. [A. W.] Thayer and Mr. [H. B.] Stanton brought the information some weeks ago, but it has only now reached us. I congratulate you with all my heart. She came to me in my dreams last night, and so charming a creature I never saw, or before imagined. I passed a few

hours in her society, and I loved her as if she had
been the most cherished friend of years. . . . We
hear that she is from Brooklyn, and that she is not
a Quakeress." [1]

On the 20th of June, 1839, an urgent call was
sent to Mr. Whittier, signed by Joshua Leavitt
and Henry B. Stanton, to attend a national anti-
slavery convention to be held at Albany, N. Y.,
July 31 of the same year. The American Anti-
Slavery Society had become a " close corporation,"
and many persons favorable to its objects did not
find opportunity for efficient work in it. This convention was called to devise means of uniting the
strength of all the friends of liberty, and Mr.
Whittier's coöperation was earnestly desired. If
he could not come, would he not write a letter that
could be sent to the convention ? He attended
the convention, and then went to Saratoga Springs,
in the height of the season. From Saratoga he
wrote to a Philadelphia friend who had accompanied him to Albany, under date of August 8,
1839 : —

" A leisure moment being afforded me, I embrace it to tell thee my adventures since I parted
with thee at the Albany Congress Hall. I went
out to Saratoga that afternoon, and arrived there
about six o'clock, in company with our abolition
friends, Hon. Amasa Walker, of Massachusetts,
and Henry B. Stanton. On board the cars was a
Mississippi lawyer and slaveholder, with his servant. He seemed to take a fancy to me, as a
Quaker, and entered into conversation on ' the

[1] This reference is probably to Lucy Hooper.

vexed question' at once. It was maintained very warmly but pleasantly until our arrival at the Springs. We found the best hotels crowded to suffocation, and finally took lodgings at the Pavilion. Here I found Dr. Farnsworth, of Massachusetts, and his daughter, and several other acquaintances, among others two young South Carolinians, upon whom I had formerly bestowed some attention, during their summer sojourn, some years ago, in my native town. They were apparently as pleased to meet me as if I had not been opposed to their 'peculiar institution.' Our Mississippi friend was full of politeness and good nature, and I believe would have been ready to lynch on the spot any one who should have assailed his Quaker friend. He came to the conclusion that the abolitionists were shamefully libeled, and that we were the *true* friends of the South. Many of my Massachusetts friends have arrived at the Springs, during the last two or three days. I am on the whole enjoying myself quite well, and my health is, I think, most decidedly improved, not by drinking the rascally drugged water here, but by travel, exercise, and open air. I wish thee was here, that we might laugh together at the ten thousand ridiculous things which are constantly occurring around us. As it is, I have laughed alone, and that is hard business. It is an admirable place here to study human nature; to watch the manifestations of its pride, vanity, and jealousy; to note the early developments of love, the agony of disappointment, of baffled aims, of wasted affections, of unshared sympathies; Hope

and Despair, Love and Hatred, chastened Desire
and unbridled Passion, — all crowded together beneath the light of the same astrals, mingling in the
same dance and promenade. For myself, I have
been somewhat of a laughing philosopher, and
have found amusement wherever I could. . . .
Thou wilt perceive that my ink is of a new color,
in explanation whereof I will just state that since
the above was written, I have been floating New
England-ward, and am now writing in the parlor
of 'mine own inn,' at Newport, R. I., on the first
day of the week and between meetings. I arrived
here last night in company with a friend, Judge
Hunt, of Rensselaer County, New York, who has
been my traveling companion for some days past.
Last night, by dint of pushing and scolding, I
obtained a berth (not a trifling matter when at
least one third of the passengers were left without
any accommodations for sleeping whatever), but
on going to take possession of it, I found a sturdy
six-footer snoring away as regularly as if he had n't
stolen his quarters. I gave him a punch in the
ribs by way of admonition, and worried him off
the premises. He growled like a bear disturbed
in his hollow log. I threatened to call the captain,
and he set me at defiance. The captain came,
and was about to administer lynch law on the spot,
when the fellow thrust his berth card in the captain's face and bade him rectify his own blunders.
It turned out that the captain had assigned us
both one and the same lodging-place, whereupon
he pointed to the first empty berth he saw and
bade me occupy it. I did so, not without some

compunctious visitations, however, for not long after I had thrown myself upon it, a little bald-headed Frenchman came and looked in upon me and then at his card. He bowed, grinned, and muttered his bad English at me. I made no reply, and he left me. ' Diable ! ' said he, ' vat vill I do for my sleep ? ' Headache and weariness made me selfish, and I held possession and left the poor Frenchman to his fate.

" I shall spend a day or two at Newport with my cousins, the Wendells, of Philadelphia. There are a good many of our *orthodox* Friends here at the present time. It is of course pleasant to meet them, only I wish there was less formality and precision among them.

" I was vexed with myself that I did not have more of thy company at Albany. The vexatious business of the convention, and one circumstance and another, prevented me. I feel as if I had been cheated, or, what is still worse, cheated myself out of a great deal of pleasure. But the past may not be recalled. Probably the circumstances which vexed me saved thee from vexation. Was it not so ? — I am desirous of hearing from thee an account of thy excursion to Lebanon, Catskill, etc., and shall expect thee to sit down at once and answer this incoherent scrawl."

In August, 1839, his sister Elizabeth thus writes to her friend, Harriet Minot, the anti-slavery war to which she refers being the contest in regard to the " new organization : " —

" Greenleaf has left his paper with cousin Moses Cartland, and gone to Saratoga and elsewhere for

his health.   He was at the Albany meeting, which,
by the way, I hear was good, quite rational.   Does
thee ever see the 'Pennsylvania Freeman'?
Cousin Moses does nobly in his new station as
editor. . . . I want to tell thee about the state
meeting at Concord, and to ask on which side thee
stands in regard to the anti-slavery war, — it deserves no milder name.   I am very sorry for this
sort of bitterness among us, and the dividing cry
of 'Every man to his tent, O Israel,' is abroad,
and each individual, however humble, is summoned now, I think, to the place of decision."

In a letter to the paper Mr. Whittier says he
" met many Southern people, had many opportunities of laying our principles before them, and
hoped had made favorable impression." From
New York he returned to his home in Amesbury,
and remained in Massachusetts until October.
On the 10th of that month he was again at his
desk in Philadelphia, much refreshed and strength-
ened by his travels.   His sister Elizabeth accompanied him on his return.   While he was absent
Joseph Healy made this announcement in the
paper: "In the absence of the editor, we take the
liberty of announcing that we have obtained a good
likeness of him, with facsimiles of his signature,
and that a few (and only a few) copies are for sale
at this office, the profits, if any, to go to the cause
in which this estimable individual is so effectively
engaged."

In the summer of 1839,[1] Henry B. Stanton and

---

[1] Mr. Stanton in his *Random Recollections* makes this date
1836, but he is in error.

John G. Whittier were deputed by the American Anti-Slavery Society to go through Pennsylvania and employ seventy public speakers, if they could find as many, who should go out to awaken the conscience of the nation in the matter of slavery. They went to the theological schools and other institutions of learning, in the hope to enlist young men in the work. Their mission brought them, among other places, to the Lutheran Institution on Seminary Ridge at Gettysburg. They were charmed with the lovely landscape in view from this lofty outlook, which included the now famous heights known as Cemetery Ridge, Culp's Hill, and the Round Top; but they little dreamed that twenty-four years later these landmarks would have a world - wide celebrity in connection with one of the bloodiest and most decisive battles of modern times, waged for the cause they were there to promote. Mr. Stanton, in his "Random Recollections," says of Whittier in connection with this trip : —

"He cheered me with his genial presence and wise counsel. . . . I am not so beside myself as to imagine that any encomium from me could add to Whittier's literary fame. But having toiled by his side for several years, and spent many a delightful hour in his cottage at Amesbury, it may become me to record that he rendered valuable aid to the anti-slavery cause by his brave example, while his pen sent ringing words of encouragement and shed unfading lustre over the field where the battle raged."

The following extracts from letters to Miss

Elizabeth J. Neall (afterward Mrs. Sidney Howard Gay), daughter of his friend Daniel Neall, of Philadelphia, illustrate some attractive phases of his character. They show how the deep earnestness of that heroic time was lightened and cheered by his sunny humor. He wrote from Carlisle, Pa., July 8, 1839, while he was making the excursion with Mr. Stanton, to which reference has been made : —

"Here we are, or rather here I am, sitting in the front parlor of our friend McKim's, solitary and alone, a stranger in a strange place. Over 'the mountains round about,' especially those which skirt the northwestern horizon, a part of that mountain-wall which girdles the great Cumberland valley, broods a thick thunder-cloud, the lightning flashing with keen brightness over woodland and church-tower, and the thunder uttering its voices, and as our friend Ralph Smith would say, ' reverberating through the valleys.' Miller McKim and H. B. Stanton have gone out in the storm, and I am left alone, an occasional light and cautious step in an adjoining room only reminding me that I am not the sole occupant of the mansion. That step I feel persuaded, nay, I would make my Quaker affirmation of it, is the step of Eliza McKim, a sister of James, whom we met at the tea-table. Why on earth don't she take pity on my forlorn condition and bend her steps this way? What can she be doing? Is she afraid to look upon me? Did she never see a live Quaker before? Maybe she has heard horrible stories of the Yankees, and takes me to be a lineal descend-

ant of one of the Salem witches! Perhaps her
household duties detain her; perhaps she is another
Martha 'troubled about many things.' Notable
must she be as a housewife, famous for her attention to 'the domestic relations' of the pantry and
supper dishes. Well, let her have her own way,
and I'll have mine; so here goes for a letter to
thee, and whether welcome or unwelcome, a letter
thee shall have.

"Why didn't we get the breakfast at 325 Arch,
according to promise? Why, for a very good reason, nay, perhaps, for *two* good reasons. 1. *We*
lay abed too late. 2. Perhaps *thee* did also, and
if we had called at the hour specified, and inquired for thee and the breakfast, the report in
regard to both might have been '*non est inventus.*'
We had hardly time as it was to get to the car
office and secure our seats. We rode about two
hours, and stopped at a dirty Dutch tavern for
breakfast. An execrable cup of tea, which would
have poisoned a Chinese mandarin; ham, tough
and solid as sheet iron, which had probably been
smoked and salted annually for the last twenty
years; and some hot cakes saturated with bad butter, greasy and heavy, and anti-Grahamish, con-
stituted our wretched fare. It was such a 'trick
upon travelers' as Yankee landlords even would
have been ashamed of. We pursued our way till
about one o'clock, when we stopped to dine. A
tremendous thunder - storm was raging, and the
rain falling in torrents. It would have given thee
a high opinion of our gallantry if thee could have
seen us wait upon the ladies out of the cars, into

the house. We got to Harrisburg about three
o'clock, and stopped at the splendid Hotel Wilson,
on Market Street. Yesterday Stanton lectured
twice, and I made some visits. This morning we
spent in looking up some anti-slavery matters,
and at three o'clock we again took the cars for
Carlisle. To-morrow, if nothing happens, we shall
go to Governor Ritner's, and from thence we shall
push on to Gettysburg in search of some one or
more lecturers to talk Dutch abolition. We have
been recommended to some half-dozen Schloshen-
burgers, and Quackenbosches, and Kakerspergers,
and Slambangers, with unpronounceable Dutch
names enough to crack the jaws of any Anglo-
Saxons, whom we hope to interest in our cause.
We must get the Germans with us, by some means
or other. These middle counties are full of Germans, and they are on this subject ' thrice dead
and plucked up by the roots.' They must be
roused up at all events.

" 9th, Third-day morning. We have just returned from a ride to Governor Ritner's farm,
about nine miles from Carlisle. The old man was
out on his farm, and his wife and daughters wel-
comed us with great hospitality. The governor
soon came in in his working dress. We stayed
about one hour and a half, and then rode back to
Carlisle, where we now are. This afternoon we
start for Chambersburg and Gettysburg."

In January, 1840, he made a short visit to
Washington, and was in the gallery of the House
of Representatives during the great debate on the
right of petition, which ended in the shutting out

of all petitions upon the subject of slavery. On
the 28th of January he wrote from Washington to
Joseph Healy, the publisher of the " Freeman : " —

" We arrived here safe and well to-day, having
stopped last night at Baltimore. I have seen
Adams, Cushing, etc., and had some conversation
with several Southern as well as Northern members, I hope with some effect. I feel better than
when I left ; expect to be at home on Seventh day.
You will see by the ' Globe ' of to-day that the
right of petition has been denied to us. Northern
subserviency has yielded *all* to the demands of the
South."

His friends had now become alarmed at the
condition of his health, and a skillful physician who
was consulted decided that there was serious
trouble with his heart, and that he must give up at
once the labor and anxiety of editorial life. On
the 20th of February he published his valedictory
as editor of the "Freeman," and the next week,
with his sister Elizabeth, he started for his home
in Amesbury, where they arrived after the journey
of a week.

CHAPTER VII.

A DECADE OF WORK AT HOME.

1840–1850.

WHEN Whittier resigned his editorial position he planned to attend the world's anti-slavery convention to be held in London, in the month of June, 1840. It was hoped the sea voyage would benefit him. He went so far as to procure his outfit and to engage his passage. But upon consulting his intimate friend, the skillful physician, Dr. Henry I. Bowditch, he was told that while the voyage might prove beneficial if he could avoid all the excitements of society, there was a chance of serious consequences from any mental or physical exertion, and it would be advisable to remain at home. He spent the summer of 1840 in visits among friends, and before he returned to Amesbury attended the Yearly Meeting of Friends at Newport.

TO ELIZABETH H. WHITTIER.

BUCKS COUNTY, PA., 5th mo., 1840.

I have been promising to write thee for some days, but a severe cold from which I have as yet but partially recovered has disinclined me to exertion of every kind. My general health is about as usual; I fear not better. I have much pain in chest and head. I have been now for some time at J. Healy's " Spring Grove Farm," on the banks of the Delaware, or rather on a high bluff overlooking the river, with a fine view of the New Jersey side. Cousin Joseph Cartland came up with me, and stayed five days. There are a great number of Hicksites in this vicinity ; they have possession of the old Friends' meeting-houses all through the county. The " Orthodox " have meetings at Solebury, three miles from Joseph Healy's, and at Buckingham, five miles. We attended meeting yesterday at the latter place, in a large new stone building, beautifully situated in a fine grove of forest trees. Some excellent remarks were made by Christopher Healy, who intends to visit New England Yearly Meeting. I expect myself to return by way of Newport, although my health is not equal to a constant attendance of the meetings. I think I shall go back to Philadelphia in a day or two, and after a short visit in Wilmington, return to New York. It is, I believe, well that I did not go to England. It was a great disappointment to me, but it is all right. I wish I could feel wholly resigned to all the allotments of All-Wise Providence, and be more thankful for the blessings still reserved to me. It sometimes seems strange that I cannot do as others around me, but I try to suppress any feeling of repining or murmuring. I feel that I have not deserved the least of the bounties bestowed on me.

On reaching New York we received an accession
to our company, Joseph John Gurney, Richard
Mott, Samuel Parsons, and a large number of
younger friends, among them my young abolition
friend Mary Murray, who in course of the evening
drew out J. J. Gurney upon the subject of his late
West Indian tour, much to the edification of ourselves and other passengers. The evening was the
most beautiful I ever spent upon the water, warm
enough to keep on deck, in view of the heavens
glorious with a sunset such as our stranger companions had never seen flushing the cold gray sky
or reflected on the shingly beaches and white cliffs
of England. Landing at Newport I met a most
kind welcome at our friend David Gould's. On
First day J. J. Gurney spoke at great length upon
the Principles of our Religious Society, and in the
course of his remarks made an allusion to the
departure of a dear friend, Daniel Wheeler. He
spoke of the lips, now cold, which had been touched
by a coal from the Lord's altar, of the kind and
generous and benevolent heart which had ceased
to beat, of the eye of sympathy and love closed up
forever. Yet he trusted it was with the eye of
faith that he looked into the world of spirits, and
felt that the reward of the righteous was sure.
He closed with a solemn and earnest appeal to the
younger class to prepare themselves by a surrender of all to Christ, for the work of sustaining
those principles and testimonies which the dear
departed had loved and been faithful to unto the

last. I never saw or felt a more solemn meeting. The immense audience, at least three thousand, were silent as if the building had been closed and tenantless, and tears in the eyes of many told how deeply their hearts had been touched.

C. C. Burleigh, who succeeded Whittier as the editor of the "Pennsylvania Freeman," declined to publish an article sent him by Whittier in regard to the exclusion of women delegates by the London convention. Commenting upon it in a letter to his cousin, Moses Cartland, he said: "Burleigh has written me, declining to publish my article. Very well, I shall not trouble him in future. He says he has reason for believing that had Lucretia Mott been Orthodox (instead of a Hicksite Friend) she would have been admitted. *I* don't believe it." It was difference of opinion upon this unimportant matter which made the first considerable break in the anti-slavery ranks. Whittier agreed with Garrison as to the appropriateness of giving public positions to women capable of holding them, but did not approve of the attempt to force this issue upon a convention, a majority of the delegates to which did not approve of it. He would not drive out of the anti-slavery ranks those who were not ready for the enfranchisement of women. His steadfastness to the anti-slavery cause was too deeply rooted to give way before any factional quarrel or misconception of his attitude.

TO MOSES A. CARTLAND.

AMESBURY, 7th mo., 2, 1840.

I wish to contradict in terms as explicit as possible the rumor which thou mentions from Newport Yearly Meeting. It is most preposterously absurd. My abolitionism grows daily stronger, my faith in its principles is deepening amidst all difficulties and trials and perplexities and vexations of our organizations. Like the pine of Vich Alpine, "Firmer it roots the louder it blow." But I do fear that my faith in our organizations is not of the "saving kind." I have just sent a letter to Joshua Leavitt, declining to act as one of the executive committee of the American and Foreign Anti-Slavery Society, and another to the anti-slavery convention in this State, declining to allow my name to be on the electoral ticket for Birney and Earle. I am now free from all trammels, and I feel more at ease. Strong in my confidence in the justice of our cause, in the beauty and excellence of our principles, and in the wisdom and expediency of our prominent measures, I am still, as far as my failing health admits of, ready to do and suffer, if need be, for abolitionism. As a man, if not as an abolitionist, I have a right to agree or disagree with the " no government " people, without giving up my faith that a man *is* a man, and not a mere thing! At Newport, and at Philadelphia, and at Lynn, I have spoken as freely in disapprobation of the lukewarm course of a portion of our Friends as the truth would justify, while at the same time I am not prepared to give up Quakerism, to throw myself body and soul into

the antisectarian *sect* about Boston. Free I am
to say that I feel a deeper interest than formerly
in supporting the religious doctrines and testimonies of our Society, and I hope I shall find
strength to manifest that interest; but the cause
of the slave still rises solemnly before me, and
from the warfare of the oppressed I feel no release, I ask for none. For me, I am sick, but to
see thee would get me well again almost. We
have now a great excitement here about a parcel
of blacks, supposed to be runaways, landed from
some vessel on our coast, who are now in the great
swamp in this town and South Hampton. I have
been out to-day after them, and have seen a boy,
but he refuses to tell where he comes from.
Depend upon it, we shall get up a great negro
hunt here, and try to catch and tame them.

On the 13th of July, 1840, Mr. Whittier left
Amesbury for Boston, intending to take the
steamship Britannia for Halifax, in the hope of
benefit to his health; but the excursion was given
up, as were so many projected trips for health
and pleasure during his whole life, because he
found himself not strong enough to undertake
them. In September of the same year he again
made preparation for an excursion to Halifax by
an ocean steamship, and again was stopped by
the delicacy of his health. As he was leaving
home on the first occasion, his sister wrote to a
friend : —

" It will be lonely when he is away. I am not
homesick in Amesbury, but it never seems like

home when Greenleaf is away. We have had a grand ' negro hunt ' through our woods, four poor hunted slaves having found their way to our neighborhood. Our people became alarmed; their cows were milked, and sometimes to the frontier farmhouses came stealing, from the woods, a weak suffering man, asking for food, and fleeing when the coarsest crust was given him. A fortnight ago a boy of the gang was caught, but he was too frightened to be able to tell anything, so they sent him Canada-wards. I wish we could find his father and brothers, now in the woods."

TO ANN E. WENDELL.

7th mo., 13, 1840.

Did I mention to thee in my letter from Newport a circumstance in relation to Richard Mott? On Fifth day evening, I called to see J. J. Gurney, agreeable to his request, in reference to abolition matters. After our interview was over, Richard Mott followed me to the door and wished to accompany me to my lodgings. During our walk he told me he knew not how it was or why, but that his mind had been drawn into a deep and extraordinary exercise of sympathy with me; that he had been sensible of a deep trial and exercise in my own mind; that he had felt it so strongly that he could not rest easy without informing me of it, although he had heard nothing and seen nothing to produce this conviction in his mind. He felt desirous to offer me the language of encouragement, to urge me to put aside every weight that encumbers, and to look unto Him who was

able to deliver from every trial. I confess I was
startled. Firmly as I believed the Quaker doctrine on this subject, its personal application to
myself in a manner so utterly inexplicable by
merely human reasoning awed me. I said little
to him, but enough to show him something of the
state of my mind. Pray for me that I may not
suffer this most evident day of the Lord's visita-
tion to pass over and leave me as before. The
suggestion of some lines on the death of Daniel
Wheeler seemed to strengthen a feeling in my
own mind which has resulted in my penning some
the other day. If I can publish it I will send it
to thee. I have no time to copy it now.

The following extract from a letter to Richard
Mott indicates a deep sense of his own spiritual
needs, and his desire to be in closer communion
with Him who alone could supply them. The
letter was written in November, 1840 : —

"I have to lament over protracted seasons of
doubt and darkness, to shrink back from the dis-
covery of some latent unfaithfulness and insincerity, to find evil at the bottom of seeming good,
to abhor myself for selfishness and pride and
vanity, which at times manifest themselves, — in
short, to find the law of sin and death still binding
me. My temperament, ardent, impetuous, imaginative, powerfully acted upon from without, keenly
susceptible to all influences from the intellectual
world, as well as to those of nature, in her varied manifestations, is, I fear, ill adapted to that
quiet, submissive, introverted state of patient and

passive waiting for direction and support under
these trials and difficulties. I think often of our
meeting at Rhode Island, and at times something of
a feeling of regret comes over me, that I am so
situated as not to be permitted to enjoy the company and the care and watchful ministrations of
those whose labors have been signally owned by
the Great Head of the church. Sitting down in
our small meeting, and feeling in myself and in
the meeting generally a want of life, and of the
renewing baptism of that Spirit which alone can
soften the hardness and warm the coldness of the
heart, I sigh for the presence and the voices of the
eminent and faithful laborers in the Lord's vine-
yard. I know that this out-looking of the spirit,
this craving of the eye and of the ear, is wrong,
but in the depths of spiritual weakness, is it not
natural to crave the support even of an earthly
arm ?''

In the article given below, and hitherto unpub-
lished, he defines his belief upon several doctrinal
points : —

"The central thought, the root-idea of Quakerism, so called, is as old as human needs. Not
only is it affirmed in the venerable Jewish Scriptures, but with more or less distinctness also in
the remarkable Vedas of India, coming down to
us from the solemn remoteness of ages ; and in the
utterances of prophets, poets, priests, and philosophers, of all peoples and times, which remain to
testify that at no period, and in no nation, God
hath left himself without witnesses. Its fitting
expression may be found in the word *Immanuel*,
God with us.

" God is One ; just, holy, merciful, eternal, and almighty Creator, Father of all things. Christ, the same eternal One, manifested in our Humanity, and in Time ; and the Holy Spirit, the same Christ, manifested within us, the Divine Teacher, the Living Word, the Light that lighteth every man that cometh into the world.

" The Scriptures are *a* rule, not *the* rule of faith and practice, which is none other than the living omnipresent spirit of God. The Scriptures are a subordinate, secondary, and declaratory rule, the reason of our obedience to which is mainly that we find in them the eternal precepts of the Divine Spirit, declared and repeated, to which our conscience bears witness. . . . They testify of Christ within. We believe in the Scriptures, because they believe in us, because they repeat the warnings and admonitions and promises of the indwelling Light and Truth, because we find the law and prophets in our souls. We agree with Luther, that ' the Scriptures are not to be understood but by that very spirit by which they were written,' and with Calvin, that ' it is necessary that the same spirit which spoke by the mouth of the prophets should convince our hearts that they faithfully delivered that which God committed to them.' "

While thus emphasizing the " Immanence of the Holy Spirit," the spiritual work of Christ in the heart, with its converting, sanctifying power, several of his poems, especially " The Crucifixion," indicate that he accepted with reverent gratitude the solemn significance of the outward sacrifice, the manifestation of the Father's infinite love for his children, thus opening the way for their redemption from the guilt and power of sin. In a letter to " The Friend," written in 1866, to correct an error as to his religious belief, made by a lecturer, he says : —

" My ground of hope for myself and for humanity is in that Divine fullness of love which was manifested in the life, teachings, and self-sacrifice of Christ. In the infinite mercy of God so revealed, and not in any work or merit of our nature, I humbly, yet very hopefully trust. I regard Christianity as a life, rather than a creed; and in judging of my fellow-men I can use no other standard than that which our Lord and Master has given us, ' By their fruits ye shall know them.' The only orthodoxy that I am especially interested in is that of life and practice."

With regard to our condition in the future life, Whittier thus replies to a letter from an inquiring friend : —

" I think I understand thy inquiry. I am not a Universalist, for I believe in the possibility of the perpetual loss of the soul that persistently turns away from God, in the next life as in this. But I do believe that the Divine love and compassion follow us in all worlds, and that the Heavenly Father will do the best that is possible for every creature He has made. What that will be must be left to his infinite wisdom and goodness. I would refer thee to a poem of mine, ' The Answer,' as containing in few words my belief in this matter."

I was in Boston this week, and looked in twice upon the queer gathering of heterogeneous spirits at the Chardon Street chapel assembled under a call issued by Maria W. Chapman, Abby Kelley, and others, to discuss the subjects of the Sabbath, ministry, and church organizations, and some twenty other collateral subjects. When I was present the chapel was crowded, a motley-opinioned company, from the Calvinist of the straitest sect to the infidel and scoffer. Half of the forenoon of the first day was spent in debating whether the convention should be organized by the choice of president and secretary, or whether these old-fashioned restraints should be set aside as unworthy of advocates of " the largest liberty," leaving each member to do and say what seemed right in his own eyes! It was finally decided to have a president. Then came on a discussion about the Sabbath, in which Garrison and two transcendental Unitarians, and a woman by the name of Folsom, argued that every day should be held sacred; that it was not a rest from labor but from sin that was wanted; that keeping First day as holy was not required, etc. On the other hand, Amos A. Phelps, Dr. Osgood, and some others contended for the Calvinistic and generally received views of the subject. Dr. Channing, John Pierpont, and many other distinguished men were present, but took no part in the discussions. No Friends were members of the convention, although there were several lookers-on. Judging from the little I saw and heard, I do not think the world will be much the wiser for the debate. It may have a tendency to unsettle some minds.

Mr. Whittier remained at home in Amesbury during the winter of 1840–41. In March, 1841, he wrote to Miss Minot, of Haverhill : —

"Thy letter was heartily welcome, for I had been for some days too stupid and dull to feel any interest in things present, and naturally enough my mind wandered back to the past, and scenes which are now but memories and the old familiar faces have been with me. I should have been glad to make Haverhill a visit in the winter, but the extremely delicate state of my health has compelled me to forego the pleasure. I feel now somewhat better, but I have little confidence in it. Well, I am in God's hands, and striving to resign myself to his will, not however, I fear, as I ought to. With all my suffering, I have many blessings, infinitely more than I deserve. . . . I now think some of going next week to New York and Philadelphia, partly to escape our east winds which I dread. I think sickness has a wonderful effect in fanning into life the half-extinguished conscience. It is doubtless better for me and for my friends that the hand of sickness is sometimes laid heavily upon me. Who knows what either thou or I should have been had we always enjoyed good health?"

In April, 1841, Mr. Whittier was in New York, and here he met for the first time the eminent English philanthropist, Joseph Sturge. It was in company with Mr. Sturge that Mr. Whittier visited the slave-dealing establishments of H. H. Slaughter, in Baltimore, and attended the Baptist convention in that city while it was discussing the question of eliminating all abolitionists from its missionary board.

TO HARRIET MINOT.

PHILADELPHIA, 5th mo., 26, 1841.

I have been in company with Joseph Sturge, of England, at New York, Philadelphia, Wilmington, and Baltimore, endeavoring to do something for the cause of abolition, with what success time will show. I shall go with Mr. Sturge to Washington next week. I sent the other day a copy of J. J. Gurney's " Letters on West India Emancipation " to Henry Clay. I was in Baltimore during the sitting of the great Triennial Baptist Convention, and heard the discussion on slavery, or rather upon the question of excluding Galusha and others, as abolitionists, from the Foreign Mission Board. Dr. Brisbane, of Cincinnati, late of South Carolina, took a noble stand.

From Baltimore Mr. Whittier accompanied Mr. Sturge to Wilmington, in Delaware, but from increase of indisposition was unable to go farther with him. In the following June, we find Mr. Whittier and Mr. Sturge again together at Wilmington, Delaware, attending a meeting of anti-slavery men in that slave State, who were considering a project for buying all the slaves in Delaware, and setting them free. It was calculated that a tax of a dollar an acre would be sufficient to pur-

JOSEPH STURGE.

chase every slave. From Wilmington they went
to Washington, and were favored with seats behind the speaker's chair during the famous debate
on the "gag" rule. They called together on John
Quincy Adams, and on President Tyler, who had
declined to receive a memorial from the British
Friends signed by Thomas Clarkson which Sturge
was commissioned to offer, upon the subject of
slavery. On a visit to the Senate, Henry Clay
had a conversation with them. He accused Whittier of deserting him, after being his warm friend.
Whittier gave his reasons, and Clay complained
that the abolitionists improperly interfered with
the affairs of the South. He inquired if Whittier
was a Friend in regular standing, intimating a
doubt on that point on account of his being such a
decided abolitionist. 'They went from the Senate
chamber to a slave-pen within sight of the Capitol,
and to the loathsome city jail, where Dr. Crandall
had been confined until his health broke down,
and he was liberated to die. Upon their return
to Philadelphia, Mr. Whittier accompanied his
English friend in a visit to Abraham L. Pennock,
an aged and influential Friend and devoted philanthropist, at Haverford. This visit they both
looked back upon in after years with most grateful
feelings. From Pennsylvania they proceeded to
Newport, R. I., and attended the Yearly Meeting
of Friends. But the burthen of their mission for
the slaves was as quietly as possible ignored by
the Meeting. They were not allowed the use of
the meeting-house for an anti-slavery gathering.
While in Newport they called upon Rev. Dr.

William Ellery Channing, who made the suggestion that petitions should be sent to Congress
praying that the Free States might be relieved
from all direct or indirect support of slavery.
They journeyed to Boston, by way of New Bed-
ford, where Mr. Sturge made note that for the
first time in the United States he attended a meeting at which the colored part of the audience were
placed on a level with, and sat promiscuously
among, the whites.   Mr. Whittier took his distinguished guest with him to his home in Amesbury,
where they rested for a few days, and then returned
to Boston.   A long interview was had with Garrison, and an attempt made to come to an understanding that would unite the two wings of the
anti-slavery forces.   But Garrison insisted upon
the right of women to take part equally with men
in the transactions of the Anti-Slavery Society, —
a right the Quakers of course did not deny, while
they thought the question need not then be
pressed.   On their way to New York, they stopped
at Worcester, and here Mr. Whittier became so ill
that he was obliged to return to Amesbury.   On
the 24th of July, 1841, Mr. Sturge and Mr. Whittier met again in New York, and returned together to Boston, afterward visiting Lynn and
Lowell.   The English Quaker embarked for home
in August.   The friendship between the two men
lasted until the death of Mr. Sturge, in 1859.   He
omitted no opportunity to be helpful to Whittier
when illness or financial embarrassment gave him
an opportunity to offer his purse.   Perceiving
Whittier's failing health, and his need of rest,

just as he was embarking for home, in August,
1841, he left with Lewis Tappan, of New York,
one thousand dollars, upon which he wished Mr.
Whittier to draw as he might need. This is his
memorandum of the transaction : —

Joseph Sturge places at the disposal of his
friend, J. G. Whittier, one thousand dollars, during the next twelve months, for his personal and
other current expenses of housekeeping, traveling,
etc., or a visit to a tropical climate for the sake of
his health ; and if he should not need the whole
for this purpose he will please apply the remainder
to any traveling or other expenses connected with
his labor with the " Reporter," or any other anti-
slavery object.

BOSTON, 7th month, 30th, 1841.

There is no means of ascertaining in what manner Mr. Whittier availed himself of this generous
gift, or indeed whether he accepted it for his personal needs. He certainly took no trip for his
health. We find among his papers a letter from
Lewis Tappan, dated March 14, 1842, in which he
speaks of a thousand dollars left with him by
Joseph Sturge " for the furtherance of the anti-
slavery cause," of which he has expended all but
four hundred dollars, and he asks Mr. Whittier's
advice as to the disposal of this amount. This is
probably the fund that was originally intended for
Mr. Whittier, and which he declined to accept.

While traveling with Joseph Sturge, Mr. Whittier wrote as follows to his cousin, Moses A. Cartland, from Philadelphia, May 12, 1841 : —

"I have been for the last three weeks peregrinating with Joseph Sturge, trying to fan into life the all but expiring embers of abolition. We have labored with Friends and Gentiles, Jew and Greek, and have had much to encourage us on the whole. Thee would like Joseph Sturge much, — a fine, free-hearted nobleman of nature; no pretension; a clear-headed, stout-hearted, practical philanthropist; the 'Howard of our day,' as he is called in England. Rogers and Garrison have been in Philadelphia, but I did not see them, being most of the time in Baltimore and Wilmington."

Mr. Sturge found many Quakers who, like Whittier, were ready to assist him in delivering his anti-slavery message to the American Friends, but the Society as a whole was rather cool and indifferent, both at Philadelphia and at Newport. In writing about it to a cousin in Philadelphia, some months after Sturge's return to England, Mr. Whittier says : —

"When I was in your city last, I was so anxious about J. Sturge's visit, and the course of Friends, and the little difficulties which we met with, that I was hardly myself. I recollect calling at the L——'s some two or three times, when my mind was altogether away and dwelling upon other things. What they thought of me I have often marveled at since. It was not on my own account that I felt uneasiness, — I am used to such things, — but I felt keenly for my English friend."[1]

---

[1] In a letter to Sturge, he says: "This cause [anti-slavery] has been to me what the vision on the house-top of Cornelius was to Peter — it has destroyed all narrow sectarian prejudices, and made me willing to be a man among men."

His sister Elizabeth, writing to the same cousin, refers to the same matter : —

"How we did love Joseph Sturge! His bland, kind face will be a joy in my memory forever. He *must*, he *will* do good among us. I am afraid I shall not love my own Yearly Meeting as well as I used to, now they have folded their idle hands, when so kindly requested to labor in their *own way*, thus wrapping the mantle of their own slumber which is unto death about a Christian brother's labors of love. I am a very naughty, wicked girl, I know, and I hardly dare make up my mind about such important movements. May love, charity, hope, and patience be given to all!"

Mr. Whittier, in a letter to Mr. Sturge, related this instance, which occurred under the administration of John Tyler, to illustrate the all-pervading espionage of the slave power, which dictated every appointment to office from a letter-carrier to an ambassador: "The newly appointed postmaster of Philadelphia employed among his numerous clerks and letter-carriers Joshua Coffin, who, some three years ago, aided in restoring to liberty a free colored citizen of New York, who had been kidnapped and sold into slavery. The appointment of the postmaster not being confirmed, he wrote to his friends in Congress to inquire the reason, and was told that the delay was occasioned by the fact that he had employed Coffin as one of his letter-carriers! Coffin was immediately dismissed, and in a few days the Senate confirmed the appointment!"

In another letter to his English correspondent

Mr. Whittier says: "To every well-wisher of America it must be a matter of interest and satisfaction to know, that there is a growing determination in the Free States to meet the combination of slaveholders in behalf of slavery, by one of freemen in behalf of liberty; and thus compel the party politicians, on the ground of expediency, if not of principle, to break from the thralldom of the slave power, and array themselves on the side of freedom." He has here outlined the policy to which he adhered steadily and consistently in all the political work of his life.

The following letter was written to Lucy Hooper's sisters, immediately after hearing of her death:

AMESBURY, 8th mo., 6, 1841.

I have just seen in the Boston papers a notice of the death of Lucy. The news has come to me unexpected — sudden. I was not prepared for such a termination of her illness. Sick myself, I cannot write you a very long letter, nor perhaps would you wish it; for what can I say to comfort you under your new bereavement — what condolence can I offer to those who have been able fully to understand and appreciate the purity and beauty of the spirit which has just passed from among you? He, alone, who loveth those whom He chasteneth can comfort and sustain you under such a trial as yours. To Him, who hath taken to the arms of His Love our dear Lucy, I can alone commend you.

When in New York only a few weeks ago, I *might* have seen Lucy; and I blame myself for yielding to my own feelings of sickness and lassitude, and not calling again, before I left. I intended to have spent the evening of Tuesday with you, but was confined to my room all the afternoon and evening by severe pain, and the next day I was under the necessity of leaving. At Boston, I was conversing with H. T. Tuckerman about Lucy — the very day before her death. I had never seen him before, but his acquaintance with you made him seem like an old friend. Do write me, and let me know the many particulars of her last illness, and of the last mournful scene. I am no stranger with a stranger's careless curiosity. I have had few friends so dear to me — so often in my thoughts — as Lucy.

What shadows we are! — It seems but yesterday when I used to visit you in the long winter evenings at Brooklyn — since Lucy and myself stood by her own loved Merrimac together in the rich light of a westering August sun. And can it be that she is no longer with us! — *But she is not gone.* Her pure affections, her fine intellect, her faith and love, and simple trust in her Heavenly Father, are not lost. She lives still, — a glorified dweller in the same universe with ourselves. With the deepest sympathy with your afflicted mother and with yourselves and brother, and with a warm desire that this dispensation of Providence may be blessed to us all, I am very sincerely, etc.

It has often been a matter of speculation whether passages in " The Last Eve of Summer," " A Sea Dream," " Memories," and other poems, were not the expression of a tender emotion which had been sacrificed to adverse circumstances. If there were ever any doubt that the sweet and tender poem, "Memories," was inspired by a romance of the poet's youth, that doubt was dispelled by the position Whittier has given these charming verses in his collected works. It was not without thought and deliberation that in 1888 he directed this poem should be placed at the head of his "Subjective and Reminiscent" poems. He had never before publicly acknowledged how much of his heart was wrapped up in this delightful play of poetic fancy. The poem was written in 1841, and although the romance it embalms lies far back of this date, possibly there is a heart still beating which fully understands its meaning. The biographer can do no more than make this suggestion, which has the sanction of the poet's explicit word. To a friend who told him that "Memories" was her favorite poem, he said, "I love it too; but I hardly knew whether to publish it, it was so personal, and near my heart."

To a correspondent who expressed compassion because he never married, and asked how it happened, he replied: " Circumstances — the care of an aged mother, and the duty owed to a sister in delicate health for many years — must be my excuse for living the lonely life which has called out thy pity. It is some, if a poor, consolation to think that, after all, it might have been a great deal worse. My life has been on the whole quite as happy as I deserved, or had a right to expect. I know there has something very sweet and beauti-

ful been missed, but I have no reason to complain.
I have learned, at least, to look into happiness
through the eyes of others, and to thank God for
the happy unions and holy firesides I have known."

TO ANN E. WENDELL.

WALNUT GROVE, LEE, N. H., 7th mo., 1842.[1]

I like thy remarks about the Liberty party and
its dangers, and I thank thee for thy friendly caution. I am not much affected by the whirl of politics. I act because I believe it to be my duty, decidedly and vigorously, but my inward self is calm.
The ambitions and selfish hopes of other years do
not disturb me. Why it is so, I know not, but I
can mingle in the exciting scenes of an election
without feeling the excitement to any considerable
extent. My enthusiasm has been tamed down by
that hard and cross-grained schoolmistress, Experience. . . . Moses and Anna are disputing as
usual upon metaphysics, Joseph and Jonathan
are in full blast upon politics, and I am holding a
sort of collateral sideways conversation with all
parties ; and the truth is, my head is getting into
confusion, its ideas holding a sort of internecine
war with each other. I can't get " into the quiet."
Tubal Cain, Jr., master builder on the Babel corporation, was never more bewildered by the confusion of tongues than I am at this moment.
Then, in addition to all, the thermometer has boiled
over. The heat is really oppressive, and all day I
have been ready to say with another : —

---

[1] While visiting his cousins, the Cartlands.

I wake from dreams of polar ice
On which I 'd been a slider,
Like fishes dreaming of the sea,
And waking in the spider.

P. S.   I must defer my visit to Philadelphia
until thy sister M. invites Elizabeth and myself to
her wedding.   Tell her that this fall will be a
suitable time, in our opinion.   There is such a
thing as overdoing this courting business; for my
part, were I in Elisha's place, I should get out of
all patience.   To be obliged to travel a mile and a
half every night, year in and year out, is more than
I could submit to, even for so good a girl as cousin
M.   And besides, looking at it absolutely, is n't
it rather ridiculous for two young folks?   Why
not marry at once and have done with it?

TO HARRIET MINOT.

AMESBURY, 5th mo., 5, 1842.

H. C. Wright, as I learn from the " Liberator,"
is going to England to *discuss*.   In view of the
state of things in that country, would it not be
better to spend the money required for his outfit
and salary in purchasing barrels of beef and flour
for the starving families of Manchester and Leeds?
Discussion is doubtless good, but sometimes bread
and meat are better.

TO ANN E. WENDELL.

8th mo., 19, 1842.

The serene, calm faith which breathes through
thy letters rebukes at times my own restless and
inquiring spirit.   I learn to love through them the

wise philosophy which, estimating its poor and
finite powers by the weighty and awful Idea of
Infinite Intelligence and Omnipotence, ceases to
search into the mysteries of its own being and of
the Divine economy, and bows with veiled eye and
simple submission to the will of the Universal
Father. . . . How vividly thy letter has brought
you all before me, in beautiful La Grange, and
how happy I should be to be able to look in upon
you, and to repeat my stroll up the banks of the
river, to the old church, the graveyard and its
white stones, overhung with the green forest!
How strange it is that the momentary glimpse of
a landscape, a smile, the tone of a word spoken
carelessly, a tree, the shadow of a cloud on the
hillside, should burn themselves like enamel upon
the mind, and live there ever after a part of our
conscious being!

TO THE SAME.

8th mo., 1843.

I should be heartily glad to visit Philadelphia,
to sit with cousin Ann, and discuss upon the great
problems of human life and destiny, and not upon
those high abstractions alone, but upon the household things, the simple, the tender, and the beautiful of daily life, which

> " Lie scattered at the feet of man like flowers,"

and talk with thy mother about Luther, Melanch-
thon, and Pope and Cardinal, and Fathers and
Councils. Speaking of these matters, does thee
read much of the Puseyism controversy which is
now going on? The English Episcopal Church

seems ready to go over to Popery in earnest. Has
thee noticed the general tendency towards the old
trust in man, — in priests, sacrifices, and ghostly
mummery and machinery? To me it seems to bid
fair to swallow up everything save Quakerism of
the old stamp, which has this advantage, that its
distinctive characteristic is the entire rejection of
all ceremonial, the total disbelief in the power of
pope, priest, or elder to give a ransom for the soul
of another. Well, let the world, sick of doubt and
infidelity, go back and try once more the old
superstitions which the Voltaires and Gibbons and
Humes of the last century exposed to scorn and
derision. Let the old tricks of monks and priests
again deceive and amuse self-blinded Christendom.
I have a strong faith — it seems almost like prophecy — that the result will be, ere the lapse of two
centuries, a complete and permanent change in the
entire Christian world. Weary and disgusted
with shams and shadows, with the effort to believe
a few miserable worms of the dust the sole dis-
pensers of Heaven's salvation, men will awake to
the simple beauty of practical Christianity. Love
will take the place of fast, penance, long prayers,
and heathenish sacrifices; altar, church, priest,
and ritual will pass away; but the human heart
will be the Holy of Holies, where worship will
still be performed, not in set forms, and on particular occasions, but daily and hourly a worship
meet and acceptable to Him who is not deceived
by the pomp of outward ceremonial, and who loves
mercy better than sacrifice. . . . I had a visit
from Lewis Tappan and wife and daughter, the

other day; he is just from England. He says the
Friends there were very anxious to have the pro-
slavery Methodists, Baptists, etc., of America exposed in the World's Convention, but evidently
feared to hear the truth of the course of Friends
in America disclosed. If I had nothing else to
be thankful for, I should still feel grateful that
I have not become a bigoted sectarian. To me,
Quaker and Catholic are alike, both children of
my Heavenly Father, and separated only by a
creed, to some, indeed, a barrier like a Chinese
wall, but to me frail and slight as a spider's web.
. . . I think some of attending the great anti-
slavery convention at Buffalo on the 30th and 31st
of this month.

With all his charity for other sects, Mr. Whittier
held firmly to the faith in which he was educated.
He did not like to see the Friends adopting the
evangelizing methods of other denominations. He
used to quote with approval a remark made to him
by Rev. Dr. Withington, of Newburyport, who
said: "I am a Calvinist; you are a Quaker. We
are in essentials in unity. But you will remain a
Quaker to the end, and I a Calvinist. It is better
so. I don't believe in spiritual chowder." Mr.
Whittier did not object to the lively music and
spirited exhortation of the Methodists, but he
thought that the Quakers made a "spiritual chowder" of it when they, who as a class had no ear
for music and few of the graces of oratory, undertook to imitate the methods of sects in which music
and elocution are carefully studied, and the meet-

ings of which are considered a failure if all the time is not "occupied." He loved best the old-fashioned Quaker meetings in which the silence was not broken unless some weighty word pressed for utterance. On one occasion he was discussing with a cultured Friend the inarticulate groanings which punctuated the remarks of some of the speakers of their faith. His friend said, " Let us discourage this mannerism by calling it grunting." " Thee better not do it," gravely replied 'Mr. Whittier; " if thee take away the grunt, there 's nothing left."

When reference was made to the Quaker misuse of English grammar, Mr. Whittier would say that it had been the manner of speech of his people for two centuries, and he clung to it with especial fondness because it was his mother's language. Occasionally, in talking with strangers, he would adopt the usual form, but he rarely did so in his letters, either in dates or in personal pronouns. He was accustomed to say that the Quaker costume had its use in keeping Friends from indulging in the frivolities of the world's people. He was never in a theatre or a circus in his life. He bore his testimony to the peculiarities of his sect on all occasions. When a member of the legislature, he adhered to the Quaker custom in the matter of the oath, and in addressing the chair. When a fellow member died he declined to wear crape on his arm, and the practice was given up after that time. When he became Secretary of the American Anti-Slavery Society, he succeeded a secretary who kept dates in the customary way. Lewis Tappan, looking at his neat records, was puzzled by the Quaker dates, but he laughed as he read " 12th mo., 6th," or " 2d day evening," and said he had no objection to this kind of date, " but Friend Whittier must be here to interpret."

In his later life the Quaker was shown in his dress only in his coat, all other clothing being in the prevailing fashion. This coat of black broadcloth was cut in the orthodox Quaker style. The Philadelphia tailor who supplied him during his residence in that city in 1838–1840, sent him from time to time all the coats he wore for the remainder of his life, without the slightest change in style or measurement.

Of innovations in the methods of Quakerism he would say, " Our folks have got to talking too much ; they even want a glass of water on the table, and some of them want singing in the meetings. I tell them if they want singing, they must get the world's folks to do it for them, for two hundred years of silence have taken all the sing out of our people.".

The skill and sagacity Mr. Whittier had shown in his editorial work upon political journals, in managing conventions, and in influencing legislation, together with the earnestness of his advocacy of the reforms then demanding attention, gave him prominence among the men who decided upon the necessity of a third party, since neither of the great national parties dared grapple with the issues presented by the aroused conscience of the nation.

In 1834, James G. Birney, a Kentucky slave-

holder, came out in favor of immediate emancipation, at the same time liberating his own slaves.
Finding it impossible to disseminate his views in
his own State, he moved to Cincinnati, and published a paper called the " Philanthropist," which
became a powerful instrument in forming public
opinion.   His experience as a slaveholder, his
philanthropic action as a liberator, and the readiness with which he defended his opinions with his
pen and upon the platform, gave him importance
in the ranks of the abolitionists who favored political action.   He came to New England in 1835,
and received much attention from friends of the
cause.   John G. Whittier, Moses A. Cartland, and
others of the Society of Friends, on the 28th of
May, 1835, wrote him a series of seven questions
covering the whole ground of the policy to be
adopted for the extinction of slavery, and his full
and explicit answer was widely circulated. He
thought that under the Constitution as it then
existed, operations against slavery could be undertaken with success ; that there was no need of tear-
ing down the whole structure of our political
institutions to extirpate this evil.   This led to the
formation of the Liberty party, in the organization
of which Mr. Whittier was active and efficient.
Birney was nominated for the Presidency in 1840
and 1844, and was supported by Mr. Whittier in
both these campaigns. The Liberty party of the
North Essex district nominated Mr. Whittier for
Congress, and so long as he was in no danger of
being elected he did not object to being a candidate.   But at length his party became strong

enough in the district to cause alarm to the Whigs, for a coalition with the Democrats was threatened, and such a coalition would certainly have been favored by Mr. Whittier if an anti-slavery candidate could have been found among the Democrats of North Essex who possessed such qualifications as caused the concentration of the Liberty vote of South Essex upon Robert Rantoul, and elected him. Mr. Whittier had a hand in managing this last-named combination, and had reason to be proud of the record of Rantoul in Congress, as is shown in his fine poetic tributes to his memory. In 1842, both Whigs and Democrats nominated men for Congress from whom Whittier could obtain no pledges in behalf of the cause he had at heart. He therefore prevented an election by remaining the third-party candidate during many successive trials, through the year 1843, the district in the mean time being unrepresented in Congress. At each trial Mr. Whittier's vote increased. At last, in December, 1843, an article appeared in the Boston " Courier," said to have been suggested by Daniel Webster, advising the Whigs in North Essex to drop their candidate and unite upon Whittier, as he was and always had been a Whig in principle, and was to be preferred to the Democratic candidate. Some of the friends of the Whig candidate resented this interference from outside the district, and brought up against Whittier a charge that he had on several occasions worked for the Democrats, notably in the case of Robert Rantoul when named for the senatorship and Marcus Morton for the governorship. The " Cou-

rier " had spoken of Whittier as a mechanic, and
to this a Whig paper in the district responded :
" It is true that in youth he was obliged to learn a
mechanical trade, but the editor of the ' Courier '
would recognize little of the mechanic in the sleek-
looking kid-gloved beau of the last seven years.
He has no more sympathy with mechanics than
with Whigs.   The Whigs can never come into
support of John G. Whittier until they lose all
regard for principle and all self-respect."

Notwithstanding this blast from the party organ,
as the day of election approached, it seemed probable that the advice of Webster would be heeded.
Whittier became alarmed at the prospect of being
elected, and immediately wrote a letter declining
the candidacy.   The Liberty candidate who took
his place had not his personal popularity, and the
Whigs at once elected their man.   If Whittier's
health had permitted, he would have remained
in the field, and if elected would have made an
efficient member of Congress, with an influence
upon legislation superior to that of many men
with readier tongues.   His ambition was distinctly
in that direction ; but he found it necessary to
heed the admonition of his medical adviser, and
keep on the outer circles of the maelstrom of politics.   All his life he was in touch with the political movements of the country, and was the trusted
adviser of statesmen.   A kind Providence, however, by a seeming affliction, had set him apart
for a still higher usefulness.

Rev. John Pierpont, pastor of the Hollis Street
church, Boston, was in these days causing a great

stir throughout New England by a bold and uncompromising determination to speak freely in his pulpit in favor of temperance and anti-slavery reforms, notwithstanding the opposition of many of the most influential people in his own society. The popularity thus acquired Mr. Whittier thought might be made available to the Liberty party, if Mr. Pierpont would consent to accept a nomination for Congress. Accordingly he wrote to Samuel E. Sewall, under date of February 12, 1842: —

" I wrote some days ago to John Pierpont about the nomination, *on my own responsibility*, as an individual, and have received a line from him. As I understand it, he is willing to stand as our candidate ; but thinks it due to those of his society who have so faithfully stood by him in his contest with the powers of rum to consult a little their feelings in the matter — or at least the feelings of two or three of the leading members. I understand he has consulted F. Jackson about it ; Jackson, I think, would offer no decided objection. Wilt thou immediately see Alden or Dr. Mann, and if it is judged best, call on two or three of the most prominent of the society. It would be well to have their concurrence and aid. It should be presented to them in its most favorable aspect : that it is the strongest testimony which we can render to the noble reformer and the firm and faithful friends who have sustained him in the Hollis Street pulpit ; that there is even a reasonable probability that he may be elected ; that there is perfect enthusiasm for him among all to whom the subject of his nomination has been mentioned. Has anything been done about securing the State House for our evening meetings ?   If Pierpont is at home, ask him not to leave Boston, if he can avoid it, until after the convention.[1]   I wish to see him, as if I am able I shall be in Boston before the meeting."

In March, 1842, Mr. Whittier wrote to Mr. Sewall : "I fear we shall get dragged into a war after all, — a war in defense of the vilest negro traffic existing anywhere save on the African coast !   It is unendurable !   And if Texas is to be added to us, as there are no doubtful indications, let us say, Disunion before Texas ! . . .   By letters from England I find that our minister at Paris, General Cass, has entitled himself to the Presidency by his vigorous efforts for the protection of that Democratic branch of commerce, — the foreign slave trade !"   The letter containing these passages is sealed with a wafer bearing this inscription : "The minister who defends slavery defends sin, and is false to his trust."

The "Pioneer" magazine, mentioned in the following letter from Mr. Lowell, was a literary and critical monthly, published in Boston by Leland & Whitney, and edited by James Russell Lowell

---

[1] Mr. Pierpont received the nomination for Congress from the Liberty party convention, but declined it in a letter to Mr. Whittier, in which he said that he must postpone his work for the slave until a minister of the gospel became a free man ; "for he can never be so," he adds, "so long as the pulpit is controlled by the pews.   This freedom is prior in the order of time to the freedom of the slave, and this freedom my friends and myself are endeavoring to vindicate, where it has been openly and powerfully assailed.   Let us work out *our* problem, — a labor quite severe enough for the hands engaged in it, — and *yours*, my friend, will be worked out the sooner for it."

and Robert Carter.   Only three numbers were issued, for the months of January, February, and
March, 1843.   It had a good sale at the start, and
the publishers, encouraged by this, launched into
other enterprises that proved disastrous failures,
and caused the suspension of the magazine.   It
was Lowell's first venture in editorship.   The
poem of Whittier's in the " Democratic Review "
to which he refers was in the October number,
1842, and was entitled " Lines on reading several
Pamphlets published by Clergymen against the
Abolition of the Gallows."   Lowell's sonnets, called
out by reading Wordsworth's defense of capital
punishment, appeared in the May number of the
" Review," and they must have been almost unintelligible to the readers of the magazine, for the
reason he gives.   They may be found in Lowell's
collected works.   The poem Mr. Whittier contributed to the " Pioneer," in response to the request of the ambitious young editor, was " To a
Friend, on her Return from Europe."   Mr. Lowell's letter is mutilated, his autograph signature
being cut from it in such a way as to remove the
date and a few of the first words.   The postmark
shows it was written in October, 1842 : —

. . . "January next . . . a magazine under my
editorial charge.   It will be called the ' Pioneer,'
and it is to be a *free* magazine.   I mean that it
shall take a high stand in Art, and also hold itself
free to advance or comment on all the great movements of the age.   It is to keep up with the age and
not behind it; nay, if possible, it shall run before,
as its name would indicate.   If the undertaking

succeeds, I shall pay authors higher than any other magazine in the land, regarding *things* and not *names*, and paying for an article's worth in spirit rather than its current value in specie. May I hope that you will send me something for my first number? Any little poem that you may have by you will be very acceptable to me. I cannot promise to pay you very much at first, for the expense of getting up such a work makes large holes in small capitals. But I trust that the hope of aiding a good endeavor will be enough to you. I am glad to see you down on the cassocked pleaders for murder in the 'Democratic Review.' Some sonnets of mine in the May number were written on reading Wordsworth in favor of bloodshed, though some parts of them were most unintelligible by the fact not being stated. I wish I were in your district to vote for you as member of Congress. But you must take my good hopes instead."

When the case of George Latimer, an alleged fugitive slave from Virginia, was on trial in Massachusetts, in 1842–43, the excitement throughout the State was intense. It was arranged by the friends of liberty that conventions should be held simultaneously in each county, and the 2d of January, 1843, was the day appointed. The convention for Essex County was held at Ipswich, and the occasion was made memorable by the reading of the intense, almost fierce, stanzas written for the occasion by John G. Whittier. It was the splendid poem, "Massachusetts to Virginia," which was printed in the "Liberator" of January 27, 1843, without the name of the author. But

as no other man *could* have written these powerful
lines, the public knew at once to whom to credit
them. Thomas Wentworth Higginson says that
he first met Whittier at about this time, and this
is his account of the meeting : —

"It was in 1843, when the excitement of the
'Latimer case' still echoed through Massachusetts,
and the younger abolitionists were full of 'the joy
of eventful living.' I was then nineteen, and saw
the poet for the first time at an eating-house
known as Campbell's, then quite a resort for reformers of all sorts. I saw before me a man of
striking personal appearance; tall, slender, with
olive complexion, black hair, straight black eye-
brows, brilliant eyes, and an Oriental, Semitic
cast of countenance. This was Whittier at thirty-
five. I lingered till he rose from the table, and
then advancing, I said with boyish enthusiasm
and I doubt not with boyish awkwardness also,
'I should like to shake hands with the author of
"Massachusetts to Virginia."' The poet, who was,
and is, one of the shyest of men, broke into a
kindly smile, and said briefly, 'Thy name, friend?'
I gave it, we shook hands, and that was all; but
to me it was like touching a hero's shield, and
though I have since learned to count the friendship of Whittier as one of the great privileges of
my life, yet nothing has ever displaced the recollection of that first boyish interview."

In a letter to his brother in Portland, dated
February 7, 1843, Mr. Whittier says : —

"I wrote to and visited Governor Morton and
got him to recommend the abolition of capital

punishment in his message [in 1840].   I shall try
for it this winter, not, however, with much hope of
success.   Our great Latimer petition was presented to the Legislature with 62,791 names.
The way we shall use up the Virginians is a caution to all kidnappers.   The Legislature is ready
to do anything for us ; our vote for Sewall last fall
did the business.   [The vote for the Liberty party
candidate, Samuel E. Sewall, had the effect to
secure the election of the Democratic candidate,
Governor Morton, for the second time.   On each
occasion he was elected by a vote of one, first in
the popular vote, and the second time in the Legislature.]   Tell Nathan Winslow that his son-in-law
[Sewall] came within a hair's breadth of being
governor.   But for half a dozen refractory members the Whig party in the Legislature would
have voted for him. . . . Our town meeting at
Amesbury comes off next week.   As it happens
that at this time there are all over the region
hereaway what are called ' revivals,' and as our
Liberty party active men are mostly deacons, etc.,
they will be kept much at home, and the ' enemy '
will be likely to prevail in one quarter while they
are routing him in another.   In other words, if
the Devil can't get the Church, he will take the
State, rather than nothing."

Mr. Whittier's acquaintance with and friendship
for James T. Fields dated back to 1839, and perhaps earlier.   In that year, when Whittier was
collecting material for the " North Star," in Philadelphia, Fields contributed a poem for his collection.   Upon Whittier's return to Massachusetts,

he found young Fields connected with the publishing house of Wm. D. Ticknor, with whom he
formed a partnership in 1845. The first volume
of Whittier's published by this house was " Lays
of My Home, and Other Poems," which was issued
in May, 1843. Whittier's correspondence in regard to the publication of this book was with
Fields. In April he wrote the following letter,
giving a list of the poems to be included in the
book. The "John Gilpin legend" to which he
refers was first published in the " North Star,"
the winter of 1839–40. " Lays of My Home '
was the first book from the sale of which Mr
Whittier realized any remuneration, all his previ
ous collections having been of limited circulation,
or issued in aid of " the cause : " —

" In regard to the matter of publication, — I
know little or nothing about it. I shall leave it
altogether to you, thinking that if the work meets
with a ready sale, you will do me justice, as I
should, I am free to confess, like to realize something from it. Will these terms answer? . . . I
send you the first articles, which will constitute
about one third or quarter of the book, and give it
its name, ' Lays of My Home, and Other Poems.'
There are two other poems which belong to this
part of the book, ' The Funeral Tree of the Sokokis,' and ' St. John.' I have no copies of them;
but you will find them in the collection of friend
Griswold, or in the 'Knickerbocker' for 1841,
and I wish you to procure them and publish them
in the following order: 1. The Merrimac; 2. The
Norsemen; 3. Ballads of Cassandra Southwick;

4. The Funeral Tree of the Sokokis; 5. St. John. . . . I shall have no preface, except a single page of note or direction. I will send the residue of the copy as soon as I can catch it, for it is scattered, like the flying leaves of the Sibyl, in all directions. . . . I have two MS. poems which I think are quite as good, if not better, than any I have printed, which I shall send. I send with this ' The Exiles,' a kind of John Gilpin legend. I am in doubt about it. Read it and decide for thyself whether it is worth printing. If published it should go in after ' St. John.' "

For some reason, " The Exiles " was not published in " The Lays of My Home ; " probably Mr. Fields advised against it. All the twenty-three poems in this little volume of 122 pages are retained in the latest editions of the complete works of the poet.

Thomas Macey, the hero of the ballad of " The Exiles," was a resident of Amesbury. The house in which he lived previous to 1664 is still standing, and is known as " the Obadiah Colby place." In that year he sold this house, and removed to " Amesbury Mills," the village built about the falls of the Powow. It was in 1659 that he harbored the Quakers, in defiance of the act of the General Court, passed in 1657. It was down the Powow into the Merrimac that the memorable race with the sheriff and the priest began. When Mr. Whittier wrote the ballad he evidently supposed that Macey's residence was in Haverhill, the ancient Pentucket, as is shown in the stanza : —

> " By green Pentucket's southern slope
> The small boat glided fast ;
> The watchers of the Block-house saw
> The strangers as they passed."

In this poem occurs a stanza that has puzzled some of its readers who are familiar with the scenery of the lower Merrimac : —

> " Oh, beautiful ! that rainbow span
> O'er dim Crane-neck was bended ;
> One bright foot touched the eastern hills,
> And one with ocean blended."

" Crane-neck " hill is on the Newbury side of the river, in such a position that the Maceys, in their boat, would not have seen the rainbow arching over it as described. Mr. Alfred Ordway, of Haverhill, informs the writer that happening to be on Job's Hill, close by the Whittier homestead, one summer afternoon, a shower came up, and after it he saw Crane-neck haloed by a rainbow precisely answering the description in the poem. He knew at once that the poet was remembering just such a scene when he wrote this stanza. From the hill of his boyhood the ocean is visible, as it could not have been from a boat in the Merrimac, and he had often seen the " bright foot " of a rainbow blending with it, while the top of the arch was over Crane-neck.

The ballad " The New Wife and the Old " is founded on one of many marvelous legends connected with the family of General Moulton, of Hampton, N. H., of whom Mr. Whittier says that he was regarded by his neighbors as a Yankee Faust, in league with the adversary. The mansion of General Moulton is still standing in Hampton,

and is pointed out to travelers on the Boston and
Maine Railroad.   In going westward, the hip-
roofed house is seen on the left side of the track,
soon after passing the Hampton station.   A lady
in Malden, Mass., who is the great-granddaughter
of " the new wife," wrote to Mr. Whittier in 1888,
asking him the source of his information, and
sending him a piece of the wedding silk of her
ancestress.   He replied :   " The story of the
' New Wife and the Old ' was told me a good
many years ago by an elderly lady.   Since then,
I have received a letter from a lady who at one
time was spending the summer at the old house in
Hampton.   She said strange noises were heard in
the rooms, the steps and rustling dress of a woman
unseen on the stairs, etc., and that the servants
were so frightened that Rev. Mr. Milton of Newburyport was sent for, who came and prayed, and
counseled the ghosts to depart.   I hope I have
not, unintentionally, misrepresented General Moulton in my poem."

Between the years 1837 and 1847, a large number of Mr. Whittier's best poems, and several
prose sketches, were sent by him to the " Democratic Review," published in Washington.   It was
to this magazine that for this decade he sent
nearly all his poems that did not directly touch
upon the question of slavery, and some prose
sketches.   It was a partisan magazine, with a
large proportion of its circulation at the South,
but Whittier made himself a most welcome contributor, though many a stanza expressed quite
plainly his abhorrence of slavery.

The series of "Songs of Labor" was begun in the "Review," and four of them were published in 1845 and 1846. When Mr. Whittier became connected with the "National Era," he finished the series in that paper. The poem "Texas: Voice of New England" was called for by James Russell Lowell, in a letter to Whittier, dated March 21, 1844. In this letter he is urgently entreated "to cry aloud and spare not against the cursed Texas plot." Two days before this call, Lowell had published in the Boston "Courier" his "Rallying Cry for New England against the Annexation of Texas," beginning with the lines:

> "Rise up, New England, buckle on your mail of proof sublime,
> Your stern old hate of tyranny, your deep contempt of crime;
> A plot is hatching now, more full of woe and shame
> Than ever from the iron heart of bloodiest despot came."

This poem of Lowell's appeared anonymously, except that it had as a sub-head the lines, "By a Yankee." It was at the time generally supposed to have been written by Whittier, and Whittier did not then know it was Lowell's. His first guess was that Pierpont was its author. The inspiration of his own "Texas: Voice of New England" came to him at length, and he sent the poem to Lowell, as a response to his request. It was published in the "Courier" for April 17, 1844, with the following preface written by Lowell: —

A few weeks since, some verses appeared in the "Courier," which were generally ascribed to Whittier. They were not his, however. In the present crisis of the fate of the Republic, New England listens for a trumpet-call from her Tyr-tæus. Nor will she be disappointed. Whittier has always been found faithful to the Muses' holy trust. He has not put his talent out at profitable interest, by catering to the insolent and Phari-saical self-esteem of the times; nor has he hidden it in the damask napkin of historical common-places, or a philanthropy too universal to concern itself with particular wrongs, the practical redress-ing of which is all that renders philanthropy of value. Most poets are content to follow the spirit of their age, as pigeons follow a leaky grain cart, picking a kernel here and there, out of the dry dust of the past. Not so Whittier. From the heart of the onset upon the serried mercenaries of every tyranny, the chords of his iron-strung lyre clang with a martial and triumphant cheer; and where Freedom's Spartan few maintain their invio-late mountain pass against the assaults of slavery, his voice may be heard, clear and fearless, as if the victory were already won. It is with the highest satisfaction I send you the inclosed poem, every way worthy of our truly New England poet. I trust that when this meets his eye, the few words which I could not refrain from adding by way of preface will not be deemed impertinent.   L.

Editor Buckingham " could not refrain " from adding, as a postscript to the poem, this note: " If any of our Southern readers should think Mr. Whittier's poem a little fierce, they will please to recollect Mr. Hayne's apology for South Carolina

nullification, — ' Something must be pardoned to
the spirit of liberty ! ' "

The poem as first published had only twenty
three-line stanzas, instead of twenty-nine as it now
appears, and some of the original stanzas have
been toned down.   For instance, the eighteenth
stanza of the first version reads : —

> " And when vengeance lights your skies,
> Hither shall ye turn your eyes,
> As the damned on Paradise ! "

The corresponding stanza of the poem, as it now
stands, has "clouds" for "lights" in the first
line, and "lost" for "damned" in the last line.
The fourteenth stanza was originally somewhat
stronger than the reading adopted in all later
editions : —

> "Make our Union-band a chain,
> We will snap its links in twain,
> We will stand erect again ! "

This was changed in 1846 to the following : —

> "If with added weight ye strain
> On th' already breaking chain,
> Who shall bind its links again ? "

This stanza now reads : —

> "Make our Union-band a chain,
> Weak as tow in Freedom's strain
> Link by link shall snap in twain."

The fifteenth stanza was remodeled with better
success.   In the edition of 1846 it reads : —

> " Chain of parchment ! sand-wrought rope !
> Shall they bind the planet up
> Scattered o'er the heaven's blue cope ? "

These lines are greatly improved in the latest
revision : —

> " Vainly shall your sand-wrought rope
> Bind the starry cluster up,
> Shattered over heaven's blue cope ! "

Both poems, Lowell's and Whittier's, were ablaze
with an indignation that was communicated to
receptive minds throughout the North, and although
the hour was not yet ripe for the full political
effect desired, they contributed greatly to the promotion of a feeling antagonistic to the spread of
the institution of slavery over the new territory
then soon to be acquired by an unjust war.   Whittier had sent his poem to Lowell about the first of
April, but not hearing from him, on the morning
of the 17th of that month (the very day it was
published in the " Courier ") wrote as follows : —

" Some week or ten days ago I sent thee a piece
on the Texas conspiracy, but, as I have heard nothing from it, presume thee have been absent, or that
my letter failed of reaching thee.   If not published,
let me suggest, as the 'Courier' has already published an article on the subject, that it be sent to
the ' Daily Chronicle,' Leavitt's paper.   In hastily
transcribing the piece, I omitted two verses, and
for the life of me, as I cannot recollect the remainder, I hardly know where they belong — I *believe*,
however, after the stanza ending with ' Freedom's
oath.' [1]   One of them thee will see is an *asinine*
Scriptural allusion to him who crouched beneath
burdens : —

> " ' What though Issachar be strong, —
> He hath stooped beneath your wrong [2]
> Over-much and over-long !

[1] The stanza now ends " the word befitting both."
[2] The latest version is : —
>   "Ye may load his back with wrong."

"'Patience with her cup o'errun,
　With her weary thread outspun,
　Murmurs that her work is done.

"'Make our Union-band a chain,'" etc.

"I am sorry to trouble thee with this matter.
If the letter containing the piece has not been received, please write me immediately."

When the Boston mail arrived at Amesbury that
day, he found his poem in the "Courier," and at
once sent this note to Lowell, dated in the afternoon
of the 17th : —

"I owe thee an apology for troubling thee so
often with my notes; but I write now just to say
that I have seen in the 'Courier' of to-day the
lines I sent thee, with the too flattering comments
of 'L.' I thank thee, for I value a compliment,
even if it be but a compliment, from such as thyself, and if anything of mine has given thee half
the pleasure which thy 'Burns,' 'Incident in
a Railroad Car,' and 'Glance behind the Cur-
tain' have given me, I shall not doubt the sincerity of thy kind words. I have read, since the
lines were written, the 'Rallying Cry' over again,
and as Tristram Shandy's father would say, 'I
like it hugely.' It has lines which have burned
into my memory. Whose is it? Pierpont's? I
have half suspected *thee* of the mischief. My principal reason for writing now was to tell thee that
not hearing anything from the lines I sent thee, or
from thee, and coming to the conclusion that thee
was absent from home, and being somewhat fearful that the iniquitous deed would be done before
I could utter my protest against it (not that I

expected to silence, like another Orpheus, the Cerberus of Slavery with my rhymes, but, like Balmawhapple, when he raised his horse-pistol against the Rock of Stirling, I wished to manifest my will if not my power), — I therefore this very morning sent a copy of the poem, as near as I could recollect it, with some additional verses, to the 'Morning Chronicle' (Leavitt's new daily). I mentioned to him that I had sent a copy some time before to thee. What I chiefly regret is that I did not see the 'Courier' in season for recalling the letter to Leavitt, and I fear, therefore, that he will publish it, unless he has seen the same in the 'Courier.' The alterations will look a little odd, but I do not see how it can be helped now. But enough of this. What art thou doing in a literary way? As for myself, what with cares of all sorts on my hands, the principal charge of our weekly paper here (*weakly* would be the better word), and the trouble and responsibility of an active politician of the Liberty stamp, as well as the constant drawback of ill-health, especially since these eastern winds have been blowing, I can do little or nothing in the way of rhyme or reason. Does thee see our friend Wm. H. Burleigh's paper? I have met with it occasionally, and like it; it is manly, earnest, and gentlemanly. E. Burritt's 'Christian Citizen' will also do good."

Having responded to Lowell's call for a Texas poem, Whittier soon after returned the compliment by asking his brother poet to write a song for the celebration of West India emancipation held at Salem, August 1, 1844. This is his letter, making the request: —

"We are to have a great anti-slavery meeting at Salem, on the 1st of August, at which Gerrit Smith, of New York, and Dr. Elder, the most eloquent speaker in western Pennsylvania, are expected to be present. I think thee once promised me a Liberty song, — and I now claim it for this meeting. Give me one which shall be to our cause what the song of Rouget de Lisle was to the French Republicans, — such an one as the maiden may whisper in the

> 'Asphodel flower-fleece
> She walks ankle deep in,'

and the strong man may sing at his forge and plough. Think of it, dear L., and oblige me, and do a great work for holy Liberty, by complying with my request. Let me have it soon, that I may hand it to the committee of arrangements."[1]

Mr. Whittier resided several months in Lowell, in 1844, editing the "Middlesex Standard," and soon after he persuaded the proprietor of the Amesbury "Village Transcript" to change its name to the "Essex Transcript," and to make it the county organ of the Liberty party. For about two years he virtually edited the "Transcript," writing most of the original matter it contained, although his name does not appear in it, and

---

[1] Whether Lowell responded to this call is not certain, but there is reason to suppose that a poem of his containing the following spirited stanza, written in 1844, was the one sent for the Salem celebration : —

> "We will speak out, we will be heard
> Though all earth's systems crack ;
> We will not bate a single word,
> Nor take a letter back ! "

his service was entirely gratuitous. Mr. Stephen Lamson, who was a compositor upon the paper, says : —

"He did not pretend, or wish it understood, that he was editor of the paper; but he was its god-father, and undertook to see that it went the way it should go. He did not sign his editorials. Often sickness or absence would prevent his coming into the office for some time, and Mr. Abner L. Bayley and Rev. Mr. Strickland would take his place. This continued about four years, when the proprietor, Mr. J. M. Pettengill, sold out, and the paper became the village organ again. . . . Mr. Whittier was then a man of thirty-seven, tall, straight, and spare, with sharp, good features, handsome face, black eyes, with a long-shaped head, and a towering intellectual forehead. He wore a Quaker medium hat, as well as coat, and used his 'thees' and 'thous' in conversation. He was not a fluent talker, never put on superior airs, but assumed the commonplace in his inter-course with neighbors, friends, and the villagers generally. I remember one or two stores, kept by good friends of his, — one a Baptist deacon, the other a Friend, — where he used to visit when going to the post office; and it was his wont to sit on boxes and barrels, as we have seen them crowd together in a small village grocery store, and do his visiting, and learn the news of the day, or talk over political matters, — for in these two friends he found congenial spirits. This was one of his ways of taking recreation. In my three years' acquain-tance with him, and observation of him in his

daily visits to our office to read the papers, I noticed that if something of great importance attracted his attention, he would nervously grasp a
pen, and thoughts that scintillated from his brain
would rush across the paper before him at a rapid
rate, in a clear, smooth, running hand, that would
surprise me. When the written pages went into
the copy drawer, it would be found in a beautiful
flowing hand, with seldom an emendation or any
interlining, he held his ideas in such perfect form
and control. I used to call it a 'lightning hand,'
so rapidly did the pen fly over the paper. His
sister used to have a literary circle to improve
her young friends in various ways. My father's
adopted daughter was a member of it, and was delighted to think she was worthy to belong to Miss
Whittier's circle. Mr. Whittier used to lend
sanction and help to these friends of his sister, and
became acquainted with each one. He used always, when I saw him, to have something to say
about this sister and about my father, and I was
grateful for it."

In the second number of the " Standard " began
the series of papers entitled " The Stranger in
Lowell," afterward printed in book form. They
picture the new city as seen by the stranger-poet
as he wandered in his hours of leisure about the
streets, and along the banks of the river which had
only recently been harnessed to do the work of
great manufactories. Mr. Whittier's editorial
connection with the " Standard " terminated in
March, 1845, but his actual residence in Lowell
did not extend over a period of more than six

months. In October, 1844, he induced the Hon.
C. L. Knapp, of Vermont, to come to Lowell as
his assistant in conducting the paper, and gradually left it in his charge, and returned to his
home in Amesbury, whence he sent occasional
articles. The "Standard" was consolidated with
a Worcester paper in the spring of 1845, and
published in both Worcester and Lowell.

TO JOHN P. HALE.

24th 1st mo., 1845.

Permit me, although a stranger to thee personally, to express my gratitude for and heartfelt
admiration of thy letter to thy constituents on the
annexation of Texas. I would rather be the author of that letter than the President of the United
States. Under all circumstances, it is one of the
boldest and noblest words ever spoken for Liberty.
May God give thee wisdom and firmness to maintain the glorious and most honorable position
which thou hast taken. The clamor of party, the
selfishness of office-seekers, the temporary withdrawal of popular favor, will not, I trust, move
thee. The Rubicon is passed. The hand which
has so bravely dashed its gauntlet at the feet of
Slavery must now do manly and vigorous battle.
There must be no retreat, no concession, now.
On, then, to the noblest combat ever waged with
Tyranny. The good and the true of all parties
will bid thee Godspeed. Democracy will yet
shake off the loathsome embraces of slavery.
Living as I do on the borders of New Hampshire,
I find that, after all, the better portion of the

Democracy believe thee to be right. The office-
holders and expectants, however, make all the noise.
I sent thee yesterday a copy of the "Middlesex
Standard," a paper for which I write. Believe me
with high respect and esteem thy friend.

In 1845, we find Mr. Whittier seriously considering a plan of going to the West to reside, but it
was soon given up.

During his residence in New York, Mr. Whittier attended several meetings that were broken up
by mobs, which were under the leadership of the
noted Isaiah Rynders. The plan adopted by Rynders did not involve any injury to the persons of
the anti-slavery orators, but he trained his followers to make boisterous disturbances, which would
drown the voice of any speaker. Some of the abolition leaders were disposed to pose as martyrs,
but as they were seldom in actual danger of bodily
injury, Mr. Whittier used to tell them that he
thought they were having a very jolly time of it
for a band of martyrs. It was indeed a goodly
company of able men, and if they failed to get a
hearing in the halls they leased, they had a free
press — often mobbed, but always maintained —
and brilliant writers, whose ability commanded the
attention of the whole country. Mr. Whittier
used to say, when his anti-slavery co-laborers were
complaining of the social and political ostracism
they were suffering: "They may send us to Coventry, but we will set about making Coventry an
agreeable and even a jolly place."

Mr. Whittier's correspondence with Charles

Sumner began before they had any personal acquaintance with each other. They had casually
met, as we have seen, in 1829, in the office of the
American "Manufacturer." But it was Sumner's
brilliant Fourth of July oration upon "The True
Grandeur of Nations," in 1845, that called the attention of the poet to the man who then deliberately threw aside all the alluring prospects his culture and legal attainments had opened to him, to
enter upon the career of a reformer. It was a
time when war was imminent between the United
States and Mexico, and such a plea for Peace as
this was unpopular. When Mayor Quincy was
asked what he thought of the address to which he
had just listened, he replied, " Cut his throat; he
will never be heard of again." This was the feeling of the Boston society in which Sumner had
previously been lionized. But the heart of Whittier warmed toward him, and he wrote : —

"I thank thee from my heart for thy noble address. The truths are none the less welcome for
the beautiful drapery in which they are clothed.
It will do great good. I would rather be the author of it than of all the war eloquence of Hea-
thendom and Christendom combined. . . . It will,
I doubt not, be republished in Europe. I shall be
in Boston, at the Liberty Convention, on the 1st
of next month, and shall take some pains to procure an introduction to the author of the very
best plea for peace which has ever fallen under
my notice."

Mr. Whittier wrote from Amesbury to his sister in Boston, under date of 26, 10th mo., 1845, a

letter which gives some idea of his anti-slavery labors in those days. Elizabeth was visiting her friend Harriet Minot Pitman : —

" Mother is at Haverhill. On Sixth day I carried her up, and then proceeded upon my mission among the abolitionists. Got to Haverhill, called on several of the ' Liberty men,' and finally held a meeting — a sort of impromptu affair — at which eloquent speeches were made by several gentlemen, Mr. Algernon Sydney Nichols among the rest. When it came to my turn I began with as much vehemence as Mr. Pickwick, but broke down about midway, and gradually subsided into a sort of melancholy monotone, which under other circumstances would have been very affecting. As it was, I am not very sanguine of its effect upon my audience, but, like Paul's unknown tongues, it at least edified myself. . . . From Haverhill I went to Bradford, called on Father P., heard his testimony against the come-outers ; called on the come-outers and heard theirs against Father P., — listening with patient but non-committal civility to both, — urging all parties to forego their contentions and emulate each other in the good cause of Liberty. I then drove down to Griffin's ; took dinner, and then he and I started for Newbury and Newburyport, where I trust we did good service. I had a letter a day or two ago from Hale. He is to have a great meeting at Dover on the 28th inst. Do write me a line and let me know how Harriet behaves as a housekeeper and wife, and whether thee do not think her husband deserves a good deal of sympathy ! Gerrit Smith is to be in Boston next week, and will speak, I believe, in Faneuil Hall. I wish thee could see him, but of course thee would not go to such a place. It is hard enough for a well person."

TO GERRIT SMITH.

11th mo., 1845.

There is nothing to alarm us in the overwhelming numbers of the two old parties. These parties are indeed evil and only evil, in consequence of their alliance with Slavery; but they are made up of *men*, — men with warm hearts in their bosoms, men who have consciences and moral perceptions, men who have with us a common interest in the welfare and honor of the country, men, in short, who now are just what we ourselves were a few years ago, and who can be influenced by the same truths which have had their effect on our own minds. The good and true and humane among them will soon be with us; *they are coming*, with the zeal of fresh converts, with the warm love of repentant men. I confess at times when I think of the atrocities of Slavery, and of our dear friend Torrey wearing out his life in the slaveholder's dungeon, I am almost ready to call for fire from Heaven. But better is it for us that these things, instead of calling forth idle railing on our part, stimulate us to a more faithful discharge of our duty. We are told in Scripture that when Michael, the Archangel, contended with Satan about the body of Moses, he brought against his adversary no railing accusation. Let us say to those who, like that prince of slaveholders, are striving with God and nature for the possession of the bodies of two and a half millions of our countrymen, " The Lord rebuke you ! "

To the political campaigns of the early days of the Free Soil party, Whittier's satirical pen lent a spice that was highly relished by all except the victims of his good-natured raillery. Some of the poetical sallies of those times were published anonymously, but the public soon learned that there was only one man in New England capable of producing them. While John P. Hale, at the head of the Independent Democrats of New Hampshire, aided by the Liberty party, was making the canvass that finally placed him in the United States Senate, Mr. Whittier took a lively interest in the contest, and paid off in stinging verse the insults that had been heaped upon him and George Thompson in their visit to the state capital eleven years before. At the time when "A Letter " appeared in the " Boston Chronotype," in 1846, the public was so familiar with the names and doings of the politicians satirized that explanatory notes were not needed. Whittier did not openly acknowledge the " Letter " as his own until the publication of his complete works in 1888, more than forty years after it was written, and such notes were added as were needed to explain the satire to the present generation.

TO JOHN P. HALE.

16th 9th mo., 1846.

I see by the papers that thy lecture in Faneuil Hall takes place on the 18th. There is one point which I wish to call thy attention to. We want some common ground for all who love Liberty and abhor Slavery to unite upon. May it not be found in the following : —

1. Abolition of slavery the leading and paramount political question.

2. No voting for slaveholders.

3. No voting for men who are in political fellowship with slaveholders.

Why can we not have a great League of Freedom, with the above for its watchwords and rallying cry? We have eighty thousand Liberty voters to begin with, and a majority of both the old parties are well-nigh ready to join in such a movement. Think of it. I notice that the English Liberal papers, Birmingham "Pilot," London "Non-Conformist," etc., have an eye on the New Hampshire movement, and think of it as a most encouraging fact in favor of the Rights of Man. In the late meeting of the British Anti-Slavery Society, Joseph Sturge, the President of the Free Suffrage Union, alluded to thy course with great satisfaction. The Editor of the "Democratic Record" has spoken of Sturge as the noblest and purest of the democracy of England.

The tribute to the memory of N. P. Rogers, written by Mr. Whittier in 1847, which appears in his prose works, shows the warmth of his attachment to that most brilliant of the early anti-slavery editors. One of the first letters of appreciation and encouragement Whittier received after publishing the pamphlet "Justice and Expediency," in 1833, was from Rogers, who invited him to his mountain home in the valley of the Pemigewasset. Their first personal acquaintance was two years afterward, when Whittier, accompanied by George Thompson (whom he had been hiding from the mob in the seclusion of his East Haverhill home), drove to Plymouth, N. H., and had a most cordial and hospitable reception. Thompson considered Rogers the most brilliant man he had met in America. The friendship thus begun was for a few years (from 1840 to 1846) clouded by the contest to which reference has elsewhere been made, growing out of the fact that Whittier could not follow the policy of Garrison and Rogers, in actively supporting several reforms not necessarily connected with the anti-slavery movement, and they could not follow him into the field of politics. But in the early summer of 1846, Mr. Whittier learned that Rogers was ill, had met with losses of property and friends, and he wrote him a letter full of hearty sympathy. To this letter he received a prompt reply, dated Concord, June 8, 1846, and a short extract from it may be found in Whittier's tribute to his memory referred to above.

It will be seen that up to 1847 Mr. Whittier's labors upon nearly all the newspapers he had edited had been interfered with and suspended on account of the delicacy of his health. From none of them had he received a salary exceeding five hundred dollars a year; and yet he had managed, with the help of small sums paid for his services as secretary of anti-slavery societies, to support himself and the family dependent upon him, without incurring debt.   Neither his books nor his poems had been a source of income to him, although his name had become well known throughout the country as a poet, as well as a reformer operating in the field of politics.   His eye had been single to the cause he had espoused, and all his powers had been concentrated upon it.   The North was ringing with his passionate outbursts against slavery, and the Liberty party he had helped to organize had begun to trouble the old parties, as it was at times holding the balance of power between them.   It had been decided by the American and Foreign Anti-Slavery Society, which had not been successful with the newspaper organs it had established in New York, to start a weekly paper in Washington, that should commend itself to the public by its literary as well as its political character.   A fund was raised that would insure its publication one year, and the management of it was confided to Dr. Gamaliel Bailey, who had been for eleven years editing the Cincinnati " Philanthropist," the first anti-slavery paper published in the West, founded by James G. Birney, in 1836. This paper, says Grace Greenwood, was issued with regularity, during mob intervals.   Three times its office was sacked, press and types thrown into the Ohio, and all concerned in its publication threatened with outrage and death.   In 1841 the city was disgraced by wild pro-slavery riots, the fury of the mob, when presses gave out, being vented on colored people.   The fourth press stood, for Salmon P. Chase and Tom Corwin, then gov-

ernor of the State, stood beside it and protected
it. Dr. Bailey began the publication of the " Era "
in January, 1847, and the next year he confronted
a terrible mob in Washington with the same spirit
he had displayed in Cincinnati. For three days
his office was besieged, but the city had an efficient
mayor, and he was protected. Leading citizens,
however, urged the doctor to restore peace to the
city and secure his own safety by pledging himself to discontinue the " Era," and surrender his
press to the mob. He refused to surrender any
right he possessed as an American citizen. On
the night of the third day, his house was besieged.
He sent his children and servants to a place of
safety, and with his wife confronted the angry
populace. When called upon to surrender, he
came out upon the front steps and stood there,
a fair mark for pistol shots. He said, " I am Dr.
Bailey. What is your wish? " The surrender
of his property was demanded, the alternative being a coat of tar and feathers, the materials for
which were paraded before him. He asked to be
heard in his own defense, and made a speech that
completely changed the feeling of the mob. He
was not afterwards threatened with violence.

A position was now offered Mr. Whittier which
would permit him to do all his literary work at
his home in Amesbury, under conditions more favorable for his health than was possible away from
the ministrations of his devoted mother and sister.
With his editorial labors, home cares, and other
demands, he was very closely occupied, and it is
pleasant to find him in the autumn of 1847 taking

a little rest with his Cartland cousins, at Lee, N. H., whence Elizabeth writes to her cousin Gertrude Whittier: "Just a week ago Greenleaf and I came over here. It is quiet and lovely all about. There was never a season of such glorious fall fruitage, and from my windows the view is beautiful — the greenness of June crowning these September woods and fields. I wish thee could join us this morning, there are so few of us, and I have strong family ties. I should never object to the plan of *clanship*, only I would like to exclude a few. Greenleaf has a prospect of being at the Buffalo convention, and, as it now seems, thy own great-hearted townsman, John P. Hale, will be our candidate for the Presidency."

In September, 1846, at a Whig convention in Faneuil Hall, Stephen C. Phillips offered an anti-slavery resolve which was rejected, and this resolve was defended in a speech by Charles Sumner. Whittier wrote his poem "The Pine Tree" immediately upon reading the proceedings of this convention. It contains the lines: —

"Where 's the *man* for Massachusetts! where 's the voice to speak
　　her free ?
Where 's the hand to light up bonfires from the mountain to the
　　sea ?
Beats her Pilgrim pulse no longer ? Sits she dumb in her despair ?
Has she none to break the silence ? Has she none to do and dare ?
O my God! for one right worthy to lift up her rusted shield,
And to plant again the Pine Tree in her banner's tattered field! "

This poem he inclosed in a note to Charles Sumner, which reads as follows: —

"I have just read the proceedings of your Whig convention, and the lines inclosed are a feeble expression of my feelings. I look upon the rejection of S. C. P.'s resolutions as an evidence that the end and aim of the managers of the convention was to go just far enough to scare the *party*, and no further. All thanks for the free voices of thyself, Phillips, Allen, and Adams. Notwithstanding the result, you have not spoken in vain. If thee thinks well enough of these verses hand them to the 'Whig' or 'Chronotype.' "

To this letter Sumner replied: —

" We do not despair. We are all alive to wage the fight another day, and feel that more was done than we had hoped to do. Our vote was strong; but it was at an hour when many had gone home by the early trains, whose presence would have made it stronger. Many who were present did not vote, and they were undoubtedly with us. The ball has been put in motion; it cannot be stopped. Hard words are said of us in State Street. I am grateful to you for your note of encouragement. The poem is beautiful, and must be printed."

The following letters, written as he was entering upon his connection with the paper, indicate also his activity in political affairs.

TO JOHN P. HALE.

12th mo., 18, 1846.

We are about starting our " National Era " at Washington, and should be glad of a note of encouragement from thee. Is it asking too much to request thee to drop me a line, as one of the editors, to this effect? We shall have similar letters

from others for our first number. We mean to
make the paper worthy of the best of causes, —
the cause of humanity, the Democracy of the New
Testament. So the pro-slavery Democrats have
troubles yet in their Israel. Who is Esquire
Marston? Is he a man to stick to his point and
show fight? . . . Webster and his two hopeful
sons, I see, are going for the war. Your New
Hampshire Whigs were in too much of a hurry to
nominate him.

TO ANN E. WENDELL.

2d mo., 21, 1847.

What a sad state of things in Ireland! We
have been trying to do something in this region.
Our little meeting here has raised about fifty dollars. The people of other denominations are also
moving. The cheerfulness with which almost
everybody contributes to this object looks well for
human nature. Oh, surely there is good in all;
the hardest heart is not wholly stone. The heart
that can sympathize with human suffering and
yearn to relieve it cannot be wholly depraved.
The longer I live, I see the evil in myself in a
clearer light, and more that is good in others;
and if I do not grow better, I am constrained to
be more charitable. I shudder sometimes at my
fierce rebukes of erring-doers, when I consider
my own weakness and sins of omission as well
as commission. . . . Our paper at Washington
[the "National Era"] will doubtless succeed. I
should have gone on this winter but for the state
of my health, and the difficulty of leaving home
on my mother's account. I write but little for it,

and have not been able to revise or correct that little. But, if in the Providence of God I am not to do much more for the cause of freedom, I am deeply grateful for the privilege I have enjoyed of giving the strength of my youth and manhood to it. The cause is destined to triumph ; and present appearances indicate that the triumph is near. . . . The action of the Pennsylvania legislature in relation to fugitive slaves is most gratifying. The exertions of the Committee of the Meeting for Sufferings undoubtedly contributed much to this result. Oh, that our Friends generally would feel their great responsibility in this matter. They have influence sufficient to change the whole legislation of the country, if it was only fully exercised. . . . I have of late been able to write but little, and that mostly for the papers, and I have scarcely answered a letter for a month past. I dread to touch a pen. Whenever I do it increases the dull wearing pain in my head, which I am scarcely ever free from. . . . I was very sorry to hear of thy mother's illness. Mother ! how much there is in that word ! If there is one earthly blessing for which more than another I feel thankful, it is that she is still spared to me to whom I can apply that endearing name.

TO JOHN P. HALE.

30th 7th mo., 1847.

Inclosed is a letter prepared and signed by a committee chosen at our conference the other day at East Boston. Farther reflection has convinced me that so far from throwing obstacles in thy way in the Senate the nomination would give a much stronger position, and besides it would have the effect to set at rest the stories of the Radicals and the fears of some of the Independent Democrats in other States, that thou art playing into the hands of the Whigs ; and thus thou wouldst be able to act more effectively upon the people, irrespective of party. As for the Whigs, depend upon it they will have no cause of dissatisfaction, if they see that thy new position enables thee more effectively to act upon the pro-slavery Democracy. Show them this, and they will not complain. I am naturally anxious that thy answer should be such a one as shall render the vote for thee in our convention entirely unanimous. It will not be published, but will be used at the convention, and sent in manuscript to a few of our leading friends in other States.

Pardon me for a suggestion or two. It is important that it should be understood that thou art disconnected entirely from the two old parties ; at the same time it would be right and proper for thee to avow thy Democratic faith in the doctrines of Jefferson, Leggett, and Sedgwick — the true and righteous democracy of Christianity. In regard to thy anti-slavery views : Perhaps if thou wast to copy the principal resolutions of the Newmarket convention, held a year ago, as expressive of thy sentiments, it would be well. Thee might close by avowing these as thy principles, and that if they coincide with those of the gentlemen addressing thee, and their friends generally, they are at liberty to use thy name at the convention. I take it for granted that thy answer will be favor-

able. The whole West will be shaken by thy
nomination. Dr. Bailey is sure of great accessions
from the Democratic and Whig ranks. We will
try for twenty thousand votes in Massachusetts
alone, and unless all indications are fallacious shall
get them. If agreeable to thee, I will ride over to
Dover with friend Tuck, at such time as may
suit thy convenience — only let it be soon as possible — and we can see thy answer, and perhaps
make some suggestions previous to its being sent.
Or, I will meet thee at the Cartlands' at Lee ; or,
still better, wilt thou not ride over to Amesbury?
. . . The Whigs of New Hampshire, if they are
looking for anything better than a slaveholder for
candidate, will be disappointed. Taylor will be
urged by the hurrah boys of both parties, at the
North and by the entire South. I have more hope
of the Democrats than of the Whigs in the coming
election. They are bolder, freer, and less influenced by conservatism. Still the young Whigs of
Massachusetts and Ohio will unquestionably vote
the Liberty ticket, with thee as the candidate.

TO THE SAME.

2d 10th mo., 1847.

Ere this I suppose the result of the convention
at Buffalo has reached thee. If not already, thou
wilt soon be officially informed of it, when it will
be expected of thee that thy position will be de-
fined. In thy case, the boldest course is the safest.
The Whigs are training Corwin and McLean to
go as far as possible towards Liberty principles
without actually reaching them. They will strive

to make it appear that they are more ultra than the anti-slavery candidate himself. On the other hand, the New York and western Democrats are preparing to bring out either Benton or C. C. Cambreling, or John A. Dix, as the opponent of slavery extension. The two latter are prepared to go great lengths in denunciation of slavery. The Whigs of New Hampshire will as readily go for an ultra-abolitionist, as a half one, while they would be glad of the excuse for going for Corwin or Judge McLean, that they were ready to go farther than thyself in opposition to slavery. A bold, thorough-going letter at this time from thy pen would awaken too deep an interest and enthusiasm among all classes of anti-slavery men to be set aside by the stratagems of the two old parties. I trust thee will not permit thyself to be troubled with " constitutional " difficulties. The Constitution has been a mere ruse of war in the hands of Slavery for half a century. It has been made to say and be just what the South wished. We must take it out of the custody of slavery, and construe it in the light of Liberty, — " as we understand it." We must bring it up out of the land of bondage, just as David did the ark from the Philistines to Obed-Edom. At all events, with the Constitution, or without the Constitution, *Slavery must die.* If, however, on full reflection, thou art not prepared to take the difficult and trying position proffered thee, I would not ask thee to accept the nomination. If it seems on the whole better and wiser for thee to enter the Senate entirely independent of all parties, I would not urge thee to take upon

thyself the responsibility we offer thee. I am
sorry the nomination was made this fall. At our
Essex County meeting, held the week before, I
procured the passage of a resolution suggesting
that deference should be had to the opinion of our
friends in New Hampshire and Ohio in respect to
deferring the nomination, and wrote the convention to that effect, being unable to attend. I have
volunteered this hasty letter from motives which
I trust thou wilt appreciate. Were I not confined
by ill health to my house, I should try to see thee.
As it is, I could do no less than drop thee a line
expressive of my feelings. Thy letter will be
looked for with great interest. If it is, as I trust
it will be, bold, pointed, and explicit, — if it not
only sustains the Wilmot Proviso, but, looking beyond that temporary measure, aims at the life of
slavery itself, and points out the duty of the Free
States in this crisis, to make the anti-slavery question first and paramount, — it will rally a mighty
host of true hearts around thee as Liberty's stand-
ard-bearer. If it fall short of this, it will be
greatly to be regretted, and by no one more sincerely, both as respects thyself and the cause, than
by thy sincere friend.

TO THE SAME.

11th 8th mo., 1847.

I wrote thee a hasty line the other day with
reference to the Buffalo nomination. I sincerely
hope thou wilt not feel thyself called upon to decline that nomination. Since I wrote thee I have
had letters from New York and elsewhere, all

highly animated, and encouraging as to the prospect of a large vote in 1848. Everywhere the nomination is received with enthusiasm by the Liberty men; and many influential Whigs and Democrats are regarding it with favor. The " Era" of last week contains an article originating in a Democratic paper in New York, and which has been copied into several other prints of the same stamp, suggesting that it would be well for the Democracy of the North to rally under thy nomination. Everything, in short, looks favorable, beyond our hopes. Our election took place to-day. When I left the polls the governor vote was not declared. That for representative in Amesbury stood, Liberty 103, Whig 99, Democratic 87. The Cushing vote will be small.

Mr. Whittier began his work as corresponding editor of the " National Era " with the first number issued, and continued in this position until 1860, a few months after the death of his associate and friend, Dr. Bailey. During the first years of his connection with the " Era " his contributions were to be found in nearly every number, and related to a great variety of subjects. They included poems that are still regarded as his best; reviews of work of his brother authors; comments upon public affairs, sometimes quite elaborate; letters from Amesbury and Boston about the progress of the cause in New England; and quaint and curious results of antiquarian research. He did not occupy any particular department, but his articles were scattered about the paper, in editorial or other columns, as it might happen, usually signed with his initials. The first number contained his noble tribute to "Randolph of Roanoke," a sketch of the life of Thomas Ellwood, and a letter from Amesbury, dealing with New Hampshire politics and rejoicing in the gallant and successful fight of John P. Hale. He likened Hale to the brave-hearted Indian, Hiarcormes, who trampled on the sacred medicine bag, and thus broke the spell of the medicine man who was frightening the con-verts of Eliot back to idolatry. "Hale's experi-ment was in its way equal to that of old Hiar-cormes. Slavery has come to be regarded a very sacred and democratic institution, to interfere with which was to incur political death. Hale has rudely touched it, and still lives."

There is occasionally a number of the "Era" that contains eight or nine columns of Mr. Whit-tier's writing. One after another he introduces to the public, with eulogistic comment, young writers who have since become popular favorites. Now it is a good word for Lucy Larcom, then for Alice and Phœbe Cary, Grace Greenwood, and others. These became regular contributors to the "Era." His life-long friendship for Bayard Taylor had its origin in his copying "The Norse-man's Ride" from the "Democratic Review" (in which it had appeared anonymously), prefacing it with hearty commendation. He did not then know the name of the writer he was praising, nor could he have guessed that his notice would be the beginning of a long and happy friendship.

We find among the papers Mr. Whittier preserved with care the first letter he received from his young friend, whose work he had praised, written from Phœnixville, Pa., September 16, 1847 : —

I know you will understand the feeling which prompts me, though a stranger, to address you, and pardon any liberties I may have taken in so doing. I was surprised and delighted a few weeks ago to see in the "National Era," in connection with a notice of the old Northern mythology, a poem of mine, "The Norseman's Ride," which was published last winter in the "Democratic Review." I am an enthusiastic admirer of the stirring Scandinavian Sagas, some of which Tegnér has immortalized in his Frithiof; and it was under the full influence of the spirit inspired by them that the poem was written. I was *possessed* by the subject and fancied I had given it fitting expression, but the friends to whom I showed it did not admire it, and I reluctantly concluded that my heated fancies had led my judgment astray, and made up my mind to forget it. Judge, then, how grateful and encouraging was your generous commendation. I thank you sincerely and from my heart for the confidence your words have given me. One day, I hope, I shall be able to take your hand, and tell you what happiness it is to be understood by one whom the world calls by the sacred name of poet. With every wish for your happiness and prosperity, I am, with sincere respect and esteem,

    Your friend,   J. BAYARD TAYLOR.

In examining files of the " Era " we come frequently upon poems that were adding steadily and
cumulatively to the reputation of their author, like
" Barclay of Ury," " Angels of Buena Vista,"
" Maud Muller," " Angel of Patience," " The
Crisis," " The Hill-Top," " A Sabbath Scene,"
" Burns," " Mary Garvin," " Tauler," " The Her-
mit's Chapel " (afterwards called " Chapel of the
Hermits "), and " The Prisoners of Naples." A
few weeks after Webster's 7th of March
speech, the terrible poem " Ichabod " is seen at
the head of a conspicuous column. That number
of the " Era " (May 2, 1850) must have caused
a sensation in Washington. Daniel Webster responded to it indirectly by a letter to certain citizens of Newburyport, in reply to an address by
Horace Mann. In this letter he said that the
views expressed in his 7th of March speech were
approved *by the great body of the Society of
Friends*. Whittier's reply to the claim is in the
" Era " of June 20, and in it he makes peremp-
tory denial of the statement, and brings forward
conclusive proof that the Quakers as a body disapprove of Webster's position. In this article he
speaks for the Friends in New England, and in
the next paper he says : —

" It has been suggested, that whatever might be
our opinion, or that of the Friends of New England, we had no right to speak for those of Pennsylvania, to whom the author of the letter may be
supposed to refer more immediately. We have,
however, abundant proofs of the correctness of our
statement, as applied to Pennsylvania Friends.

It is notorious that for the last half century the latter have been the friends and advisers of the colored people; and whenever a slave case was before the courts of law they have been found standing between the oppressors and the oppressed; and when the decision was against the latter, they have submitted only with the deepest sympathy for the slave, and abhorrence of the law which consigned him to hopeless bondage."

He quotes Webster's assertion that fugitives are arrested and carried away into slavery from Pennsylvania without complaint or excitement, and shows by extracts from Quaker periodicals and minutes of the Yearly Meeting that the Friends in that State were profoundly stirred by the attempt to repeal the state law granting jury trial to fugitive slaves. His two years' residence in Pennsylvania had qualified him to speak for that State as well as Massachusetts.

Mr. Whittier's second visit to Washington was in December, 1845, when, in company with Henry Wilson, he was delegated by a Liberty party convention to carry to Congress a petition containing 60,000 names against the annexation of Texas. It was after a visit to a slave prison in that city that he wrote the poem " At Washington."

He again visited Washington in February, 1848, and a few days before the death of John Quincy Adams had an interview with that statesman, of which he gave some account in the " Era " of April 13. Adams said he longed to see our government take a step which would place a seal of national disapprobation on the institution of slavery. On the 23d of February, the very day of the death of Adams, Whittier wrote to Charles Sumner from Washington as follows : —

" Ere this thou hast doubtless heard of the sudden illness of the venerable Adams. At a late hour last night he was still living, but sinking fast. I have not heard this morning. His death will be the fitting end of such a glorious life. Falling at his post, dying with his harness on, in the capitol so often shaken by his noble battle for freedom! My eyes fill with tears, but the emotion is not unmingled with a feeling of joy that such a man should thus pass from us. A few days ago I had a highly interesting conversation with him. All his old vigor seemed to reanimate him when he touched the subject of slavery. I shall never forget that interview. Even if now living, he cannot survive through the day. . . . An election will of course take place in his district. There is a feeling among our friends here that his place should be worthily filled. Who so proper, then, as his son, Charles Francis Adams ? He is virtually a resident of the district. Think of it, dear S., — think what a glorious thing it would be to see the vacant seat of the elder Adams so well filled. . . . Look at the article in the ' Era' this week on Yucatan. I have had an opportunity to acquaint myself with the object of the Yucatan commissioner. Cannot the fact of the rejection of his overtures for the admission of a *free* State be used in favor of liberty, and against the doughfaces of the North ? "

The article upon Yucatan to which reference is

made affirms that the administration turned a cold shoulder upon Yucatan, because the constitution of that State prohibits slavery. After his return to Amesbury, in March, 1848, Mr. Whittier wrote in commendation of a letter by Horace Mann, then member of Congress from Massachusetts, saying he does not know Mann, and asking if he is really all that his letter indicates. Sumner's reply must have been satisfactory, for Whittier writes : —

"I am glad to hear thy report of Horace Mann. I trust he will equal thy hopes. . . . What a glorious change in the Old World. I feel almost like going to France myself, and would if I could do anything more than gratify my own feelings by so doing. The position of Lamartine, Arago, and their colleagues, is a sublime one, but its responsibility is terrible. My friend Joseph Sturge, of Birmingham, who has just returned from a visit to Paris, places great confidence in them. He writes me that they are determined to put an end to slavery at once. He found them busily at work, greatly worn and prostrated by their severe and protracted labors. The sympathy of all friends of liberty should be with them. I wish our legislature, in its congratulations of France, would specially allude to the abolition of slavery. I have not seen whether the resolves have passed or not. 'Hale's proviso' ought to be attached to them." [1]

[1] When the United States Senate was considering the resolutions congratulating France upon securing a republican form of government, in April, 1848, Senator Hale moved to insert a clause commending the French government for "manifesting the sincerity of their purpose by instituting measures for the immediate

Here is an earnest letter of advice given in the political crisis of 1848, when the Whig party was divided over the nomination of Zachary Taylor. The "Cotton" Whigs went for Taylor, and the "Conscience" Whigs had called a convention to decide upon the course they should adopt. Whittier wrote to Sumner from Amesbury, June 20 : —

"In the mean time, what will the New York Barnburners do? Is there no hope of uniting with them, and erecting on the ruins of the old parties the great party of Christian Democracy and Progress? Why try to hold on to these old parties, even in name? . . . It strikes me that it would be best not to make a nomination at Worcester, but to appoint delegates to a general convention of the friends of Freedom and Free Soil, without distinction of party, the time and place of which not to be fixed before consultation with friends of the movement in other States. Don't stultify yourselves by boasting of your Whiggery. That died when Taylor was nominated. Judge Allen is right: the Whig party is dissolved. Let your emancipated friends now rise to the sublime altitude of men who labor for the race, for humanity. Send out from your convention, if you will, a long and careful statement of the facts in the case, but with it also an appeal to the people which shall reach and waken into

emancipation of the slaves in all the colonies of the republic." The American Senate, at this time, was hardly in the mood to consider this proposition seriously. Samuel S. Phelps, of Vermont, was the only Senator who stood by Hale in voting for it. This was the " proviso " to which Whittier referred in his letter to Sumner, as one that the state legislature ought to adopt.

vigorous life all that remains of weakness in the
North. Kindle up the latent enthusiasm of the
Yankee character, call out the grim fanaticism of
the Puritan. Dare! *dare!* DARE! as Danton told
the French ; that is the secret of successful revolt.
Oh, for a man! There is the difficulty, after all.
Who is to head the movement? Hale has many
of the martial qualities of a leader. As a stump
orator he is second only to John Van Buren, who,
by the bye, I would far rather see in nomination
for the Presidency than his father, or Judge Mc-
Lean. It would be folly and suicide to nominate a
shrinking conservative, whose heart is not with
you, and whom you must drag up to your level by
main force. . . . You must have a new and bold
man, one to whom old notions and practices on the
question of slavery are like threads of tow, breaking with the first movement of his limbs. But
this advice, however well-meant on my part, is
doubtless not needed. You have strong and noble
men, — Adams, Howe, Phillips, Wilson, Hoar,
Allen, and others. I only wish you had the power
of the French provisional government; I could
answer for the wisdom of your decrees."

In his reply to this letter Sumner said : —

"Things tend to Van Buren as our candidate;
I am willing to take him. With him we can break
the slave power : that is our first aim. We can
have a direct issue on the subject of slavery. We
hope that McLean will be Vice-President. Truly,
success seems to be within our reach. I never
supposed that I should belong to a successful
party."

On the 6th of December, 1848, Sumner wrote to Whittier, whose poem "The Wish of To-Day" had just appeared in the "Era:" —

"Your poem in the last 'Era' has touched my heart. May God preserve you in strength and courage for all good works! . . . The literature of the world is turning against slavery. We shall have it soon in a state of moral blockade. I admire Dr. Bailey as an editor very much. His articles show infinite sagacity and tact. . . . But I took my pen merely to inquire after your health. There are few to whom I would allot a larger measure of the world's blessings than to yourself, had I any control, for there are few who deserve them more."

The attitude taken by Whittier in the strait through which the political movement against slavery passed in the formation of the Free Soil party, at the time of the Buffalo convention of 1848, is shown in the following letter to Dr. Wm. F. Channing, who was an alternate delegate from Boston to the convention. It was dated July 1, 1848. Whittier's suggestion that Channing should write to Van Buren was adopted, but the wily ex-President made no reply : —

"Providence permitting, I will be with you on the 19th. In the mean time I can only add that I cannot vote for Van Buren in his present attitude, yet I greatly fear that the Buffalo convention will affirm his nomination, and that Hale will decline, as indeed he has a right to do when his party abandon him. What can be done? Van Buren is too old a sinner to hope for his conversion. Had the

Barnburners nominated John Van Buren, I would have gone for him, for he is not bound to vindicate his consistency in evil, and he is a man of *progress*. Even now, if the Conscience Whigs so will it, he might be substituted for his father, and thus all parties might unite. I see no other way. As things now stand we are likely to lose our candidate, for self-respect alone and self-preservation would induce him to withdraw his name from a divided and dissolving party.

"Would it not be well for some one — I think thee are the very person to do it — to address an earnest letter to Martin Van Buren, stating the strong desire felt to effect a union of all parties opposed to the usurpations of slavery — putting the question plainly to him whether he is willing and prepared to stand at the head of such a movement, and give his sanction to all legal and constitutional means for the limitation and overthrow of slavery. Write to him in behalf of eighty thousand Liberty voters. It is important that we should know positively how he stands. The Whigs generally, I think, will prefer Van Buren to Hale, strange as it may seem. For one, I cannot and will not go blindly and rashly into the support of such a candidate as Van Buren — let Conscience Whigs and Western Liberty men do as they will."

TO MOSES A. CARTLAND.

27th 7th mo., 1848.

I would like to go to the Buffalo convention, but my health forbids the idea. What will be done there? I would go for Van Buren — if Hale decline — if he would come out in favor of abolition in the District of Columbia. But I will never vote for him until I know that he has taken a new position on that point. How we should look if Van Buren were elected by our votes, and should veto a bill to abolish the most infernal slave market this side of Tophet! No, no. I will vote alone before I will so stultify myself and disgrace the cause. I give Van Buren all due credit for his stand against the extension of slavery; but if we may judge by his own letter, while all the world has been making progress in liberal principles, he remains just where he was in 1836. If the Buffalo convention are wise they will nominate John P. Hale; or if not, compel Van Buren or his friends for him to define his position. After having been brayed in the mortar of slavery he must be stupider than Solomon's fool if he is still disposed to act the part of a " Northern man with Southern principles." The Free Soil movement — the *animus* of it — the spirit and life which it infuses into the people — is indeed glorious. I hope much from it, and will do all I can to urge it forward. How nobly Hale behaves! His last speech is spoken of as admirable in the New York papers. I wish the Barnburners could be induced to go for him.

TO GRACE GREENWOOD.

5th mo., 10, 1849.

We have had a dreary spring — a gray haze in the sky — a dim, beam-shorn sun — a wind from the northeast, cold as if sifted through all the ices of frozen Labrador, as terrible almost as that chill

wind which the old Moslem fable says will blow
over the earth in the last days. The birds here-
about have a sorry time of it, as well as " humans."
There are now, however, indications of a change
for the better. The blossoms of the peach and
cherry are just opening, and the arbutus, anemones,
and yellow violets are making glad and beautiful
the banks of our river. I feel daily like thanking
God for the privilege of looking upon another spring.
I have written very little this spring, — the " Legend of St. Mark " is all in the line of verse that I
have attempted. I feel a growing disinclination to
pen and ink. Over-worked and tired by the long
weary years of the anti-slavery struggle, I want
mental rest. I have already lived a long life, if
thought and action constitute it. I have crowded
into a few years what should have been given to
many.

In 1849, Joseph Sturge, the eminent English
philanthropist, proposed to Mr. Whittier through
Lewis Tappan that he visit England, offering to
pay all the expenses of the journey. Mr. Whittier
replied to Mr. Tappan, under date of July 14,
1849 : —

" I have been spending some weeks in the northern part of New Hampshire, and thy kind note
relative to our friend Sturge's proposition, re-
ceives my earliest notice on my return. I wish it
were possible for me to avail myself of so generous an offer ; but in my present very weak state
of health, I could be of no real service to the cause,
without making exertions to which my strength is

inadequate. If I could visit Europe as a mere looker-on, careless and indifferent in respect to the great questions which agitate it, I might possibly be benefited by it. But this I cannot do, and I can ill bear any additional excitement. But, believe me, I feel none the less grateful to our dear and generous friend Sturge, and to thyself for your kindness.

"I am glad to hear that thou art now a 'free laborer' in the cause of freedom, and peace, and humanity. I have often marveled at the vast amount of labor performed by thee in addition to thy daily and engrossing business, in behalf of these objects; and for thy sake as well as for theirs, I am glad thou art able to bear what Charles Lamb calls 'the dull drudgery of the desk's hard wood.' Thou wilt, I apprehend, find no lack of occupation. The church is not yet right on the question of slavery. The nominal orthodoxy of the land has sorely suffered through the conduct of its leaders in opposing the cause of practical righteousness. No man can do more than thyself to change this state of things. The Free Mission movement has already done immense good; the old boards will all be compelled soon to take the same ground and maintain it.

"Then in the matter of political action, strong as is my confidence in the good intentions of the great mass of Free Soilers, and well satisfied as I am with the result of their labors thus far, I am not without fear that they may be drawn into some unworthy compromise. We need all thy vigilance and wisdom to keep us straight in the line of principle. I do not fear for the integrity of the old Liberty men, the mob-tried, church-censured confessors of '35 and '36. They may get off the track now and then, but their instincts will set them right. But we are now all abolitionists; it is as difficult to find an open pro-slavery man now as it was in '33 to find an anti-slavery one; yet I have scarcely charity enough to suppose that this marvelous conversion is altogether genuine and heartfelt. The responsibilities of the cause never rested heavier on the genuine old-fashioned abolitionists than at this time. I feel extremely anxious about the result of the attempt to unite the Barnburners with the old Hunkers in your State. If they can come together on the basis of the Vermont resolutions I shall hope for the best.

"The next Congress will settle the California and New Mexico question. I look forward with hope not wholly unmingled with fear. Can thee not spend a few weeks at Washington this winter? Depend upon it, there will be ample opportunity for the profitable exercise of all thy powers. Dr. Bailey [of the 'National Era'] is confined to his office; there must be some one always there to supply the members with necessary facts, for they are all sadly ignorant in this matter. But alas, I am laying out work for others, while I am myself well-nigh powerless! What Providence has in store for me I know not, but my heart is full of thankfulness that I have been permitted to do something for the cause of humanity, and that with all my sins and errors I have not been suffered to live wholly for myself.

"I saw the Rogers family at Plymouth. They spoke of thee with affectionate warmth. Kind, gifted, amiable, they have all the pleasant traits of their father; but the conduct of some of the church and clergy in respect to him has made them skeptical, and prejudiced them against the forms of religious observances."

In 1848, after the Buffalo convention that nominated Van Buren, the Liberty party had high hopes from the division of the Democratic party in New York, and Whittier wrote his " Pæan " with the feeling that the North was at last thoroughly aroused, and that the encroachments of slavery would be stopped. But it was found that the North was not quite ready for a full revolt. It was necessary to fill the measure of its humiliation by the passage of the fugitive slave law; and even that was not enough, as the event proved.

The " Era " had become self-supporting in the first year of its existence. Some of its readers objected to the stories, sketches of travel, and poems that had no reference to the cause in which they were interested, but Dr. Bailey informed them that it was this literary element that kept the enterprise afloat, and he should continue to draw upon it. Of course, there was no complaint from any anti-slavery reader, while " Uncle Tom's Cabin, or Life among the Lowly," was appearing as a serial, in 1851–52. Even readers principled against novels could not resist the fascination of that remarkable story, which was coming out in weekly installments, while the operations of the fugitive slave law were exciting a deep feeling of indignation throughout the North. Whittier's charming sketch of character and manners in the ancient times of New England, which, while it was appearing in the "Era," had for its title, "Stray Leaves from Margaret Smith's Diary, in the Colony of Massachusetts," was published as a serial in 1848, and was reprinted in book form in 1849, with the title "Margaret Smith's Journal." While this volume was in press, Mr. Whittier wrote the following letter to J. T. Fields, in regard to a proposed portrait of Rebecca Rawson, and the matter of following the ancient system of capitalization, which had been adopted in the original publication of the work as a serial in the "Era," but was discarded in the book. The letter was dated December 12, 1848 :

"I send herewith the engraving of R. Rawson, taken after her abandonment by her husband. She was about twenty-one when married, and about thirty-five when she died. The picture represents her at the latter age. As an authentic picture of the heroine of the 'Journal' it might be well to have it in the book. I begin to have some fears that the capitals will be a little too thick for a handsome page. It was not an invariable rule to use them at that time — in fact there was no rule about it. You can scarce find two books of the middle of the seventeenth century alike in spelling and lettering. Just get a proof of one or two pages, and see how it looks. If it is likely to disfigure the page, strike out most of them, and let us have the more important words capitalized."

As originally published in the "Era," the episode

of the wandering Milesian schoolmaster, O'Shane, with his ballad "Kathleen," does not appear in this story. It was sent to Mr. Fields to be inserted when the book was in press, and three of the best stanzas were an afterthought, as will be seen by the following letter, dated January 3, 1849 : —

"That rascally old ballad occurred to my mind last evening, and it struck me that it wanted something, although already too long. The following verses might do to follow (I quote from memory) the verse

> "'He tore his beard so gray ;
> But he was old and she was young,
> And so she had her way'—
>
> "'Sure that same night the Banshee howled
> To fright the evil dame,
> And fairy folks who loved Kathleen
> With funeral torches came.
>
> "She watched them gleaming through the trees,
> And glimmering down the hill;
> They crept before the dead-vault door,
> And then they all stood still !
>
> "'Get up, old man ! the wake-lights shine !'
> 'Ye murthering witch,' quoth he,
> 'So I 'm rid of your tongue I little care
> If they shine for you or me !'"

I think there is a touch of nature — old Adam's — in the last verse, but if it is too late let it pass. . . . The weather this morning is cold enough for an Esquimaux purgatory — terrible."

Soon after the publication of "Margaret Smith's Journal," in March, 1849, Rev. Theodore Parker wrote the following letter to Mr. Whittier : —

" Your little book of ' Leaves from Margaret Smith's Journal' emboldens me to write and ask you if you would not furnish for the ' Massachusetts Quarterly Review' a paper on the Servants, i. e., the *White Slaves*, which our fathers brought to New England, or otherwise acquired, and held in most wicked bondage. I know how well you have studied the subject of our early history, and suppose that it would not be so laborious for you as for me to do the work. The subject is new ; the matter little known, little thought of, yet it is interesting and highly important. If you will be good enough to inform me whether you will do so or not, you will much oblige me. I should not want the paper before the middle of October."

Mr. Whittier was unable to furnish the article called for. But twenty years later, in " Marguerite," and in the preface he prepared for that poem, he has referred to the subject, and also in a letter he wrote in regard to " Evangeline." Before Longfellow considered the matter of writing " Evangeline," Whittier had made a study of the history of the banishment of the Acadians, and had intended to write upon it, but he put it off until he found that Hawthorne was thinking about it, and had suggested it to Longfellow. After the appearance of " Evangeline," Mr. Whittier was glad of his delay, for he said : —

" Longfellow was just the one to write it. If I had attempted it I should have spoiled the artistic effect of the poem by my indignation at the treatment of the exiles by the Colonial Government, who had a very hard lot after coming to this country. Families were separated and scattered about, only a few of them being permitted to remain in any given locality. The children were bound out to the families in the localities in which they resided, and I wrote a poem upon finding, in the records of Haverhill, the indenture that bound an Acadian girl as a servant in one of the families of that neighborhood. Gathering the story of her death I wrote ' Marguerite.' "

The biographical sketches entitled " Old Portraits " were among Mr. Whittier's contributions to the " National Era," and also some of the papers included in his " Literary Recreations." During his connection with this paper he furnished nearly ninety poems, which, as Mr. Underwood remarks, exceed in number, power, variety, and interest any series, except, perhaps, that contributed to the " Atlantic Monthly." Nathaniel Hawthorne submitted to Whittier his story of " The Great Stone Face ; " it was accepted for the " Era," and published January 24, 1850, Hawthorne receiving twenty-five dollars for it. Theodore Parker issued his powerful address " To the People of the United States," in 1848, through the columns of this paper.

As a business venture, " Margaret Smith's Journal " had proved somewhat successful, although the amount realized for it by Mr. Whittier was not large, and Mr. Fields in the summer of 1849 was urging Whittier to get out another volume of prose, to be made up of his contributions to the " National Era." While this was being considered, Whittier wrote to Fields, under date of July 30, 1849 : —

"I can't yet make up my mind, but will let thee know in the course of the next ten days, definitely. As for a title, this will nearly express the contents of the volume, 'Old Portraits and Modern Sketches.' . . . I shall send the documents for thy inspection at any rate. I have a mass of material, but it's like Chaos, without form, and, what is worse, oftentimes *void*."

At about this time, in response to a call from Mr. Fields for a contribution to an annual, Mr. Whittier wrote : —

"In regard to your 'Boston Book' I have nothing available on hand for it, either in prose or rhyme. But some years ago I wrote a story for the 'N. E. Magazine,' called 'The Opium Eater.' I have almost forgotten about it, and I dare say everybody else has *entirely;* which might be made use of as good as new. It is wholly unlike anything else of my writing, as near as I can recollect."

Mrs. E. D. E. N. Southworth began her career as a novelist with several stories written for the "Era." Mr. Whittier met her while in Washington, in 1847, and read some of her first manuscripts. "Grace Greenwood" was a frequent contributor of both prose and verse, and she began a friendly correspondence with Mr. Whittier which lasted to the end of his life. While writing for the "Era," her name appeared on the covers of a popular Philadelphia magazine as one of its editors. But as in her letters to the organ of the Liberty party she was quite outspoken on the subject of slavery, the proprietor of the magazine began to hear complaints from the South that he was employing an abolitionist, and his publication could not be received as long as Grace Greenwood was on the editorial staff, or even an occasional contributor. Acting upon his first impulse he dropped her name from the cover, with some parade of subserviency, but he found this lost him subscribers at the North, and, without consulting her, he restored it. She refused to continue in his employment. At about the same time he had the misfortune to publish his own full-length portrait as a frontispiece to the magazine. This was the origin of the stinging poem of Whittier's, "Lines on a Portrait of a Celebrated Publisher : " —

> "A greedy Northern bottle-fly
> Preserved in Slavery's amber ! "

The original title of the poem [1] was "Lines on the portrait of a celebrated publisher who has lately saved the Union, and lost a contributor."

Mr. Whittier was always quick to resent an insult to a cause that was near his heart, or an injury to a friend, but he was kind and appreciative in his editorial reviews of the works not only of his literary friends but of strangers. Helpful paragraphs about the young writers of his time are scattered through the columns of all the papers he edited or with which he corresponded. If he had occasion to criticise, it was done in such a way as

---

[1] In a letter to J. T. Fields, written October 26, 1850, Whittier encloses this poem with the remark : " I send thee ——, done after my fashion. It was written before I heard of Calhoun's illness, or I should have substituted the name of Foote." Calhoun was not mentioned by name in the poem, but referred to as " Carolina's sage."

to leave no rankling wound.   His friends, Holmes, Longfellow, and Lowell, each published volumes of poems in 1849, and of each he wrote elaborate reviews.   That of Holmes comes under the head of " Mirth and Medicine."   In his review of Lowell he selects " The Present Crisis" as the noblest poem in the collection.   He speaks of Longfellow as " one of the sweetest poets of our time," and has especial praise for " The Fire of Driftwood " and " Resignation."

The poem " Our State," published in the " Era " in 1849, was originally entitled " Dedication of a Schoolhouse," and was written for the dedicatory services of the high school building in Newbury, Mass.   An address was delivered on that occasion by Rev. Dr. Leonard Withington, and Whittier's hymn was sung by the assembly.   The first two lines as originally published were : —

> " The South-land hath its fields of cane,
> The prairie boasts its heavy grain."

This was afterwards changed to : —

> " The South-land boasts its teeming cane,
> The prairied West its heavy grain."

CHAPTER VIII.

1850–1856.

No comprehensive edition of Whittier's poems had been published before 1849, when B. B. Mussey & Co. of Boston gave them to the public in a dignified octavo volume, which by its style was a recognition of the position attained by the poet. Mr. Mussey was in full sympathy with the poet in his anti-slavery views, and was determined, whether or not he made money out of his venture, to give the poems a setting in accordance with what he considered their intrinsic value. He surprised Mr. Whittier by offering him five hundred dollars for his copyrights, and also a percentage on his sales. With the single exception of " Lays of My Home," published by W. D. Ticknor in 1843, no book of Whittier's had up to this time paid him any royalty worth mentioning. Mussey's stout octavo volume, beautifully printed in large type on heavy paper, neatly bound, and exquisitely illustrated with steel engravings, from designs by Hammatt Billings, met with an unexpectedly large sale, and Mr. Mussey earned the gratitude of Mr. Whittier by paying him more than he had agreed. A second and a third edition were called for. In the mean time Mr. Whittier had been arranging with Mr. Fields for the publication of "Songs of Labor," which appeared in the early summer of 1850. While correspondence was going on between the poet and his publisher, Mr. Fields was married. Mr. Whittier wrote his congratulations in a postscript to a letter: —

"And now, business over, let me in all sincerity, bachelor as I am, congratulate thee on thy escape from single misery. It is the very wisest thing thee ever did. Were I autocrat I would see to it that every young man over twenty-five, and every young woman over twenty, was married without delay. Perhaps, on second thought, it might be well to keep one old maid and one old bachelor in each town, by way of warning, just as the Spartans did their drunken Helots."

On the 6th of May he returned a proof-sheet of "The Drovers," and some idea of Fields' criticism may be gleaned from the characteristic remarks of Whittier. As originally published in the "Era," in 1847, the first lines of this stanza stood as follows: —

> "From many a Northern lake and hill
>   To Ocean's far-off water
> Shall Fancy play the Drover still,
>   And make the long night shorter."

Mr. Whittier wrote: "I send thee the proof sadly disfigured, for which thank thyself. I have altered some of the rhymes; others I have left to their fate. Heaven help them, I cannot. In the verse commencing

> "'By many a Northern lake and hill,'

I don't think I have mended the matter. ' Pasture,' ' faster,' ' water,' ' shorter' — both are good Yankee rhymes, but out of New England they would be cashiered. Take thy choice, I see no difference. I have tried other ' Songs of Labor,' but I cannot get the spirit of the early ones, and I think it best to let them go by themselves. I have exhausted that vein, so far as I am concerned. . . . Kearsarge is pronounced always Ke'-ar-sarge. . . . I send ' Memories' out of respect to thy opinion and that of our friend Whipple. Is it best to print it? I humbly thank thee for thy suggestions; let me have more of them." Mr. Fields evidently preferred " pasture " and " faster " as rhymes to " water " and " shorter," and the poem has ever since had this reading : —

> " By many a Northern lake and hill,
> From many a mountain pasture,
> Shall Fancy play the Drover still,
> And speed the long night faster."

Beside the six songs of labor, there were twenty-one miscellaneous poems in this volume, including " The Lakeside," " The Hill-Top," " An Eagle's Quill," " Memories," " Legend of St. Mark," " Ichabod," " To A. K., " etc.

In a note to Fields sent with some proof-sheets of the " Songs of Labor," Whittier stands out for some rhymes which had been criticised by his publisher, but adds : " However, as they say in the East, Who is my mother's son that I should presume to dictate to thy superior wisdom? Do as seemeth best in thine own eyes, and I shall take

it for granted it *is* best. I have had no leisure
when in tolerable health for any polishing of my
rhymes.   I suppose under such circumstances I
ought not to have made any, but *I could not help it*."

In another note he follows a suggestion to
substitute " farmer girls " for " corn-fed girls " in
" The Huskers," although himself preferring the
latter phrase, and justifying it by referring to
Allan Ramsay's " kail-fed lassies."   The stanza
in the Dedication of the " Songs of Labor " beginning, " The doom which to the guilty pair," was
an afterthought, sent with the proof-sheet, accompanied by a note containing this sentence : " Pray
get out the book as soon as possible, for your own
sake ; I have a terrible propensity, always after it
is too late, to see something which I ought to
have seen before."

When Whittier was preparing the copy for the
volume " Old Portraits and Modern Sketches,"
published in 1850, he placed the articles he proposed to use in a portfolio, upon a fly-leaf of which
we find in pencil these lines, which were apparently intended for a preface or inscription to the
work : —

> " For whatever here is wrong I crave
>   Forgiveness ; and if haply there be found
>   Sweet flower or healing herb where weeds abound.
>   How shall I dare to claim
>   As mine the gifts the Heavenly Father gave,
>   Or without guilty shame
>   From His own blessings frame
>   A pagan temple for the idol Fame ? "

One of the poems included in the volume has an
interest as a sort of confession of faith : for once,

when asked by what poem he would wish to be most remembered, he waited a moment, and then thoughtfully and seriously answered, "I think 'The Reformer' embodies my sentiments."

In 1850, Mr. Whittier was active in bringing about the coalition between the Free-Soilers and the Democrats, which resulted in the election of George S. Boutwell as governor of Massachusetts, with the understanding that the Free-Soilers should name the United States Senator and some of the state officials. Mr. Whittier insisted that Sumner should be named as the Free-Soil candidate for Senator, to fill the place made vacant by the resignation of Daniel Webster, who entered the cabinet of President Fillmore. Whittier went to Phillips Beach, Swampscott, to consult Sumner about the matter, and to induce him to accept the nomination for the senatorship, in case the coalition of Free-Soilers and Democrats carried the State. Sumner was unwilling, but listened to his arguments, and at length consented. It was to this visit that the poet referred in his poem "To Charles Sumner:"

> "Thou knowest my heart, dear friend, and well canst guess
> That, even though silent, I have not the less
> Rejoiced to see thy actual life agree
> With the large future which I shaped for thee,
> When, years ago, beside the summer sea,
> White in the moon, we saw the long waves fall
> Baffled and broken from the rocky wall,
> That, to the menace of the brawling flood,
> Opposed alone its massive quietude,
> Calm as a fate; with not a leaf nor vine
> Nor birch-spray trembling in the still moonshine,
> Crowning it like God's peace."

After the governor and his council had been

elected in conformity with the terms of the coalition, some of the Democrats refused to vote for Sumner, and the result was a prolonged contest. The Whigs voted for Robert C. Winthrop, and the Democrats whose consciences would not allow them to vote for a Free-Soiler scattered their votes. Caleb Cushing led the anti-Sumner Democrats. Governor Boutwell's inaugural address gave offense to his Free-Soil allies. When Mr. Whittier saw that the Democrats were not disposed to do as they had agreed, he wrote this letter to Sumner in the first heat of his indignation : —

"Illness, severe and protracted, confines me at home, or I should have seen thee. I have read the message of Governor B.; it is, under the circumstances, insulting and monstrous. May God forgive us for permitting his election. I have watched the balloting with intense anxiety. I see now no hope of our success. I think it is determined by both branches of the Democracy to defeat our purposes. Under these circumstances, dear Sumner, I, who urged the nomination so strongly and imperatively, must now confess I see no other course for thee than to *decline at once*. And Wilson, Knapp, Walker, and the three councilors should at once resign their places. Think of a Free-Soiler in Governor B.'s council! As the election of one of our own men is hopeless, if I were in the legislature I would vote Governor G. N. Briggs right into the United States Senate, as an anti-Webster, anti-Fugitive Slave Law candidate. We have done him an injustice ; and he is at heart right on the great questions in which we feel an interest. I write, as thou wilt see, in haste, and with the roused feeling incidental upon the perusal of that detestable message, and the vote in the House. I wish thee to consult at once with our friends, Sewall, Adams, S. G. Howe, and others, and with Earle and others in the legislature. Thus far thy position has been manly and honorable. There is now, as it seems to me, a new state of things, requiring a new course of action. Pardon the abruptness of this note; it is the result of *feeling* rather than deliberate reflection."

Sumner's own wish was in accordance with Whittier's suggestion, but in the councils of the party it was decided he should continue his candidacy. The popular feeling against the Fugitive Slave Law was increasing in intensity, and began to have its effect upon the legislature. Towards the last of March, Sumner wished to consult with Whittier, and urged him to come to Boston. If he had been in good health he would have been at work on the floor of the House during the whole contest. But he was compelled to write the following letter : —

" Thy letter, most welcome, was received yesterday, and would have been answered in person had I been able to leave here. I can only assure thee that were I able to visit Boston just now I should need no other inducement than thy request. I have watched with deep interest the proceedings in our legislature, and have, I think, fully comprehended thy feelings, and sympathized with thee in the peculiar and difficult position in which thou hast been placed. As matters now stand, I cannot venture to offer advice. I fear there would be no prospect of electing any true man if thou shouldst withdraw, as it would somewhat remove obligation from the Democrats to vote with us. On the other hand, I should be sorry to have the election thrown upon the next legislature, as the Whigs will be sure of a majority in that body. We could not again unite with the Democrats, if this legislature adjourns without thy election. We could not trust them; it would be folly to think of it. But I am talking at arm's length and without data. Need I tell thee that I should be right glad to see thee at Amesbury. Why not come and spend First day with us? Thou canst go back by the seven o'clock train on Second day (Monday) morning. I shall expect thee. Do not disappoint me."

Sumner went to Amesbury and consulted with his friend and adviser. At last, on the 24th day of April, upon the twenty-sixth ballot, Sumner by a majority of one was elected United States Senator, a position he held continuously until his death. Here is Whittier's letter of congratulation: —

"I take earliest moment of ability, after a sudden and severe attack of illness, to congratulate thee, not so much on thy election, as upon the proof which it offers of the turning of the tide — the recoil of the popular feeling — the near and certain doom of the wicked Slave Law. My heart is full of gratitude to God. For when 1 consider the circumstances of this election, I am constrained to regard it as His work. And I re-

joice that thy position is so distinct and emphatic;
that thy triumph is such a direct rebuke to politicians, hoary with years of political chicanery and
fraud ; that unpledged, free, and without a single
concession or compromise, thou art enabled to
take thy place in the United States Senate. May
the good Providence which has overruled the purposes of thy life, in this matter, give thee strength
and grace to do great things for humanity. I
never knew such a general feeling of real heart-
pleasure and satisfaction as is manifested by all
except inveterate Hunkers, in view of thy election.
The whole country is electrified by it. Sick abed,
I heard the guns — Quaker as I am — with real
satisfaction."

A letter written on the 18th of May, 1851, to
his friend Grace Greenwood, has so full an expression of his feeling in regard to the election of
Sumner, that it is here inserted : —

"I am slowly recovering from the severest illness I have known for years, the issue of which,
at one time, was to me exceedingly doubtful.
Indeed, I scarcely know now how to report myself,
but I am better, and full of gratitude to God that
I am permitted once more to go abroad and enjoy
this beautiful springtime. The weather now is
delightfully warm and bright, and the soft green
of the meadows is climbing our hills. It is luxury
to live. One feels at such times terribly rooted to
this world : old Mother Earth seems sufficient for
us. . . . After a long trial and much anxiety, our
grand object in Massachusetts has been attained.
We have sent Charles Sumner into the United

States Senate, — a man physically and spiritually head and shoulders above the old hackneyed politicians of that body. The plan for this was worked out last summer at Phillips Beach, and I sounded Sumner upon it the evening we left you at that place. He really did not want the office, but we forced it upon him. I am proud of old Massachusetts, and thankful that I have had an humble share in securing her so true and worthy a representative of her honor, her freedom, and intellect, as Charles Sumner. He is a noble and gifted man, earnest and truthful. I hope great things of him, and I do not fear for his integrity and fidelity, under any trial. That Sims case was particularly mean on the part of the Boston shopkeepers. I never felt so indignant as when I saw the courthouse in chains."

The " soberer piece " referred to in the following letter was " Moloch in State Street," which was published in the " National Era " of May 22, 1851. The rendition of the fugitive slave, Thomas Sims, by United States officials, aided by the armed police of Boston, and abetted by State Street merchants, at night, by stealth, while the state officials who would have prevented it slept, occurred a few days before the election of Sumner, and caused an outburst of popular feeling which probably hastened the election. .The " bit of doggerel," referred to below, has never appeared in any edition of Whittier's works ; it served its turn as a bit of poetical fireworks, for an evening's amusement. Many such " occasional " poems were written by him, with no expectation that they would be printed. He wrote to Sumner : —

CHARLES SUMNER.

" The bit of doggerel[1] on the other page might answer to raise a laugh at our friend Gilbert Gore's party to-morrow evening, which I expect I cannot enjoy in person. Give it, if there is nothing objectionable in it, to friend Burlingame, or some one who will be at the party, as the anonymous contribution of a friend who could not be present. My soberer piece was sent to the 'Era' a fortnight ago, but when it will appear, if at all, is uncertain. I quite approve of thy decision in respect to public speaking to any great extent. Thy letter of acceptance gives great satisfaction to all except the inveterate Hunkers. I feel exceedingly anxious for Palfrey's success, and I do not think it would be any way improper for

---

[1] WHAT STATE STREET SAID TO SOUTH CARO-LINA, AND WHAT SOUTH CAROLINA SAID TO STATE STREET.

Muttering "fine upland staple," "prime Sea Island finer,"
With cotton bales pictured on either retina,
"Your pardon!" said State Street to South Carolina;
"We feel and acknowledge your laws are diviner
Than any promulgated by the thunders of Sinai!
Sorely pricked in the sensitive conscience of business
We own and repent of our sins of remissness:
Our honor we 've yielded, our words we have swallowed;
And quenching the lights which our forefathers followed,
And turning from graves by their memories hallowed,
With teeth on ball-cartridge, and finger on trigger,
Reversed Boston Notions, and sent back a nigger!"

"Get away!" cried the Chivalry, busy a-drumming,
And fifing and drilling, and such Quattle-bumming;
"With your April-fool slave hunt! Just wait till December
Shall see your new Senator stalk through the Chamber,
And Puritan heresy prove neither dumb nor
Blind in that pestilent Anakim, Sumner!"

thee to speak once or twice in his district.[1] Your relation and personal friendship alone would justify it — say in Cambridge, or some other large town. Think of it, and act. Rantoul will unquestionably be chosen."

It is seldom that the world has seen such an example of the poetic and devotional temperament, combined with preëminent political sagacity and business judgment, as in the case of Whittier. He was a safe counselor for every emergency. The anti-slavery movement needed just such a balance wheel as he proved to be. He could work without quarreling with any one who was earnestly seeking to benefit the race. When he came to the parting of the roads, and could not walk with one with whom he had been in general agreement, he took his own way quietly, bidding his companion God speed. In every church and in every political party he found men he loved, and he did not insist upon their agreement with his opinions on any subject as a condition of friendship. He looked for the best points in the characters of all with whom he came in contact, and without being blind to their failings made the most of their fairest side. Positive in his own convictions, he had the widest charity for every honest difference of opinion he encountered. But he had no patience with insincerity and heartlessness in any form. With all the indignation of the Hebrew prophets, as one has well said of him, he never lost sight of that love of God and love of man, which tempers even the hatred of evil.

---

[1] Sumner did not speak for Palfrey, but he wrote a letter of earnest support, in which he added a good word for Rantoul.

Many of Whittier's notes to Fields contain reference to current events and to the new books of other authors, as in the following, — written April 7, 1851: "So your Union tinkers have really caught a 'nigger' at last! A very pretty and refreshing sight it must have been to Sabbath-going Christians, yesterday, — that chained court-house of yours. And Bunker Hill monument looking down upon all. But the matter is too sad for irony. God forgive the miserable politicians who gamble for office with dice loaded with human hearts! Thoreau's 'Walden' is capital reading, but very wicked and heathenish. The practical moral of it seems to be that if a man is willing to sink himself into a woodchuck he can live as cheaply as that quadruped; but after all, for me, I prefer walking on two legs."

Whenever friends of Mr. Whittier were traveling in this country or any other, he followed them in their journeys with the keenest interest, and greatly enjoyed such letters from them as described the scenes through which they were passing. Every book of travel that came in his way was thoroughly read, and his memory held accurate pictures of scenery and people, a fact that must impress every reader of his poetry. The local coloring of those poems which relate to countries he never saw is as faithful to the reality as if he had not been compelled to rely upon the eyes of others. We have elsewhere seen how his friendship for Bayard Taylor began. It was not alone the poet soul he recognized, but he enjoyed the charming stories of his travels, and as he read

" The Norseman's Ride " his imagination was led into regions that had great attractions for him. A half page of the " Era " is filled with a lively review of Taylor's " Eldorado," dealing especially with the chapters concerning the new State of California, and concluding with this suggestion: " In taking leave of his volumes, we cannot forbear venturing a suggestion to the author, that he may find a field of travel, less known and quite as interesting at the present time, in the vast Territory of New Mexico — the valley of the Del Norte, with its old Castilian and Aztec monuments and associations ; the Great Salt Lake, and the unexplored regions of the great valley of the Colorado, between the mountain ranges of the Sierra Madre and the Sierra Nevada. We know of no one better fitted for such an enterprise, or for whom, judging from the spirit of his California narrative, it would present more attractions." Mr. Taylor's pleasure at this kind reception of his work is expressed in the following letter from New York, bearing date July 9, 1850 : —

" I owe you a world of thanks for your surpassing notice of ' Eldorado ' in the ' National Era.' I have read it with the most genuine pleasure, not on account of the life it will give to my literary reputation, but because you seem to have so thoroughly appreciated and enjoyed my work. I care but little for the general praise or censure, but I *do* value that of my friends, and if I satisfy them, there is no higher reward. Would you had been with me in California! I often recalled, while there, those lines from ' The Crisis ' describing the scenery of our central wilderness. The next trip you propose for me is the very one which I have often wished to make, and if it was not time that I should stop from roving, and build up a home for myself, I would go there next year. I am going to Boston next week, for a few days, and hope to be able to pay another flying visit to Amesbury. I have not forgotten the view I had from the hill-top."

The visit suggested in this note was in a few days made in company with James Russell Lowell, as we find in a letter Taylor wrote to a friend, dated July 22, 1850 : —

"Friday morning early, Lowell and I started for Amesbury, which we reached in a terrible northeaster. What a capital time we had with Whittier, in his nook of a study, with the rain pouring on the roof, and the wind howling at the door ! "

These visits of Taylor to Amesbury are referred to in a stanza of " The Last Walk in Autumn : "

> " Here, too, of answering love secure,
>   Have I not welcomed to my hearth
>   The gentle pilgrim troubadour,
>   Whose songs have girdled half the earth ;
>   Whose pages, like the magic mat
>   Whereon the Eastern lover sat,
> Have borne me over Rhineland's purple vines,
> And Nubia's tawny sands, and Phrygia's mountain pines."

A meeting to express sympathy for Hungary was held in Boston, August 20, 1851, and Sumner made a speech. On that day, Whittier wrote to him : —

"I wish I felt able to take the cars to Boston and hear thy speech this evening. I was glad to hear of thy meeting, although I greatly fear it is too late to be of any service to poor Hungary. She will be crushed under the avalanche of Russian barbarism, and the sympathies and congratulations of the friends of freedom abroad will be to her ' like delicates poured upon a mouth shut up, or as meats set upon a grave.' I wish, either in resolutions or speeches, the disgraceful conduct of the United States Consul at Paris [1] could be noticed as it deserves.   Through him our government commits itself in favor of the kings and priests of Europe in their barbarous measures suppressing the growth of free principles.   We are made parties to the usurpations of Bonaparte the Less, the bombardment of Rome, the bloody rule of Naples, the atrocities of Austria and Russia in Hungary.   The miserable fellow would be nothing by himself, but as an official of our government he can do a great deal to disgrace us. . . . The New York conference ended as I expected, after the late elections.   The South always contrives to control the North, by throwing itself on the Whig or Democratic side, just as these parties are inclined towards abolition.   For instance, in 1839 the Whigs talked anti-slavery at the North. The slaveholders deserted their faithful allies, and went over to the abolition Whig, and the Whigs, as in duty bound, eschewed abolition.   In 1843–44, they set aside Van Buren, and got a place-holder nominated by the Democrats, who was for Texas annexation with slavery, and voted him into

[1] Robert Walsh, who was also correspondent of several American journals.

power. He did his work, and the Whigs in their exasperation again threatened to become abolitionists; and the South silenced them by voting for General Taylor. Now, the Democrats are forming coalitions with the abolitionists, and the South must change in their favor. This is the way that the two parties at the North are managed. I have been desirous to see thee and others of our Free-Soil friends, but have been confined at home by illness."

In the fall of 1851, Sumner desired a continuance of the alliance with the Democrats, but many men of the Free-Soil party were opposed to it. He wrote to Whittier on the 7th of October: "Will not Higginson see the matter in a practical light? I respect him so much, and honor his principles so supremely, that I am pained to differ from him; but I do feel that we must not neglect the opportunity afforded by alliance — not fusion — with the Democrats to prevent the Whigs from establishing themselves in the State. Palfrey is now earnestly of this inclining; so is Hopkins; also Burlingame,— and all these stood out before."

In December, 1851, Kossuth arrived in this country, and from his anxiety to propitiate all classes of our people in favor of his cause, in his first speech, in New York, he took pains to say that he did not propose to interfere with our domestic institutions. Whittier wrote Sumner the letter that follows, which is without date, but its contents show that it was written early in December, 1851: —

"On thy way to Washington pray see W. C.

Bryant, Seward, and some other leading men, —
Greeley, for instance — and caution them to see to
it that the 'Union savers' do not thrust their notions upon Kossuth, and call out from him speeches
of the Castle Garden stamp. Naturally he would
deprecate a dissolution of this Union — but he
ought to understand that it is not in the slightest
jeopardy — that the solicitude of the 'Union
savers' is all for political effect. I wish he could
have a half hour's talk with Benton. I do not
wish him to be mixed up in *any way* with our domestic matters. He has his mission; we ours.
I hope thou wilt see the great Hungarian's reception in New York, and take part in it. I have just
finished reading his English speeches, and I am
deeply impressed by his wisdom and ability. God
bless thee, my friend, in thy new and difficult,
but glorious position."

Sumner was nine months in the Senate before
he found an opportunity to make a speech on
the great issue upon which he was elected. There
was a conspiracy among the Senators of both parties to prevent any chance being offered him.
Whittier refers to this in the following letter : —

"I am by no means surprised at the refusal of
the Senate to hear thee. It is simply carrying out
the resolutions of the two Baltimore conventions.
Never mind. The right time will come for thee,
if not this session, the next certainly. I think our
proper place for speaking now is to the people
directly, rather than to Congress. I want thee to
put on thy harness this fall and do battle as in '48.
. . . The sad intelligence of the death of Robert

Rantoul [1] has just reached me. I have lost an old and valued friend, and the State and country a noble man. How little did I expect to outlive him. I have just read thy tribute to him. It is a relief to me to hear the right words spoken of my friend."

Mr. Sumner's reply to this letter was written in the Senate Chamber, August 13, 1852: —

" I am grateful for your words of cheer and confidence. I have never desired to come here, as you well know. Since I have been here, our cause has never been out of my mind. In the exercise of my best discretion I have postponed speaking until now. To this course I was advised by friends also. Should I not succeed before the close of the session, I shall feel sad; but I cannot feel that I have failed in a duty. *But I shall speak* on an amendment of the Civil Appropriation Bill. Thus far, whenever I have spoken I have been listened to. On this occasion I may not have the attention; but the speech shall be made. For a long time I have been prepared to handle the Fugitive Slave Bill at length. By the blessing of God it shall be done. . . . With you I deplore Rantoul. I pray you read my remarks *as corrected* in the ' National Era.' . . . I cannot make any lyceum engagements for the coming season, and I shrink from the political labors to which you beckon me. I have been in my seat every day this session. I long for repose and an opportunity for quiet labors. But more than all things I long to declare

[1] Robert Rantoul died at Washington, August 7, 1852, while representing the Essex district in Congress.

myself here against the Fugitive Slave Bill. Then
I shall be happy for a while. At this moment I
can say nothing. My ship is in a *terrible calm*,
like that of the Ancient Mariner. But it will
move yet. . . . I notice the withdrawal of confidence from me. Well-a-day! I never courted it.
I will be content without it. But I shall claim
yours."

TO RALPH WALDO EMERSON.

AMESBURY, 21st 10th mo., 1853.

What marvelous weather! Amidst the autum-
nal opulence of the last two weeks, I have lived
more than royally. How poor and mean in com-
parison seem all the pomps and shows of kings and
priests! And what folly to run abroad over the
Old World, when all that is beautiful may be seen
from our own door-stone! Munich, the Louvre,
and the Vatican are doubtless well worth seeing,
but I fancy I see all and much more in my own
painted woodlands. At any rate, I am satisfied.
Oh, that I could put into words the hymn of gratitude and unspeakable love which at such a season
as this is sung in my heart. I wish thee could
have been with us the other day on the Merrimac. We wanted an interpreter of the mystery
of the glory about us.

When Taylor returned from Africa, Japan, and
China, in 1853, he received from his Amesbury
friend this greeting : —

"Give me thy hand! Welcome home again, and
a happy New Year to thee! We are fellow travelers. I have followed thee all the way over the

world, without any share of thy expenses, trouble, or fatigue. I wish, though, we could have reached the snowy African mountains. *Thou* wast there, in spirit, however, beyond doubt, as thy splendid poem testifies. But to the point: Canst thou not steal away a day or two, — see Whipple, Samuel Longfellow, and Fields, — run up and spend the night with me, and talk an hour or so to our lyceum on what thee saw in Africa and Japan? Don't refuse — there is no need of a formal lecture — our folks only want to see thee and hear thee talk a little. Don't rank this with a thousand and one other applications — but drop me a line and say *yes*. Say a good word for Phœbe Cary's poem, and Mrs. Howe's memorable ' Passion Flowers,' just out from Ticknor's."

The Amesbury Lyceum secured many a firstrate lecturer it could not otherwise have obtained, by such an application as this from Whittier. As for himself, he never attended an evening lecture, even when Beecher and Phillips went from his tea-table to the platform. The great orators would come to this little village to meet their friend and enjoy his hospitality.

" For Righteousness' Sake," originally entitled " Lines inscribed to Friends under Arrest for Treason against the Slave Power," was written in the winter of 1854–55, when Theodore Parker, with others, was indicted in the United States Circuit Court in Boston, for resisting the process for the rendition of the fugitive slave, Anthony Burns, the alleged act of resistance in Parker's case being a speech he had delivered in Faneuil Hall.

The poem now known as "The Rendition," originally published in the "Era" in 1854, was then entitled "Ichabod," the same title given four years earlier to the famous philippic upon Webster. Many of the titles of Whittier's poems were thus duplicated, and even triplicated, as in the case of "Stanzas for the Times." The name Ichabod seemed to have a fascination for him. Several of his early poems, published while in the Academy, had it for signature.

"Maud Muller" was first published in the "National Era" in 1854. Whittier sent this note to the printer, with his manuscript: "The term 'chimney lug' which occurs in this poem refers to the old custom in New England of hanging a pole with hooks attached to it down the chimney, to hang pots and kettles on. It is called a 'lug-pole.' I mention this for fear the word would not be understood, and taken by the printers for something else."

To a correspondent who asked of him the pronunciation of "Muller;" about the word "but" in the nineteenth couplet of the poem ; and the meaning of one of the last couplets, Mr. Whittier replied: "I don't think 'Maud Muller' worth serious analysis, but in answer to thy questions I would say: 1. Pronounce the name with either the Yankee or the German accent —·it matters not which. [He always pronounced the *u* as in gull.] 2. 'But' should have been 'And.' 'For all of us a sweet hope lies' is the prose version."

The following passage occurs in a letter written to Fields in 1854: "I met Holmes for the first

time at Haverhill the other night. There is rare
humor in him, and I like him. I inclose thee
a jingle of mine — not published — and therefore
only for thy private reading. It is one of those
pieces that make themselves, and come to you un-
called for. My 'Singletary Papers' still drag
their slow length along." The "jingle" was
"Official Piety."

In 1854, Messrs. Ticknor & Fields published a
collection of Mr. Whittier's prose essays under the
title of "Literary Recreations," most of the articles in which were copied from his contributions to
the "National Era."

Mr. Sumner was at last heard in the Senate
upon themes that aroused him to his best oratori-
cal efforts. The speeches made in the summer of
1854, upon the Kansas and Nebraska questions,
are referred to by Mr. Whittier in the letter here
given : —

"I will not trouble thee with a long letter : but
I cannot forbear to thank thee, in the name of
humanity, and our dear old Commonwealth, for
thy late noble efforts. I have never seen such an
effect produced by any speech in Congress before.
Everybody has read the newspaper reports of the
encounter, and everybody, save a few desperate
office-holders, commends thy course in terms of
warm admiration. Thy first speech on the Nebraska crime was everywhere commended. Indeed,
all things considered, I think it the best speech of
the session. It was the fitting word — it entirely
satisfied me, and with a glow of heart I thank God
that its author was my friend. . . . What a pity

—— could not see the path clear before him to stand forward at this crisis, and bring his party up to the desired point! It has occurred to me that a letter from thee — kind, generous, and earnest — might move him. However, I only throw out the hint; there may be good reasons against it. Just now, the people of Massachusetts will hear and indeed approve of almost anything against the Fugitive Slave Law. One more Burns case would make Hunkerism an unsafe commodity in any part of the State."

TO LUCY LARCOM.

1855.

Elizabeth has been reading Browning's poem (" Men and Women"), and she tells me it is great. I have only dipped into it, here and there, but it is not exactly comfortable reading. It seemed to me like a galvanic battery in full play — its spasmodic utterances and intense passion make me feel as if I had been taking a bath among electric eels. But I have not read enough to criticise.

The repeal of the Missouri Compromise added to the irritation at the North caused by frequent slave hunts in communities that had no patience with them. The determination to colonize Kansas with men who would make it a free State grew out of this repeal, and it was Whittier again who spoke for the North, with a voice heard farther at the time than the speech of any orator, and which will not be silent while our language endures. In a brilliant magazine article,[1] Hon. James J.

[1] In *Harper's Monthly*, April, 1893.

Ingalls has given a spirited account of the efforts made to colonize Kansas with free labor, so as to secure by popular vote the exclusion of slavery hitherto effected by the Missouri Compromise. After referring to the appeals of the Northern press, he adds : —

" The journalists were reinforced by the poets, artists, novelists, and orators of an age distinguished for genius, learning, and inspiration. Lincoln, Douglas, Seward, and Sumner delivered their most memorable speeches upon the theme. Phillips and Beecher, then at the meridian of their powers, appealed to the passions and the conscience of the nation by unrivaled eloquence and invective. Prizes were offered for lyrics, that were obtained, so profound was the impulse, by obscure and unknown competitors. Lowell, Bryant, Holmes, Longfellow, and Emerson lent the magic of their verse. Whittier was the laureate of the era. His ' Burial of Barbour ' and ' Marais du Cygne ' seemed like a prophet's cry for vengeance to the immigrants, who marched to the inspiring strains of ' Suoni la Tromba,' or chanted to the measure of ' Auld Lang Syne,'

> " ' We crossed the prairies, as of old
>   Our fathers crossed the sea.'

The contagion spread to foreign lands, and alien torches were lighted at the flame. Walter Savage Landor wrote an ode to free Kansas. Lady Byron collected money which she sent to the author of ' Uncle Tom's Cabin ' for the relief of the sufferers in Kansas. Volunteers from Italy, France, and Germany, revolutionists and exiles, served in

the desultory war, many of whom afterwards
fought with distinction in the armies of the Union.
It was the romance of history. The indescribable
agitation which always attends the introduction of
a great moral question into politics pervaded the
souls of men, transforming the commonplace into
ideal, and inaugurating a heroic epoch. The
raptures that swelled the hearts of the pioneers
yet thrill and vibrate in the blood of their posterity, like the chords of a smitten harp when the
player has departed."

When bands of ruffians from Missouri crossed
the border and committed atrocious barbarities
upon these anti-slavery pioneers, a mighty wave of
indignation stirred the whole North, and Whittier
gave voice to it in his poem " Le Marais du
Cygne." Some of the details of the massacre of
Swan's Marsh will explain to younger readers who
have no memory of these stirring times the reason of the deep feeling displayed in this poem.
" Chouteau's Trading Post," as it was called at
the time of the massacre, is on the old military
road, now disused, from Fort Leavenworth to Fort
Scott, on the south bank of the Marais du Cygne
River, three miles from the Missouri line. On the
morning of May 19, the settlers at the Post were
engaged in their usual pursuits, unarmed, and
without thought of danger. A band of twenty-
five or thirty Missourians, mounted, and under
command of Captain Charles A. Hamilton, crossed
the border, and captured twelve men, several of
them the heads of families. They were bound and
taken to a ravine, where they were placed in line,

and fired upon at close range. Five were killed,
and all the others wounded, except one. He fell
with the others, feigned death, and escaped injury.
All the wounded recovered, and some of them became influential citizens in the free State they had
helped to found. Whittier's verses were written
while the soil was yet red with the blood of the
victims. The last stanza proved prophetical : —

> " On the lintels of Kansas
>   That blood shall not dry ;
> Henceforth the Bad Angel
>   Shall harmless go by ;
> Henceforth to the sunset,
>   Unchecked on her way,
> Shall Liberty follow
>   The march of the day."

The assassins were well-known Missourians, not
disguised. Only one was arrested that year, and
he escaped. But in 1863, while the civil war was
in progress, another of the murderers was captured
and hanged. One of the wounded men acted as
his executioner.

As Whittier watched the progress of the cause
of liberty, and recognized the surety of its triumph,
he became less impatient of the wrongs which were
so surely to be overruled for good, and returned
less frequently to the theme that in former days
aroused his righteous wrath, and nerved him to the
utterance of his passionate " Voices of Freedom."

In July, 1854, he was invited by Ralph Waldo
Emerson and others to join them at a meeting in
Boston, called to consider the political situation,
and to devise a way to bring together the men of
all parties who were opposed to the encroachments

of slavery. His reply is dated Amesbury, 3d 7th mo., and is addressed to Mr. Emerson: —

"The circular signed by thyself and others, inviting me to meet you at Boston on the 7th inst., has just reached me. If I am able to visit Boston on that day I shall be glad to comply with the invitation. Your movement I regard as every way timely and expedient. I am quite sure good will come of it, in some way. I have been for some time past engaged in efforts tending to the same object, — the consolidation of the anti-slavery sentiment of the North. For myself, I am more than willing to take the humblest place in a new organization made up from Whigs, anti-Nebraska Democrats, and Free-Soilers. I care nothing for names; I have no prejudices against Whig or Democrat; show me a party cutting itself loose from slavery, repudiating its treacherous professed allies of the South, and making the *protection of Man* the paramount object, and I am ready to go with it, heart and soul. The great body of the people of all parties here are ready to unite in the formation of a new party. The Whigs especially only wait for the movement of the men to whom they have been accustomed to look for direction. I may be mistaken, but I fully believe that Robert C. Winthrop holds in his hands the destiny of the North. By throwing himself on the side of this movement he could carry with him the Whig strength of New England. The Democrats here, with the exception of two or three office-holders and their dependents, defend the course of Banks, and applaud the manly speeches of Sumner."

"The Panorama" was written by Mr. Whittier, to be read at the opening of a course of lectures on slavery, delivered in Tremont Temple, Boston, during the winter of 1855–56. The plan of this course provided that both sides of the question should be given, and leading Southern statesmen were invited to alternate with eminent Northern philanthropists in presenting their views. Among the men not in sympathy with the anti-slavery movement who were asked to speak from this platform were Henry W. Hilliard of Alabama, A. P. Butler of South Carolina, Wm. A. Smith of Virginia, Robert Toombs of Georgia, David R. Atchison of Missouri, and Stephen A. Douglas of Illinois. Dr. Samuel G. Howe was chairman of the lecture committee. William Lloyd Garrison was invited to give one of the lectures, but he declined, not being in sympathy with the management. The first lecture in the course was announced as to be given November 22, 1855, by Horace Mann, to be followed by a poem by John G. Whittier. Mr. Whittier asked Rev. Thomas Starr King to read his poem, and gave him the manuscript of "The Panorama." The following letter by Mr. King, written November 30, 1855, and found among Mr. Whittier's papers, gives some idea of the enthusiastic spirit with which he performed the task assigned him. The reading occupied forty minutes. Charles Sumner was upon the platform, and the reference to his name and "fresh renown" in the poem was greeted with much applause : —

"I have hardly been in Boston since the evening when my voice was honored, as never before, in being the medium of your genius. I beg you therefore to accept this fact as an explanation of the delay in sending you my thanks for the compliment you paid me in asking my poor service as your interpreter. The poem is admirably adapted to lecture utterance. It is so broad in its plan, so vivid, so stirring, so practical in its appeal, that it needs two thousand ears, and the wide atmosphere of the public heart, to allow the proportions of its power to appear, and its eloquence to find sea room to disport itself. I have heard the heartiest encomiums of it, even from men not specially interested in the anti-slavery cause, who were swept by it. Inadequate as the reading was, I am suspicious that the soul of the piece possessed my voice, and lifted it above its natural poverty. If possible, I shall read it in Worcester, some time during the week. Would that Mrs. Webb might give it wings! Though I think it needs a man's throat and passion. I have been invited to read it in Manchester, but could not go. I shall mention this fact to Dr. Stone when I see him. God bless you, my dear friend, and preserve you for many such Tyrtæan songs. I thank you, and remain cordially yours."

The allusion to Mrs. M. E. Webb is due to the fact that she was to read Mrs. Harriet Beecher Stowe's drama the next evening in the course. She was a colored dramatic reader.

"The Panorama" was written with a view to political effect in the presidential campaign of 1856, and Mr. Whittier desired it to be published at once, as a book. Mr. Fields suggested that it was so late that it could not appear until after the holiday season, and had better be postponed until the next fall. Whittier made reply in a letter dated January 6, 1856. The poem to which he referred as being in manuscript was either " The Barefoot Boy," or " The Ranger," which was originally named " Martha Mason, a Song of the Old French War ; " or possibly it might have been " Mary Garvin," which was published in the " National Era " in the month of January, 1856. These three poems were in manuscript at about this time.

"The wisdom of thy suggestion is very manifest. I have only one objection to it. ' The Panorama ' is a poem for the present time ; it is like Pierce's Message — it won't keep. But if it could be put at once through the press, with the other poems, it would answer my purpose. Now, if you have nothing better to do, just inform me, and you shall have the other pieces at once, as I have them, for a wonder, at hand, including one in MS. which I like better than ' Maud Muller.' But I don't think much of my own judgment in such matters, and it may be a very poor affair in reality."

In compliance with this request the book was put to press at once, and among the poems and ballads with which it was enriched were " A Memory," " Maud Muller," " Mary Garvin," " The Ranger," " Summer by the Lakeside," " Burns," " Tauler," " The Barefoot Boy," and " The Kansas Emigrants." The proof sheets came to Amesbury in the winter, and the poet was not in the mood to make so many changes as usual. He wrote : —

" I should perhaps make some other changes in the poem — but brain and hand are numb with frost. Whatever poetical fancies garnered up in more genial weather may be left within me, they are frozen up before reaching my finger-tips, like the tunes in Munchausen's horn, and I cannot, like the veracious hunter, get up a fire sufficient to thaw them out."

The origin of the poem " A Memory " is given in the following extract from a letter written by Mrs. Mary Rogers Kimball, daughter of Whittier's early and dear friend, N. P. Rogers : —

" We all loved Mr. Whittier, and before we left our home near Plymouth, N. H., for the West, in 1853, I think, he spent a week with us. With what delight we wandered, talked, read, and played with him! We sang to him; and of all the songs, English, Scotch, or Irish, he loved the negro melodies best. How well I remember his creeping softly behind me and shaking into my neck the dew from a branch of cinnamon rose he had picked and carried a long distance that early morning, ' for this express purpose,' as he said. I cherished the precious twig for many years. . . . The little poem entitled ' A Memory ' was of my next older sister, Ellen, who was spending a few days with friends at Wolfborough, N. H. She was a singer, and one evening the poet wrapped a white shawl about her, and put a Quaker bonnet on her head, and made her sing through the long twilight the songs he loved. The little event is immortalized; the Singer and the Poet have ' passed on.' "

When "Mary Garvin" was published in the "Era" in 1856, Mr. Whittier received a pleasant letter from his friend Dr. H. I. Bowditch, inclosing one from his young daughter Olivia, then not old enough to write, but who printed a letter in childish fashion. She had taken much pleasure in hearing the poem read by her father, and wished to send her thanks. This is Mr. Whittier's reply to the child's note, dated Amesbury, 28th 1st mo., 1856 : —

MY DEAR FRIEND OLIVIA, — I thank thee for thy kind note ; and am sure some good angel bade thee write it. I was very glad to know that my "Mary Garvin" gave thee so much pleasure. I know of no better way of being happy than in making others so. And then too, as an author, I was gratified by thy praise of my verses, because I was sure it was the honest expression of thy feeling. I remember that after Bernardin St. Pierre had written his beautiful story of "Paul and Virginia" (which I hope thou hast not read yet, because in that case there is so much more pleasure in store for thee), he was afraid it was not good enough for publication, and was on the point of laying it aside, when he chanced to read it to a group of children, whose evident delight and tearful sympathy encouraged him to print it, and thus please and sadden the hearts of young and old from that time to this. Following St. Pierre's example, I think I shall print "Mary Garvin" in a book with some other pieces. If my young critics are pleased I can well afford to let the older ones

find fault. I thank thee and thy dear father and
mother for the invitation, and hope I shall be able
to accept it when spring brings back the green
grass, the bright flowers, and these wintry drifts
are only a memory.

Mr. Whittier's interest in the movement for
woman suffrage is shown in this letter to a Woman's Rights Convention, held in Worcester: —

" Come what may, Nature is inexorable; she will
reverse none of her laws at the bidding of male or
female conventions; and men and women, with or
without the right of suffrage, will continue to be
men and women still. In the event of the repeal
of certain ungenerous, not to say unmanly, enact-
ments, limiting and abridging the rights and privileges of women, we may safely confide in the
adaptive powers of Nature. She will take care of
the new fact in her own way, and reconcile it to
the old, through the operation of her attractive or
repellent forces. Let us, then, not be afraid to
listen to the claims and demands of those who, in
some sort at least, represent the feelings and interests of those nearest and dearest to us. Let Oliver
ask for more. It is scarcely consistent with our
assumed superiority to imitate the horror and
wide-orbed consternation of Mr. Bumble and his
parochial associates, on a similar occasion."

On the 23d day of May, 1856, Sumner was
struck down in the Senate chamber, by Preston S.
Brooks, of South Carolina, for words uttered in
debate. This is the letter Whittier wrote to him
when he learned that his injuries were not likely
to deprive him of life: —

" I have been longing to write to thee, or rather to see thee (if I had strength I should now be in Washington) for the last fortnight. God knows my heart has been with thee, through thy season of trial and suffering; and now it is full of gratitude and joy that thy life has been spared to us and to Freedom. I have read and reread thy speech, and I look upon it as thy best. A grand and terrible philippic, worthy of the great occasion, — the severe and awful Truth which the sharp agony of the national crisis demanded. It is enough for immortality. So far as thy own reputation is concerned, nothing more is needed. But this is of small importance. We cannot see as yet the entire results of that speech, but everything now indicates that it has *saved the country.* If at the coming election a Free State President is secured it will be solely through the influence of that speech, and the mad fury which its unanswerable logic and fearless exposure of official criminals provoked. Thank God, then, dear Sumner, even in thy sufferings, that He has 'made the wrath of man to praise Him, and that the remainder of wrath He will restrain.' My heart is full and I have much to say; but I will not weary thee with words. Permit me a word of caution. Do not try to go back to thy senatorial duties this session. Avoid, as far as possible, all excitement; get out of Washington as soon as thee is able to travel. I almost dread to have thee come North, the feelings of all classes of our people are so wrought up; they so long to manifest to thee their love and admiration that I fear we should retard thy recovery by our demonstrations. Thy brother George must take care of thee, and prevent thy being 'killed by kindness'! My mother and sister join me in love to thee. And now, dear Sumner, I can only say, Heaven bless and preserve thee."

The intensity of Mr. Whittier's feeling in regard to the outrage upon Mr. Sumner is shown in the following letter of his, read at a meeting of the citizens of Amesbury and Salisbury, held on the 2d of June, 1856 : —

"Fearing I may not be able to attend the meeting this evening, I beg leave to say a word to my fellow-citizens. I need not say how fully I sympathize with the object of the meeting, nor speak of my grief for the sufferings and danger of a beloved friend, now nearer and dearer than ever, stricken down at his post of duty, for his manly defense of freedom ; nor of my mingled pity, horror, and indignation in view of the atrocities in Kansas. It seems to me to be no time for the indulgence of mere emotions. Neither railing nor threats befit the occasion. It is our first duty to inquire, why it is that the bad men in power have been emboldened to commit the outrages of which we complain. Why is it that the South has dared to make such experiments upon us ? The North is not united for freedom, as the South is for slavery. We are split into factions, we get up paltry side issues, and quarrel with and abuse each other, and the Slave Power, as a matter of course, takes advantage of our folly. That evil power is only strong through our dissensions. It could do nothing against a united North. The one indispensable thing for us is Union. Can we not have it? Can we not set an example in this very neighborhood, — Whigs, Democrats, Free-Soilers, and Americans, joining hands in defense of our common liberties? We must forget, *forgive*, and UNITE. I feel a solemn impression that the present opportunity is the last that will be offered us for the peaceful and constitutional remedy of the evil which afflicts us. The crisis in our destiny has come : the hour is striking of our final and irrevocable choice. God grant that it may be rightfully made. Let us not be betrayed into threats. Leave violence where it belongs, with the wrong-doer. It is worse than folly to talk of fighting Slavery, when we have not yet agreed to vote against it. Our business is with poll-boxes, not cartridge-boxes; with ballots, not bullets. The path of duty is plain : God's providence calls us to walk in it. Let me close by repeating, Forget, *forgive*, and UNITE."

In a letter to Emerson dated June 13, 1856, Mr. Whittier urged him to attend the convention that nominated Frémont. He wrote : "I see this morning that Governor Boutwell is not able to attend the Philadelphia convention. I believe thou art one of the substitutes, and I drop this line to urge thee to go in his place. It is a great occasion : the most important public duty which can occur in a lifetime. By all means, go. A thousand thanks for thy speech at the Concord meeting!"

Elizabeth Whittier was in full sympathy with

her brother in his political and anti-slavery work. In a letter to her friend Lucy Larcom, written June 19, 1856, she says : —

"Our poor land ! What can we do ? I know what *thee* can do — write a ringing song for freedom and Frémont. Frémont is my hero of years ; his wild ranger life has had the greatest charm for me. I used to envy Kit Carson, who was always near him, helping bravely in the trials and dangers of his young leader. I wish I was somebody — I would do great things now — write songs, first of all. Will not some one set the present heart-beat of the people to music ? Those were dark days for Greenleaf, when his noblest and dearest friend was in great danger. I, too, passed under the shadow. Sumner's position seems very grand and solemn — the charged prophet of freedom. His great work is before him."

This call for a campaign song was responded to by Miss Larcom. It is easy to believe that Elizabeth's enthusiasm was also the inspiration of her brother's political work in the same year. In addition to the deep interest Mr. Whittier took in the contest for Free Soil involved in the Frémont campaign of 1856, was a strong personal feeling for the "Pathfinder," whose way across the continent he had followed with the enthusiasm and sympathy he gave to all explorers. He hardly needed the summons Charles A. Dana, then one of the editors of the "New York Tribune," sent him to write a campaign song for his favorite. Dana wrote, under date of June 8, 1856: "A powerful means of exciting and maintaining the spirit of freedom in the coming decisive contest must be songs. If we are to conquer, as I trust in God we are, a great deal must be done by that genial and inspiring stimulus. They should be written to popular and stirring tunes, such as the Star-Spangled Banner, God Save the King, the Marseillaise, Tippecanoe and Tyler too, Old Dan Tucker, and the like. In this case we of course appeal to you for help." In response to this call from Mr. Dana, Whittier wrote several lyrics, of which one is here given, written to be sung to the music of " Suoni la Tromba " in " I Puritani :"—

" Sound now the trumpet warningly !
The storm is rolling nearer,
The hour is striking clearer,
  In the dusky dome of sky.
If dark and wild the morning be,
A darker morn before us
Shall fling its shadows o'er us
  If we let the hour go by.
Sound we then the trumpet chorus !
Sound the onset wild and high !
  Country and Liberty !
  Freedom and Victory !
These words shall be our cry, —
  Frémont and Victory !

" Sound, sound the trumpet fearlessly !
Each arm its vigor lending,
Bravely with wrong contending,
  And shouting Freedom's cry !
The Kansas homes stand cheerlessly,
The sky with flame is ruddy,
The prairie turf is bloody,
  Where the brave and gentle die.
Sound the trumpet stern and steady !
Sound the trumpet strong and high !
  Country and Liberty !
  Freedom and Victory !
These words shall be our cry, —
  Frémont and Victory !

" Sound now the trumpet cheerily !
　Nor dream of Heaven's forsaking
　The issue of its making,
　　That Right with Wrong must try.
The cloud that hung so drearily
　The Northern winds are breaking ;
　The Northern Lights are shaking
　　Their fire-flags in the sky.
Sound the signal of awaking ;
　Sound the onset wild and high !
　　Country and Liberty !
　　Freedom and Victory !
　These words shall be our cry, —
　　Frémont and Victory ! "

At a Frémont meeting in Amesbury in July, 1856, Mr. Whittier was chairman of a committee on resolutions, and introduced a series which express the belief that " the Divine Providence has not mocked us with this great occasion, without the means to meet it." And Frémont is spoken of as " a man whose romantic achievements stir the blood of the young, and whose modesty, prudence, and sound principles commend him to the favor of the conservative, as one whose middle years are rich in varied experience, and to whom wisdom is gray hairs, and an unspotted life old age."

In a moment of sanguine hope of the success of the Free-Soil movement in 1856, Mr. Whittier wrote to Moses A. Cartland : " Ah me ! I wish I had strength to do what I see should be done ! But all I *can* do shall be done. I am not apt to be very sanguine, but I certainly have strong hopes of Frémont's election. I think I see the finger of Providence in his nomination. It appeals to all that is good and generous in Young America. It touches the popular heart." On the same sheet his sister Elizabeth wrote, beginning with a reference to the assault upon Sumner: "What sad, strange times are these! We have felt that the splendid life, so precious, has been in extreme danger. And then, poor Kansas! With the noble men and women doing far more than the old times ever called for, it would be very dark and sad, only for the hope we have in our brave young leader. The music of Freedom is in his very name. We shall surely find our way again, with Frémont at our head. I send thee this Quaker song of Greenleaf's — it was sung at our Frémont meeting." The song which was inclosed has not been found or identified. This letter was written in July, and "Sound the Trumpet" was not published until September.

The poem "What of the Day?" was written in the height of the excitement of the presidential contest, when the friends of Freedom were feeling somewhat confident of winning the day. It shows that Whittier did not share the bright hopes of those who expected to crush the barbaric institution of slavery without resort to anything harsher than the ballot. There is in it a prophetic intimation of the deadly war which was to rage five years later, and he expresses his gratitude that he had lived to take part in the preparatory struggle, while the gathering hosts were in "the Valley of Decision:"—

"I fain would thank Thee that my mortal life
  Has reached the hour (albeit through care and pain)
When Good and Evil, as for final strife,
  Close dim and vast on Armageddon's plain;
  And Michael and his angels once again

> Drive howling back the Spirits of the Night.
> Oh, for the faith to read the signs aright
> And from the angle of Thy perfect sight
> See Truth's white banner floating on before,
> And the Good Cause, despite of venal friends
> And base expedients, move to noble ends:
> See Peace with Freedom make to Time amends,
> And, through its cloud of dust, the threshing-floor,
> Flailed by the thunder, heaped with chaffless grain!"

The other poems which belong to this campaign are "The Pass of the Sierra," "To Pennsylvania," "A Song for the Time," and the song beginning, "Beneath thy Skies, November." The following interesting reference to "The Pass of the Sierra" is made in a letter written by Jessie Benton Frémont to Mr. Whittier, from Pocaho, N. Y., March 5, 1868: —

"The General had a case before the Supreme Court which has kept him some weeks in Washington, and yesterday, when he made time for a day at home with us, among other things he had to tell us was that a young lady has been introduced to him who had been on quite a tour in the California mountains, — to the Yo Semite, and into the Sierra Nevada. The point of it to us was that she told the General that on the first night they camped out in the Yo Semite mountains she could not sleep for the wildness and beauty made by the 'camp-fire's wall of dark.' When we lived two dreary years of enforced patience, waiting for the law's delay, in that same mountain country, I cut out and pasted to the wall, by the General's dressing-glass, where he had to see it daily, those lines of yours. Many and many a time when the

troubles of business depressed him, these words
with their grand ideas, and the memories of a
nobler life, put fresh heart into him. The young
lady's quotation [from " The Pass of the Sierra "]
reminded us of those times, and we talked them
over, sitting again by a country home fireside —
the wood fire, the dogs lying on the hearth, the
pines loaded with snow, all as it used to be in the
mountains, but within — health and peace and
rest."

The earnest abolitionists of these days made
public the confession of their faith in every possible way. One device was to print anti-slavery
pictures and mottoes upon the envelopes of their
letters, which gave offense to postmasters, who were
usually pro-slavery in their sentiments, and there
was complaint that many letters adorned with
these " incendiary " legends failed to reach their
destination. During the Kansas troubles the
phrase " Border Ruffian " came to be applied to
the party of the administration. This explains an
allusion in the following letter from Mr. Whittier
to Lydia Maria Child, written June 12, 1856 : —

" Thy book, most welcome of itself, was received a day or two ago, with the kind note accompanying it. I have never received the letter to
which thee alluded. The Border Ruffian official,
perhaps, withheld it on account of its 'image and
superstition.' I shall try and find it, however, for
I am not willing to lose a word of love and kindness from one I have so long loved and honored. I
the more regret the destruction of the letter, as
I see by thy note that my silence gave thee pain.

God forbid that I should forget or neglect an early
and much loved friend!   When we have reached
middle years, and begin to tread the sunset declen-
sion of life, it is not easy to make new friends or
give up old ones.   Long before I knew thee I had
read thy writings, and honored thee for thy noble
efforts in the cause of freedom.   Since then I have
had no occasion to qualify my respect and admiration, or to regard thy friendship as anything less
than one of the blessings which the Divine Providence has bestowed upon me — in more than compensation for whatever trifling sacrifices I have
made for the welfare of my fellow-men."

The following letter to Mrs. Child was written
in reply to one suggesting that he offer consolation to a mutual friend then in affliction : " I
thank thee for thy kind letter.   I had before seeing
thee anticipated thy suggestion as respects Mrs.
L——.   I called on her just as she was leaving
Beverly, urged to do so by an impulse which I
could not resist.   Her great sorrow and its holy
consolations deeply impressed me.   I was truly
glad to meet thee, in Boston.   It is the pleasantest
reminiscence of my visit.   My sister joins with me
in hoping we may see thee under our roof."

The poem " The Mayflowers " was written in
1856, and the concluding stanzas of it show that
a thought of the impending presidential campaign
was in the poet's mind as he wrote it : —

> " The Pilgrim's wild and wintry day
>   Its shadow round us draws ;
> The Mayflower of his stormy bay,
>   Our Freedom's struggling cause.

"But warmer suns erelong shall bring
  To life the frozen sod;
And through dead leaves of hope shall spring
  Afresh the flowers of God!"

This poem was suggested by a gift of mayflowers sent Mr. Whittier by a friend residing in Plymouth, Mass., on the 30th of April, 1856. The note accompanying the flowers has this passage, from which the poem grew: "You know the mayflower with us is *the* flower, and all our people gather them at this season and send them to their friends who have them not. There is such meaning in the mayflower to all descendants of the Pilgrims and to all lovers of freedom."

After the election, he wrote the "Song inscribed to the Frémont Clubs," in which he took a cheerful view of the situation, foretelling the success that was to come in 1860 : —

"For God be praised! New England
  Takes once more her ancient place;
Again the Pilgrim banner
  Leads the vanguard of the race.

"Then sound again the bugles,
  Call the muster-roll anew;
If months have well-nigh won the field,
  What may not four years do?"

After the death of Mr. Mussey the plates and copyright of the illustrated edition of Whittier's poems came into the hands of Sanborn, Carter, Bazin & Co. In 1857, Mr. Whittier, who was pleased with the blue and gold edition of Longfellow, wished to make a complete collection of his own works, to be published in the same neat and

popular form. He had written much since he had
sold his copyrights of all earlier poems to Mussey,
but it would be necessary for him to regain possession of these old copyrights before the new complete edition could be published. He had not the
means at the time to make the purchase, but the
matter was negotiated for him by Mr. Fields, and
the blue and gold edition was published in 1857.
The first correspondence in regard to it which is
before us is a letter of Whittier's dated January
4, probably written upon receipt of Longfellow's
blue and gold volumes: "Longfellow's poems are
always welcome. I like your new edition exceedingly, and wish some means can be devised to get
my verses into a similar shape. I wish I could
get hold of the Mussey volume. I would prefer
to have one publisher, of course. . . . A great
many thanks, dear F., for thy kind response to
my verses ["The Last Walk in Autumn"]. The
poem was written for thee and such as thee, for
the friends the good God has given me. I did
not expect the public at large to see much in it.
The weather deals harshly with me, and I cannot
leave home without suffering a great deal. The
worst of it is that a large part of the time I can
neither write nor read."

Fields replied in regard to the Mussey book, on
the 12th of January: "I have been trying for a
long time to get that big volume of your poems
out of Mussey's hands, with reference to bringing
you out complete, as we have done Longfellow.
Your poems are now held by Sanborn, Carter,
Bazin & Co., the successors of Mussey, and I

have failed as yet to bring them to terms. In whatever I have attempted to do, I have had your interest in mind. I am still negotiating, and hope I may yet be successful. You had better not write to them at present on the subject."

In a few weeks the matter was arranged, and Mr. Whittier at once set about the revision of his works. On the 5th of March he wrote : —

"I have marked for *omission* some eight or ten pieces, and have a great desire to wipe out others. Indeed, if I could have my way I would strike out the long Indian poem. In other words, I would kill Mogg Megone over again. I think the poem has some degree of merit, but it is not in good taste, and the subject is by no means such as I would now choose. I have objections to it not merely from an artistic point of view, but a moral one also. But I refer the matter to thee, whether Mogg can be omitted. I send an ambrotype just taken in this village, which my friends think an excellent likeness, barring a slight grip of the mouth, giving it a little twist by way of variety. Never mind that; twists are natural to men of one idea."

The portrait in the first volume of the blue and gold edition is from the ambrotype to which reference is made in the letter just quoted. On the 11th of March he wrote to Fields, who had objected to the omissions he proposed : —

"So, then, I must still carry the burden of my poetical sins ! Is there no way to lay the ghosts of unlucky rhymes ? As for Mogg Megone, he is

very far from pleasant company, but I see by thy
letter that it is idle to think of shaking the tough
old rascal off. Let him ride then — bad luck to
the ugly face of him! I had no business to make
him, and it is doubtless poetical justice that he
should haunt me like another Frankenstein. But
I insist on dropping 'The Response,' 'Stanzas
for the Times, 1844,' 'Address at the Opening
of Pennsylvania Hall,' and 'The Album.' Their
place is more than filled by the pieces added
and sent with the book. I have some eight or
ten pieces written within the past year which I
will send as soon as I can get them together. . . .
[He refers again to the ambrotype sent, from
which to engrave a portrait.] The ambrotype
process gives the hair and complexion a blanched
look, whereas my hair is black and but sprinkled
with gray sufficiently to give me the *external* sign
of wisdom."

The four poems named in this letter, which he
insists on dropping, are omitted from the blue and
gold volumes, but two of them may be found in
the edition of 1888. Of these two one is the
"Address at the Opening of Pennsylvania Hall,"
and the other is "Stanzas for the Times, 1844,"
which is now entitled "The Sentence of John L.
Brown."

Even when Whittier was in his most pressing
pecuniary straits, he was devising liberal things
for his friends who were more needy than he. Beside putting his hand in his own pocket, he called
upon his more prosperous friends for contributions, and among those upon whom he found he

could always rely were Mr. Fields, his publisher, and Mr. Haskell, editor of the Boston "Evening Transcript." In later years, George W. Childs, of Philadelphia, with characteristic generosity desired Whittier to draw upon him for any charity in which he was interested. Here is a letter to, Fields of May 1, 1857, asking help for a friend who had been dear to Whittier from childhood : —

"As thee is not one who wearies in well-doing, let me ask of thee to see friend Haskell of the 'Transcript,' and ask him to help set on foot a subscription for the benefit of ——, the historian, who is now sick in mind and body, at W. A kinder-hearted, quainter, and more genial man never lived than he. He has done a great deal of good in collecting material for the future historian and novelist. Let the subscription take the shape of a testimonial for his eminent services as a historian and antiquarian. If Haskell will act as treasurer, I will send my subscription to him."

Fields replied the same day : —

"I will speak to Haskell to-morrow about poor Mr. ——, whom I never saw but once or twice ; but as he is your friend, he shall have five dollars from a friend of yours, whose name is synonymous with *Meadows*. I will stir Haskell up to write of him in the 'Transcript,'

> "'And he shall say a good word for him,
>   Igo and ago ;
> Else may Old Nick to shoe-strings chew him,
>   Iram, coram, dago.'

Let me whisper to you, if at any time you find your pockets light, it will give me great pleasure per-

sonally to shovel in a few ' rocks,' to be returned
at any time when most convenient to you — or if
they should never come back it would be better
still. My hand is still lame, but I can sign a check
at any time, if a friend needs it."

To this Whittier replied : —

" I am sorry for thy lame hand, but be thankful
that thee are not an old bachelor, and lame all
over with rheumatism, as I am. Emerson's ' May
Day' is charming, — full of wisdom and sweetness.
Thy parody of Captain Grose set me rhyming
when I sat down to write to thee : —

> "Dear F. will take a friendly pride in
> The absent hand and heart confiding,
> And if then any are deriding
> That plea of Haskell's,
> We 'll count the cautious robes they hide in
> As sheer wrap rascals !
>
> " Oh, well-paid author, fat-fed scholar,
> Whose pockets jingle with the dollar!
> No sheriff's hand upon your collar,
> No duns to bother,
> Think on 't ; a tithe of what you swallow
> Would save your brother !
>
> " More blest is he among the living
> Who gives than he who is receiving:
> And that last robe which Time is weaving
> To bear us off in
> Shall be the lighter for our giving
> A lift to —— .
>
> " And now Heaven help the old and poor
> And keep the gaunt wolf from his door !
> I send for lack of silver ore
> These paper shadows :
> Thou 'lt add, I 'm sure, as many more,
> My dear friend — *Meadows.*

James T. Fields

" So shall the public crowd and mingle
Where'er thou hangest out thy shingle,
And all the joys the happy ingle
    Of human love yields
Be thine, and blessings never single
    Add Fields to Fields ! "

A few days later Mr. Whittier wrote: "I am
rejoiced to hear of the success of the subscription.
Some ladies from —— have just called on me with
the agreeable intelligence that our worthy old
friend has so far recovered as to be able to return
to his home. If now we can raise $200 for him it
will enable him to hold the old house where his
ancestors for many generations have lived, and set
the old man on his legs again, and warm and
gladden his heart. His bodily and mental health
seems now very nearly restored, and he fully ap-
preciates every kindness."

The ballad of " The Sycamores," which tells the
legend of the row of trees planted by the merry
Irishman, Hugh Tallant, on the left bank of the
Merrimac, below Haverhill, was published in
1857. Very soon after its publication a descendant of Tallant, Caroline L. Tallant of Nantucket,
Mass., wrote to Mr. Whittier making inquiries.
As first printed, the name was spelled " Talent,"
and the writer of the letter was not quite sure that
her ancestor was the person referred to in the
poem. She wrote for information on this point,
and added : —

" It is traditionary lore in our family, that three
Tallant brothers, of whom one was Hugh, came
over from Ireland and settled in New Hampshire,
and that from them descended all who bear the

name of Tallant in America. My grandfather, Andrew Tallant, was the son of Hugh. He died last spring in Pelham, N. H., on the old homestead which was left him by his father. I remember having seen one other son of Hugh. When I was quite young one of my uncles took me to ride from Concord to Pelham, and on the way he stopped at an old brown house, quite in the woods, that I might see his uncle Hugh. That Hugh Tallant was living, when last we knew anything of him, in Pembroke, N. H., and must be now about eighty-eight years old. Then my uncle has told me of another uncle of his, George, whom he remembers as having some skill in ' fiddle ' playing. That is one of the links in my chain of evidence, because he must have inherited the gift from his father. Hugh and George are all my grandfather's brothers of whom I know. On the back of a coat of arms, I have found the date of Hugh Tallant's death as 1795, and his *supposed* age 108 or 110 years. My grandfather used to tell us story-loving children that his father was a ' spry old man ' — ' over a hundred when he died,' and then he would relate to our great pride and satisfaction, how he had seen his father, when over seventy years old, leap over, by putting his hand on the neck of one of them, two horses placed side by side. He used to tell us too that his father saw the ' Battle of the Boyne ' in old Ireland, and Hugh Tallant was almost as much a hero for admiration as Washington. But it was with young eyes he saw the bloodshed of his countrymen, for he was held a child in arms on the battle-field.

The battle of the Boyne was July 1, 1690, which would make Hugh Tallant only 105 in 1795 — not agreeing exactly with the statement on the coat of arms. Your ballad says, —

> " ' One long century hath been numbered,
> And another half way told,
> Since the rustic Irish gleeman
> Broke for them the virgin mould.'

" Hugh Tallant, a hundred and fifty years ago, was an Irish youth of seventeen or twenty, with all the poetry of his nature fresh and uncrushed within him — and so it was just the age for him to disclose his musical and fun-loving disposition. Did your Hugh wander round from town to town with his fiddle and his pack? I know scarcely anything excepting what I have told of my great-grandfather. He lived in Atkinson at one time, and then he lived in Pelham. He owned at one time thousands of acres of land in and about the latter town, but he sold them carelessly away for almost nothing."

To this Mr. Whittier replied : —

" Thy letter took me almost as much by surprise as the entrance of the veritable and venerable Hugh himself would have done. When I wrote the poem in question, I never expected that a fair descendant of the Milesian tree-planter would be called up. In fact, Hugh Talent was to me a pleasant myth, a shadowy phantom of tradition only. Since receiving thy letter I have ascertained for a certainty that the Hugh of my ballad and thy great-grandfather are one and the same. I am not sure of the date of planting the trees, but it was certainly in the early part of the eighteenth century. Hugh at that time was a resident of Haverhill, on the Merrimac, now a town of some ten thousand inhabitants. The trees, twenty of which are now standing, he planted on the river bank, before the mansion of Colonel Richard Saltonstall, brother of Governor Saltonstall, of Connecticut.

" The tradition of him is pretty correctly given in the ballad. After leaving Atkinson [N. H.], then a part of Haverhill, he moved to Pelham or Windham, became a considerable landholder, and was noted for his love of fun and lawsuits. He took the Tory side in the Revolution, was outlawed, shot at, and driven off by his neighbors, but soon managed to return. These latter facts I have just learned. I wish they had been before me, as well as those of thy own letter, when I was writing ' The Sycamores.' The trees are about twelve miles up the river from my residence [in Amesbury]. I should like to show them to a descendant of the merry troubadour who planted them. I give the name as it stands in the Haverhill records, — Talent. I presume it should be Tallant. Of course, thou art at liberty to alter it in the poem. The incident of Washington is true."

Miss Caroline Tallant made the following lively response : —

" Very few of *old* Hugh's many-acred farms have descended to us, but I am more than content with *young* Hugh's bequest to me. How thoughtful in the youth to look down the long future and know of the poet yet to come, whose song and own handwriting and special message I should be

most pleased with, and then with his Irish wit
to set about gaining them for me by planting trees
on the river-side. My matronly sister insists upon
dashing my enthusiasm by reminding me that possibly Hugh may have planted the trees with no
higher aim than that of earning his dinner by his
labor. I scorn that idea, however, and will not be
convinced that the young man would as content-
edly have dug post-holes all day. He planted the
trees because he loved trees and flowers, and birds,
and everything beautiful, natural, and free, and I
am going to have him sainted for it, and a day
awarded on the family calendar. Saint Hugh's
day shall be duly honored with Thanksgiving fes-
tivities. His ballad shall be read, and we will not
forget, with our toast to his memory, the memory
of the singer who has sung both of him and of the
'sea-beat island,' — the only spot we call our
home."

In Mirick's " History of Haverhill," under date
of 1739, may be found this item, which evidently
gave the suggestion of the ballad to the poet, as we
find in Mr. Whittier's copy of the book the first
draft of a stanza of the poem written on the mar-
gin of the page that contains this passage : —

"About this time, the sycamore-trees, now standing before Widow Samuel W. Duncan's mansion,
were set out. The work was done by one Hugh
Talent, a wanderer from the green fields of Erin,
and who was a famous fiddler. He lived with
Colonel Richard Saltonstall, in the capacity of
a servant, and tradition says that he frequently
made harmonious sounds with his cat-gut and rosin

for the gratification of the village swains and lasses."

In the edition of 1873, there is an error in the twenty-eighth stanza of "The Sycamores:" —

> " But the trees the gleeman planted,
>   Through the changes, changeless stand,
>   As the marble calm of Tadmor
>   *Marks* the desert's shifting sand."

The word should be " mocks," and this is the reading in the latest editions.